Chicken Soup for the Soul.

Miraculous
Messages from Heaven

Chicken Soup for the Soul: Miraculous Messages from Heaven
101 Stories of Eternal Love, Powerful Connections, and Divine Signs from Beyond
Jack Canfield, Mark Victor Hansen, Amy Newmark
Published by Chicken Soup for the Soul Publishing, LLC www.chickensoup.com

The publisher gratefully acknowledges the many publishers and individuals who granted Chicken Soup for the Soul permission to reprint the cited material.

Front cover photo courtesy of iStockPhoto.com/ Milanares (© Milanares).
Back cover and interior photo courtesy of iStockPhoto.com/ Irochka_T (© Irochka_T).

Cover and Interior Design & Layout by Brian Taylor, Pneuma Books, LLC

Distributed to the booktrade by Simon & Schuster. SAN: 200-2442

Publisher's Cataloging-in-Publication Data
(Prepared by The Donohue Group)

Chicken soup for the soul : miraculous messages from heaven : 101 stories
   of eternal love, powerful connections, and divine signs from beyond /
   [compiled by] Jack Canfield, Mark Victor Hansen, [and] Amy Newmark.

      p. ; cm.

   ISBN: 978-1-61159-926-8

   1. Spiritualism--Literary collections. 2. Spiritualism--Anecdotes. 3. Supernatural--Literary collections. 4. Supernatural--Anecdotes. 5. Anecdotes. I. Canfield, Jack, 1944- II. Hansen, Mark Victor. III. Newmark, Amy. IV. Title: Miraculous messages from heaven : 101 stories of eternal love, powerful connections, and divine signs from beyond

PN6071.S9 C452 2013
810.2/02/37   2013937413

PRINTED IN THE UNITED STATES OF AMERICA
on acid∞free paper

22 21 20 19 18 17 16 15 14 13   01 02 03 04 05 06 07 08 09 10

Chicken Soup for the Soul

Miraculous Messages from Heaven

101 Stories of Eternal Love,
Powerful Connections,
and Divine Signs from Beyond

Jack Canfield, Mark Victor Hansen & Amy Newmark

Chicken Soup for the Soul Publishing, LLC
Cos Cob, CT

Contents

1

~Answered Prayers~

2

~Saying Goodbye~

❸

~Love that Doesn't Die~

❹

~Heaven Sent~

❺

~Heavenly Comfort~

❻
~Miracles of Love~

❼
~Miraculous Messengers~

8

~Dreams and Premonitions~

9

~Divine Connections~

10

~The Power of Love~

Chapter 1

Miraculous
Messages from Heaven

Answered Prayers

Our Roots Are Forever

Every December Sky must lose its faith in leaves,
and dream of the spring inside the trees.
~Beth Neilson Chapman

had been looking and hoping for a sign from my mom for months. She had died suddenly in mid-December and here it was almost the end of May. Still no sign. I was starting to think it would never happen. I'd been missing her so much, irrationally wishing I could somehow see her again. I was having a hard time moving on.

My father had passed away five years earlier. When you lose the second parent it can bring up a lot of unexpressed grief about the first, and I was finding my mother's death much harder to get through. With my dad's death I had also been shocked and bereft, but I had received a sign from him that had helped me. On the day of his funeral a little grey-feathered robin came to the tree outside one of my upstairs windows and immediately I knew it was him. The bird seemed so peaceful and calm. As I stopped and watched, I felt sure that he was communicating with me. In that moment I knew my dad was still there, that he was okay and I felt the sadness lift as I watched the bird fly away minutes later. My family name is Robinson, so it was even more meaningful. To this day there is almost always a robin on my lawn, and whenever I see it I always say, "Hi, Dad." I feel like he's still watching over me.

But back to my mom.

My mother was truly one in a million. A huge personality and character. A real sugar-cured ham, as she liked to call herself. She was born an identical triplet in Brantford, Ontario in 1927, and let me tell you those were three wild and crazy gals.

Growing up, I almost felt like I had three moms, and I think mine was the kookiest of them all. Everyone loved my mom—she was the warmest, most engaging, and more-the-merrier parent of all my friends. On the domestic side she was not the best housekeeper. As she would say, "A Suzy Homemaker I'm not." When we were kids, the joke was if she ever got the vacuum cleaner out, my brother and I would ask, "Who's coming over?" But, there was always an open door at the Robinsons'.

She threw a fabulous party and was extremely creative, smart, and funny. She was writing her memoirs when she died—a 200-page tome à la Erma Bombeck entitled *I Married an Idiot*. The opening line said that it was *she* who was the "idiot," not my dad. She ran him in circles but they had so many great times and laughs during their marriage. They loved their life together, in spite of all the shenanigans and arguments. In her book she joked that they had had the same breakfast for fifty years… a piece of toast and a fight… and sometimes no toast!

They instilled their love of music and theater and films in my brother and me, and one of the things we loved to do was watch movies together. I remember watching an old W.C. Fields movie with a hilarious scene where Fields is riding in the back of a Model T Ford, swerving down a county road followed by gangsters, all shooting at him. W.C. was just sitting back, smoking his trademark cigar, looking up at the foliage arching over the winding road, calmly observing, "Ah, look at the beautiful Catalpa trees." Now, none of us had the faintest idea what a Catalpa tree was but for some unknown reason, that odd little quote became a favorite in my family. We took a lot of road trips together and at some point, one of us, usually my mom, would imitate W.C. Fields and say, "Ah, look at the beautiful Catalpa trees," while miming the cigar. Don't ask me why—we just did, and we always laughed. It became one of our family "things."

When I went away to university my mom and dad travelled every few months to come to my stage performances and they became friends with all of my fellow actors. My mom especially was like the honorary den mother of my class. She kept everyone in stitches, telling jokes, adlibbing little skits and doing her famous W.C. Fields impersonation. One of my best friends even gave her the nickname "W.C."—and he called her that for all the years to follow.

So now here I was, the last weekend in May and, against our better judgment, my husband and I decided to have a garage sale. We had accumulated so much as our kids had grown and had piles of "junk" from both our families, especially lots of things from my mother's house, as she was the last remaining parent. Saturday morning I was out on our driveway, bright and early, trying to get the last few boxes sorted, items priced and displayed. It was a gorgeous spring day, and the flowers and trees on our property were just staring to bloom.

Some of the "early birds" you hear about—the super-motivated insomniacs that read the paper and show up before the allotted time to try to scoop up the best deals—had started to arrive. One in particular really caught my attention. He was a sweet, older gentleman, wiry and small, with a dry sense of humor—a real conversationalist. He was talking a blue streak to me and I was patient for a while, but I finally had to turn away from him and get back to my work. The sale was starting to get busy and noisy. I had my head down in a box, trying to see what I could find to bring out next when I faintly heard a voice say, "Oh, look at the beautiful Catalpa tree."

I couldn't believe my ears.

I slowly looked up from the box, turned back to see the little man standing there again and asked in a half-whisper, "What did you say?"

"I said look at that Catalpa tree."

"What are you talking about… where?"

"Right there," he said, pointing to this huge tree in the middle of my front yard.

"Those are really rare here in Canada. I can't remember seeing one in Toronto."

"How would you know that?" I stammered.

"Well, I *should* know," he said. "I'm a tree expert."

I had never known what a Catalpa tree looked like, or that we had one on our lawn, nor had my mom, who was quite an accomplished gardener and had been to my house countless times.

"They have giant heart-shaped leaves, right, and they are kind of messy, aren't they?"

This time I could not answer him because I was suddenly filled with my mom's spirit.

Of *course* she was here. And she had found a way to let me know. My mom had the biggest heart of anyone in this or the next world. And she absolutely loved garage sales!

At last I had my sign.

Sometimes when I'm lying in bed I look out my bedroom window and see that tree… and somewhere in my head I can hear her say, "Ah, look at the beautiful Catalpa tree."

Thanks, Mom.

~Laura Robinson

One Final Goodbye

I cannot forget my mother. She is my bridge.
~Renita Weems

Maybe I was wrong for not going back this time, but my mother had been dying for nine years. When we first learned of her disease, she'd been given nine months to live. I lived 3,000 miles away and had a young family. How many times over these nine years had I received the same phone call, "Your mother is in the hospital, in intensive care. You need to come home immediately if you want to see her again."

In the beginning, I'd fly back as often as I could. I'd stand at her bedside crying and willing myself to let her go. Each time I'd leave, I was certain this was our last goodbye.

When my mother moved in with my brother and his family, I felt a huge relief. Now, they'd take care of her, and I wouldn't have to go back as often.

Calloused as it may sound, I'd grown to dread those visits. The repeated goodbyes were tearing me apart.

With my mother's sixty-sixth birthday coming up, I took a friend's advice to go see her. I decided my visit would be the perfect gift.

She was frailer than I'd ever seen her, and during my visit, we rushed her to the emergency room, a too familiar experience. By now, she was worn out from the disease that had ravaged her body. She seemed ready to face death. But was I willing to let her go?

Inwardly, I sighed in relief when the doctor released her to return to the assisted living home.

After a two-week visit and one more goodbye, I returned to my family in California. Six weeks later, my uncle called. "Your mom is back in the hospital. If you want to see her alive, you need to come now."

My brother was with her, and with my recent visit, I decided not to go. Besides, she'd told me not to rush back. "You need to take care of your own family and your health," she'd said. And I knew she'd rebound, like all the other times.

I went about my normal routine, but I was uneasy. Had I made the right decision? What if she really was dying? I needed my mother's reassurance.

One week after she'd been admitted to the hospital, I felt compelled to stop everything I was doing and pray for her. Not the prayers I'd been praying over nine years, but a different kind of prayer. Something seemed to say, "You need to pray for your mother's transition from this life into eternity. It's time."

A picture came to my mind of a woman laboring to give birth to a child. My mother needed me to pray for her delivery into God's waiting arms.

Shutting the door to my bedroom, I fell to my knees. I saw myself standing next to her bed, holding her hand. Through my prayers, I was there with her. A presence filled my bedroom, and a warm sense of peace settled over me. "Lord Jesus," I prayed, "I ask you to release my mother from her earthly body. Please fill that hospital room with your ministering angels and allow her to feel Your Presence."

When the prayers felt complete, I said, "It's okay to go, Mom. I love you so much."

For a brief moment, I felt my mother's spirit with me, assuring me that she loved me and understood. Then, she was gone.

I picked up the phone and called my mother's hospital room. My brother answered. "She's gone," he said.

"When?" I asked.

"Just minutes ago," he answered.

I know, I wanted to say, but didn't.

Tears started to flow, but I knew I'd be okay. God had allowed my mother and me to have this one final goodbye. I wouldn't sink into a bottomless pit of despair, as I had feared. I hoped she'd seen angels, heard celestial music, and died with a youthful glow on her face.

Standing in my bedroom, I said one last time, "I love you, Mom. Goodbye."

~Jeanne Getz Pallos

A Walk in the Park

Faith is not without worry or care,
but faith is fear that has said a prayer.
~Author Unknown

am not a person who puts too much faith in dreams. I always seem to find a logical explanation for them. However, something happened that made me realize that God talks to us in dreams, as do our loved ones who have passed away.

It happened when things were at an all-time low for us. We had become homeless just months before, and we finally were able to save enough to get back into a house. My husband had not found work, and we had no money. Many times I went to the Dumpsters in the back of grocery stores to find food for my family. It was a dark time.

I wanted to give up and throw in the towel. It was hard to see how things would improve. When you're eating from garbage cans, it's hard to stay positive. However, my faith in God and reading the Bible kept me strong even in difficult times.

We were living in Oregon in a two-bedroom house with six children and no utilities. With no running water, I had to get water in a bucket from a neighbor's house. I needed $150, as a deposit, to turn on the water and lights. I just could not come up with the money.

On a Sunday night I poured out my heart to God and told him

how much money I needed for the utilities. I felt as if I was at the end of my rope. I did not know what to do. That night I had a very strange dream. In the distance I saw a campfire with men sitting around it. As I walked closer, I saw tents and horses as well. It looked like they were soldiers in the Civil War. All the men wore uniforms that fit the time period. The men were looking down at the fire as I walked up to them. Then one man looked up at me and smiled. He had a very big smile and he acted as if he knew me. I just stared at him. He had a pleasant face, but he looked tired. We looked at one another for a moment or two before he spoke.

"Take a walk in the park," he said. His voice was strong.

"What did you say?" I asked.

He repeated, "Take a walk in the park."

"Who are you?"

"Parkhurst," he said. "I am called Parkhurst. It's a family name." And he laughed.

I woke up and remembered every detail of the dream.

The next morning I walked to the store to return some bottles for the deposit, and right next to the store was a little park off to the side. I froze as I stared at it and recalled my dream. I walked away, into the store. As I headed home, Parkhurst's words came to me. I turned around and went back to the park. I did not see anyone in the park, so I started on the walking trail. Around the corner I saw a woman jogging toward me so I moved over for her to pass. I kept walking and looking for some reason I was there, but found none. Then someone touched me on my back and I turned to see the jogger.

"Hello," she said. "You must be the one."

"I don't understand," I told her.

"I dreamt last night that someone needed some money, and I handed it to them at a park," she said.

My mouth fell open but I did not say a word. She handed me an envelope, said "God bless you," and off she went. I yelled "thank you" when I could talk again. I opened the envelope, and there was $150. I had to sit down.

I went over and over what had happened. I prayed and had a

dream with a message from a strange man, and this woman had a dream and knew how much money I needed. I could not believe it, for nothing like that had ever happened to me. I hurried home to tell everyone.

It was not until twenty years later, when I took up genealogy, that I discovered a man named Parkhurst Shurlock who served in the Civil War. He was a sergeant in the 100th Co. D. I could not believe what I was reading. He was my great-great-grandfather.

As I did more research I learned the name Parkhurst was a family name, and to keep it alive they used it as a first name. About three years ago I found a photo tintype of Parkhurst Shurlock. It was without a doubt the man in my dream. I had come face to face with my great-great-grandfather.

~Judy Ann Eichstedt

Hi, from Dad

*Miracles are a retelling in small letters of the very same story
which is written across the whole world in letters too large
for some of us to see.*
~C.S. Lewis

After a short run outside, I started to give my dad a little "report," as he called it, on how things were going in my life. I sat down on the only dry spot—his headstone—longing for this to be more than a one-sided conversation. It was exactly one year after Dad passed away. I looked out over the clouded valley, recalling his two-year battle with brain cancer.

"I hope I can come see you after I've passed on," Dad told me during one of our last conversations before the tumor inhibited his speech entirely. "I hope I can come see how you are and give you a little report on what I'm doing."

I desperately wanted that visit now, and I had the faith that it was possible. Nineteen was too young to lose a father, and one year seemed so long. One year without seeing my dad, one of my best friends. I even said a prayer and asked God to let me see him.

"I just wish you could come see me again, Dad," I whispered after my prayer.

I sat and I sat. Exercising all the faith I knew how, I waited for what felt like forever until I finally accepted a hard fact: he wasn't coming. Yet as I stood to leave, I heard a man's voice. I looked up to see someone walking through the empty cemetery toward me, someone I had never seen before.

"This looks like a special day for you," he said.

We both looked down at the headstone which stated that my dad's date of death was exactly one year ago.

"Yes, it is," I replied, not sure what else to say to this stranger who had so unexpectedly shown up.

He stood in silence for a moment before continuing, "I was driving by, and when I saw you here in the cemetery, something touched my heart. You see, I've learned throughout my life that when the Spirit tells you to stop, you don't just keep on driving. I hope I haven't intruded on any special moment for you, but the Spirit told me to stop and tell you, 'Hi, from Dad.'"

I assured him of my appreciation before he got back into his car, and as I jogged back home I couldn't stop the tears from falling. I hadn't seen my dad, but God had heard my prayer, and he loved me enough to send this timely message of comfort from Dad.

~Laura Johnston

A New Home

Peace — that was the other name for home.
~Kathleen Norris

It had been four months since my niece Karen was tragically snatched from our lives. Four months of regular visits to my sister Lydia's home and to my niece's grave to place fresh flowers. I dreaded today's visit with Lydia. It was Karen's eighteenth birthday and I knew this day would be especially difficult.

Strangely, Lydia's spirits were high when I arrived at her house.

"I dreamed of her last night," she said. "It was so amazing and so real, I'm sure I was actually there."

I was excited for her, knowing how much she had longed to see her daughter one more time. She had been praying for this every day for four months.

We sat down on the couch with a cup of coffee. "Tell me more," I urged.

"I went to bed around eleven last night. I cried fresh tears and prayed the same prayer." She handed me her journal and opened it to the last written pages. I looked at the date and time. She'd penned her last entry just before two that morning.

I looked up at her, hesitant. These were her private thoughts on a journey no mother ever wishes to take. It was where she wrote her letters and thoughts to Karen as she worked through the tragedy of her sudden death in a car accident.

"Read," she encouraged.

I read aloud. "My dearest child… it's Wednesday morning, quarter to two, and it's your birthday. Happy birthday! Today you're eighteen years old—in heaven. I've been praying every night since the day you died that Jesus would let me dream of you. I've pleaded to see you again but to no avail. And then today, on your birthday, God granted my heart's desire. I had the most wonderful dream of you."

I wiped away the tears that had started to fall. Lydia was crying too, but today her tears were different. These tears came with a smile on her face. I continued to read.

"I stood beside you as you lay on a lush pink Victorian couch, book in hand. I knew you were in a deep study. Curled up beside you was your beloved dog, Tara. We were in the sitting room of your home. The room was overgrown with plants, and on one side stood the biggest sound system I've ever seen. The most beautiful music filled the room. Behind you an enormous white and marble staircase spiraled to the next floor. You didn't seem to know that I was there.

"Suddenly we were outside and you were seated on a low wall. From this vantage point I could see how big your home really was—four stories high, built on a mountain. It's amazing, the garden beautiful. I don't have words to describe it all.

"I couldn't believe I was with you, seeing you. But then I heard your father and brother-in-law's voices, calling me, telling me we needed to go. I didn't want to leave. When I looked at you, that beautiful, familiar smile swept across your face. You didn't speak, and yet we communicated—without you uttering a word, I heard what you were saying. 'You need to go now, Mommy, otherwise you won't catch up with Daddy and Martin.' I wrapped my arms around you and held you tight. Your arms embraced me too and we kissed each other on the cheek, over and over, before I turned to walk away. I called back as I waved, 'I love you so much. Remember how much I love and miss you.' I reminded you to wait, that one day I would come to you. Again you smiled, and without a word the message came: 'I know, Mommy, I know. And I'm waiting for you—there's plenty of space here. I love you all too. Thank you for everything. My grave is beautiful; I really like it.'

"I caught a final glimpse of you sitting, cross-legged, on the wall shadowed by the mansion behind you and I'm filled with joy and peace. How privileged you are to be where you are. What a wonderful, indescribable place.

"Somehow, you've matured so much. You still look the same — small and petite, the same twinkle in your brown eyes — but your hair is straight and shoulder length. You're so beautiful, your skin almost translucent, and I can't describe the joy and peace that emanates from your very being. The best I can offer is that you have truly reached perfection and glory.

"I'm so thankful to God that he honored my prayers on your birthday, and with every fiber of my being, I look forward to seeing you again."

The letter comes to an end signed, "All my love, Mommy."

Wet-face and red-eyed, I closed the journal and hugged my sister.

She turned to me and said, "Sis, it was incredible. When I woke, I could still feel her kiss on my cheek. It had been so powerful, like she was drawing the very life from me. But perhaps she was filling me with the life that she now has. It was all so... real."

"I believe you were really there, with her. What an incredible answer to prayer. And God could not have timed it better."

"That's not all!"

"There's more?"

Lydia nodded. "When I got to the bottom of the hill, Hennie and Martin were examining a big book. Martin pointed at the book and exclaimed, 'Here it is. Here's Karen's house.' As he touched the page, I caught a glimpse of the word his finger had landed on. And then I woke up. It was about 1 a.m. It was Karen's birthday."

"So, what was the word?"

Lydia's eyes filled again with tears. "Mizpah. After I woke, I got up, wrote this letter to Karen, and then I searched my Bible for the meaning of this word. On finding it, I'm convinced this is the name of Karen's new home in heaven."

Mizpah — a watchtower; a look-out — its meaning derived from the scripture, "May the Lord keep watch between you and me when we are away from each other."

Lydia smiled. "My daughter lives at Mizpah, her mansion set upon a hill. And God is watching over us while we're apart."

~Marion Ueckermann

All I Had to Do Was Ask

*Grieving is a necessary passage and a difficult transition
to finally letting go of sorrow—
it is not a permanent rest stop.*
~Dodinsky

t had been three years since the loss of my husband. I was not able to utter the word "died." I couldn't think of him as dead. I just had lost him. To him, it was cancer. To me, it was a heart-ectomy.

I thought I was getting on with my life. I had been dating. I had made new friends who were older and single, like me. I had joined Toastmasters. In fact, I had even won an award from my club for being The Most Inspirational Speaker.

But I was a fraud. I knew I was a fraud when I went to hang up that award on the wall in the hall. The hallway led to the master bedroom, a bedroom I had not entered for three years. How could I be inspirational when I couldn't even sleep in my own bedroom?

After Vern passed, I moved into a smaller bedroom off the kitchen. I moved my clothes from the master bedroom into the closet of that room. My life changed. I missed him just as much every single day. But I was learning to live with that loss as one learns to live with the amputation of a limb. The living part was getting easier. The loss part was not.

There truly is no loss in the world comparable to the loss of a spouse. I cried buckets. I cried so much that I should not have been able to pee for a month. But once the guestbook closed and the people went home, I knew it was time to restock my emotional self. However, it took me three years to restock, as I didn't want to use the master bedroom. All I did was look down the hall at that closed bedroom door.

Eventually, I was determined to move back into that bedroom. I was going to do it! I saw myself as a fraud, and now I was determined to live up to being "inspirational." In a demon-like frenzy I marched down the hall and threw open the door and dusted the furniture. I changed the bed sheets and began moving my clothes into the closet. And I prayed.

With each step I took I asked God for strength. I asked for a sign so that I would know I was moving in the right direction. I was gaining strength even in small steps. Then I realized this was the "growth" that was talked about. This was the "growing through grief" that I needed. But I still wanted a sign.

I remember the day my garage door wouldn't open. I had to learn how to open it manually. It was a nuisance that made me late for an appointment. Within a few days, the electricity went off. Guess what? I did not panic. I already knew how to get the door open. The day that happened, I truly felt like I had arrived. I knew that God was teaching me lesson after lesson every day of my life. I only needed to be awake and alert enough to learn them.

Today I was opening myself up to another lesson. I was cleaning the bathroom in the master bedroom when it happened. I was throwing out all the old pills in the medicine cabinet. I opened a small container that contained my allergy medication and saw my Mikimoto pearl ring. This ring had been missing since before my husband had passed away.

Vern made jewelry. And he was a perfectionist. Prior to his last stint in the hospital I had lost a pearl from the ring. He said it was no problem; as soon as he could, he would get a matched pearl and set it for me. The problem was that he went into the hospital and never came out. He never got to search for that pearl. And he did not tell me where he had put the ring. I had torn the house apart looking for it. My sister Marilyn had helped me search. We had checked the linings of the drapes, his jackets, and everywhere we thought he might have put it before going into the hospital the last time. We had finally given up.

Finding the ring was the sign. It was the sign that I was doing the right thing. I was in tears when I called my sister. I explained that I was moving back into the bedroom. She heard my tears and immediately suggested maybe this was too soon.

"No, Sis. It's not too soon. You will never guess what I just found," I sobbed.

"What?"

"The pearl ring."

"No way! We searched that room from top to bottom," she replied.

"And you will never guess. Remember the pearl that was missing? The one I wanted Vern to match?"

"Yes," she said.

"Well, the ring is perfect. No pearls are missing. They are all there. I can't even remember which one was missing. But the ring is perfect, just like new."

My grief was not eased at once by moving back into the master bedroom. But I slept that night knowing The Teacher above was continuing to provide life lessons with every step I took. All I had to do was ask.

~Linda Lohman

Pennies from Heaven

*What greater thing is there for human souls than to feel that they are joined
for life — to be with each other in silent unspeakable memories.*
~George Eliot

I t all began one Friday when I was at lunch with some of my
coworkers. I had just sat down at the table when my cell phone
rang. It was my mother.

"David is dead!"

"What?" I said. "David is dead? What happened?"

Mom said she didn't know, but the coroner's office had just left
the house. I told her I would be there as soon as possible. I prayed
for God to please send me a "penny from Heaven" to let me know my
brother was in Heaven.

My husband drove me to my parents' house. Pastor Zechiel was
already there comforting my parents. We still didn't know the actual
cause of death. My parents told me the coroner only said he thought
that David died of natural causes. Later that evening, my cousin had
broken the news to my siblings and me. David had shot himself. It
took me a while but I finally told my parents later that evening. Of
course, everyone started to blame themselves — we knew David was
depressed and we failed to help him.

On Saturday I cleaned and vacuumed my parents' van just to
have something to do. My parents did not drive or ride in this vehicle
the entire weekend. I constantly prayed to God to send me that penny
from Heaven.

The funeral was the following Monday morning at Immanuel Lutheran Church in Campbell Hill, Illinois. Of course the family was at the church early. My husband Ken and I entered the room where everyone was gathering before the ceremony. A lot of friends and relatives were there, and Ken sat at the table in front of the restrooms. I have no idea why I didn't make an effort to sit by Ken, but for some reason the pew along the wall caught my attention. I sat in the corner of this pew, not sure why I chose that particular spot. I saw a small prayer book lying there and picked it up so I could sit down. To my surprise, I found not one penny, but two pennies in the corner of this pew! I still get goose bumps when I think about this. I know God was answering my prayers and letting me know that David was in Heaven.

My sister Karrie called me late the next morning. "You will never believe what just happened," she said. I thought something was wrong because she sounded so upset, almost to the point of tears. Karrie told me she went home Monday night and prayed to God to send her a penny. She found a penny on the floor of her second bathroom.

My mother finally drove their van a day or two after the funeral. She called to tell me there was a penny stuck to the carpet in a wide-open area. I had not seen that penny when I vacuumed the van.

Tuesday, the day after the funeral, David's daughter Kayla and I went to the gravesite to say a prayer. We took six of the roses off the gravesite and brought them back to my mother. I grabbed what I thought was a vase from their mantel and took it to the kitchen sink to fill it with water. I didn't realize when I picked up the crystal, it was actually two pieces (which obviously would not hold any water). I placed the crystal back on the mantel. To my surprise, there was a penny sitting right in front of where the crystal was!

A few days after the funeral, my husband called me at work and told me his penny story. Ken was walking barefoot in the kitchen and kept hearing cling cling cling on the bottom of his foot. He said he could not feel anything but rubbed the bottom of his foot. He started walking again and he heard this cling cling cling noise again.

He rubbed the bottom of his foot a second time and a penny fell to the floor.

While on the phone with Ken, I was looking at some change on my desk. I was thinking to myself that when I get off the phone I would ask God to let one of those four pennies be the year 1974—the year David was born. Then the very first penny I pulled out was dated 1974!

There is no doubt in my mind that God is sending these pennies to me—assuring me my brother is in Heaven!

~Shelly S. Shevlin

The Miracle of a Precious Stone

I miss thee, my Mother! Thy image is still
The deepest impressed on my heart.
~Eliza Cook

should have been happier. It was two days before Christmas and I was driving alone on a country road in our small mountain community delivering homemade cookies to shut-ins. A light dusting of snow covered the barren cornfields, giving hope to every child who prayed for a white Christmas.

I had spent the last couple of days with church friends, mixing dough, shaping date balls, melting chocolate, baking dozens and dozens of different Christmas cookies. We had covered every surface in my kitchen with cookies, laughing uproariously at our own jokes, singing off-key one familiar Christmas carol after another.

Driving along the familiar roads that late afternoon, I was having a conversation with my Lord about the death of my mother four months earlier. We had had this conversation before, and each time God had provided a measure of peace.

And yet, the same questions surfaced again and again. Why did my mother have to endure so many years of mind-numbing pain before her death? Why didn't I have peace about where she was?

I delivered all of my cookies, warmly greeting the shut-ins. Their homes were decorated with small white pines or blue spruce cut from the deep forests surrounding the community.

At my final stop, Miss Ruby, a beloved eighty-three-year-old known for her quiet benevolence, was slow to respond to my persistent knock on her front door. I started to get concerned because she had fallen on Thanksgiving Eve while preparing dinner for several neighbors who would be alone that holiday.

Finally, I heard the steady rhythm of her wooden cane as she slowly made her way to the door.

"I guessed you'd be coming by, my dear, so I've made some hot chocolate to entice you to stay a little longer. It gets lonely here on Long Bottom Road in the winter, and even more so now that I can't get outside in this cold weather while my hip is healing."

We chatted while I balanced my cup on my knee and found myself wishing her grown children lived nearer to provide companionship and care for her. As I was leaving, she put her arms around me, kissed me on the check and whispered, "You're an angel, do you know that?" I was hardly an angel, but I thanked her and promised to visit again after Christmas when the holiday rush was over.

Back in the car, I drove a short distance down the dirt road before easing to a stop next to a weathered split-rail fence. No farmhouses were in view.

I laid my head down on the steering wheel and wept.

"I miss you, Mother," I cried out, looking heavenward to the overcast skies, hoping she heard me.

This was my first Christmas season without her. I knew well the verse, "to be absent from the body is to be present with the Lord." Still, I wept alone on that country road, unable to accept the peace that God was so willing to give me.

Finally, in desperation, and with no thought of Biblical precedent, I asked the Lord for a sign, a sign that He cared, a sign that He heard me, a sign that He loved me, a sign that my mother was safe in heaven with Him.

Wiping my eyes, I returned to our country home where I quietly prepared dinner for my husband. We were alone; our sons were married and living in another part of the state. This was their year to spend Christmas with their wives' families.

The next morning, while dressing for church, my husband turned to me in surprise and asked, "Where on earth did you find this?"

"Find what?" I asked, straightening my skirt before the mirror.

"The ruby!" he replied. "Isn't that your ruby there on the bedspread?"

I rushed to the bed, picked up the ruby, held it close to my breast and began to weep.

It had become a custom for my parents' seven children to pool our resources each time one of us celebrated a fortieth anniversary and to present the happy couple each with a ruby, the stone traditionally associated with that anniversary. On our anniversary the previous year, I was given a lovely ruby set in a pendant on a simple gold chain.

The first week I wore it, the stone had come loose from its setting and was never found, leaving me distraught.

I had searched for nearly a year, combing the carpets, checking our closets, looking in the most unlikely places for this ruby which had lovingly tied me to my siblings.

And now, on this Sunday morning, the ruby appeared from nowhere in the center of our bedspread. More curiously, I had made the bed less than a half hour before.

My husband, sensing my suspicion, placed his hands firmly on my shoulders. "I know you must think I found the ruby and laid it on the bedspread where you'd quickly see it. But I can assure you before God that this is the first I've seen it since you lost it last year. I promise you!"

It was my sign. There could be no other explanation. And I sought none.

~Mariane Holbrook

From Mourning to Morning

God can heal a broken heart, but He has to have all the pieces.
~Author Unknown

t had been several sad and lonely months since my three-month-old son Travis had died from congenital heart disease. I was so angry with God for taking my son that I vowed to never pray to Him again.

There was just one problem. My four-year-old son Aaron missed his brother dearly and would ask me questions every day like, "Mommy, what's Heaven like?" "Mommy, can I go to Heaven and see Travis?" Or, "Mommy, why can't Daddy go get Travis and bring him home?" These are tough questions, especially when you are mad at God.

I couldn't stand the thought of infecting Aaron with the bitterness that was consuming me. I had taught him every day of his young life that Jesus loved him. I could not destroy that faith. I knew I had to find peace beyond my grief so that I could be a good mother to Aaron.

Finally, one night, as I lay alone on my bed, I poured out my heart to God—my anger, bitterness and pain. I prayed, "Lord, I have tried to change, but I can't; so if you want me whole again, you will have to do it."

Suddenly, the room was filled with an almost palpable peace

and I heard God speak to my heart, "Louise, Travis is with me." Then, to my amazement, I felt the weight of my baby son placed against my breast and could almost feel his soft, baby hair brush against my cheek. I couldn't open my eyes as tears streamed across my temples, soaking my hair. I lay absolutely still, allowing God to comfort me in a way I had never known as I continued listening to His gentle whisper: "Travis is okay. He's with me."

When I awoke the next morning, the bitterness and anger were gone. I still missed my son terribly. I still had no explanation as to why he was taken. But I had the most intimate encounter with God's love and presence that I had ever experienced in my entire life.

~Louise Tucker Jones

A Handwritten Message from Heaven

While we are mourning the loss of our friend,
others are rejoicing to meet him behind the veil.
~John Taylor

t was a beautiful Tuesday morning but my mood did not match the day. I was in a solemn and reflective mood, grieving the loss of someone very dear to me. I'd had almost four months to grieve and deal with the reality of her death, but something else nagged at me this morning. I realized suddenly that I didn't know about her salvation. And although we were very close, that was something we had never discussed.

Although we were not blood kin, Shirley had been in my family and like a second mother to me for twenty-five years. My mother and father had divorced when I was fourteen, and my mama was struggling to raise us four kids alone. Shirley was from Richmond, Virginia and had been transferred to Atlanta, Georgia several years before and had no family here. She and my mother worked for the same company but different departments, and so did not know each other well. Their worlds were miles apart. Shirley had no family close by. She had lost her mother when she was a child; her father had deserted the family when she was a baby. She had no children of her own and had never been married. She and her only sibling, a half-sister, were split up when their mother died, and were raised in different homes. Her sister, Peggy, had been taken to live with her father and Shirley was raised by an "old maid" aunt and her granny.

One particularly stressful day she found my mother crying in the lounge and offered her help. My mother thanked her but told her no one could solve the problems she had. She was required to work late and her four kids were at home alone with no dinner. Shirley opened her heart and said, "Well I certainly can help with that! I will be glad to go over and cook dinner and stay with the children until you get off work." My mother, stunned, couldn't say no. And that was the beginning of our new and very different family, one that included Shirley for the next twenty-five years.

Shirley had died from multiple errors during what should have been a simple heart procedure. She was on life support for four months before they turned the machines off. It was a heart-wrenching four months, and I went to see her every single day on my lunch hour. I fed her, read to her and met with doctors to discuss her care. We were all with her the day she died.

Over the years we talked a lot. We talked dogs, we talked kids, and we talked cooking. Shirley and I shared a love for cooking as she patiently taught me my way around the kitchen. She taught me how to pay bills when I married and how to stretch food dollars on healthy inexpensive meals. She taught me how to balance a checkbook and make a budget. Over the years, we talked about a million things, but today I was having regrets that we never talked about her relationship to God.

After she died, my mother told me that Shirley had asked questions and worried a lot about her spiritual condition. She worried as she aged about the fact that she had never been baptized and the fact that she had never regularly attended Church service. She asked a lot of questions and began to read the Bible. But as far as I knew she had never made a conscious decision to give her heart to God. I found myself crying for her yet again and praying that she was okay.

Three years earlier, Shirley had given me a beautiful antique oak sideboard that had been in her family for several generations and was left to her when her aunt passed on. She and my mother had cleaned all of their belongings out of it, and I checked to make sure before we moved it. It had been in my living room for the past three years. I had polished it, wiped out all the drawers and replaced a broken glass handle. Since the drawers were old and rickety I kept a few little household items in it, but primarily it was still empty. Over the past three years I had been in it dozens of times and it held mainly my old feather duster and a few orphaned keys.

This morning, after I got over my crying spell and long talk with God, I washed my face. Determined to get my mind off the grief, I got busy around the house. The first thing I did was wrestle with the top drawer of the old sideboard where I kept my old orange feather duster. When I finally tugged the drawer open and picked up the duster, I saw something clinging to the bottom. It was a piece of cardboard found on the back of a small 5x7 pad. I noticed something written on it; not a word or two but an entire page — a poem — carefully transcribed on the piece of cardboard most people throw away. I noticed the tiny, precise lettering and immediately recognized the handwriting as Shirley's. It stopped me in my tracks, mystified as to how it got there when I knew the drawer had been emptied of all of its belongings three years ago.

It was a poem by her favorite poet — Helen Steiner Rice. I realized that in less than fifteen minutes after my request, in her own handwriting, she had sent me the message that I had asked for. Through tear-dimmed eyes I read the poem to the bottom and then back up to the title. In big bold letters were the words: Good Morning God.

~Andrea Peebles

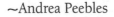

Chapter 2

Miraculous
Messages from Heaven

Saying Goodbye

One Last Hello

There are things that we don't want to happen but have to accept,
things we don't want to know but have to learn,
and people we can't live without but have to let go.
~Author Unknown

My brother Michael James was a beacon of light in a dark world. He was always smiling, and there never seemed to be a day that he was in a sour mood. He was a generous man who would never hesitate to give everything he had if he knew you needed it more. Always there to lend a shoulder to cry on or tell a joke to lift your spirits, he truly was one of a kind.

Michael was tragically killed on impact when a teenager running from the police in a stolen car hit him at over 100 miles per hour. The police came to our home in the middle of the night to tell us the shattering news.

The night before Michael was laid to rest, we viewed his beautiful face one final time at the funeral home. A heart-wrenching ordeal, we solemnly went home to grieve. Once home, I curled up in the family room with my brother Thomas and my future husband Jason. We had the television on, but we were not really watching it. My parents had gone to bed as soon as we got home.

After maybe an hour, I heard heavy footsteps in the upstairs hallway, and assumed it was my father coming downstairs to get a drink of water. The kitchen door did not open, so I shrugged it off and didn't think much of it. The footsteps continued into the kitchen. I looked up but still did not see anyone.

I turned to Thomas and asked him if he saw anyone. He glanced quickly and shook his head. Suddenly, the stained glass sun catchers on the sliding glass door started swinging for no apparent reason! Shocked, I turned to Thomas and Jason to see if they also saw what I was seeing. Their eyes were wide as they looked at me in disbelief.

Thomas cleared his throat, and asked "Michael, are you here?" The sun catchers continued to swing, and somewhat faster. Grins spread across all three of our faces. Without warning, the swinging stopped. Our shoulders drooped, because we figured Michael must have left.

The dogs however seemed to know he was still there, because they both jumped off Jason and Thomas's laps to mount the couch next to the sliding door. This was astounding because for whatever reason they only would sit on that particular couch when Michael was there.

We all laughed and tears of joy filled our eyes, as we knew Michael was there to say hello and let us know he was still with us. We all told him that we loved him and that we missed him.

Soon, the dogs retreated from the couch and got back onto Jason and Thomas's laps. We heard the floorboards creak upstairs in my parents' room and we knew Michael had gone to visit them.

The next morning, my mother told us about how she had the most wonderful dream that Michael had been in their room. He had hugged her and told her not to worry. Thomas, Jason and I looked at each other knowingly, and said, "Hey Mom, want to hear something amazing?"

~Megan LeeAnn Waterman-Fouch

Namesake

God pours life into death and death into life without a drop being spilled.
~Author Unknown

woke up when I felt someone sit on the side of the bed. I glanced at the clock and saw that it was the middle of the night. I pushed my pregnant body up on my elbows expecting to see my five-year-old daughter in need of comfort or refuge from a nightmare. Instead I was surprised to see my Italian grandfather sitting there looking at me. "Pop! What are you doing here?" I said.

He smiled and patted my leg. "I come to tell you something and to ask a favor," he said.

"Oh, okay," I said still groggy from sleep.

He put his hand on my rounded stomach and smiled at me. "You will have a boy coming soon," he said.

My jaw dropped. "How do you know?" I asked.

He nodded and tapped his finger against the side of his head and smiled. A gesture he always made to assure me of his wisdom. "Now I ask a favor since I never had a son, for you to give him my name as part of his," he said.

I could never refuse my "Pop" any favor he asked of me and least of all this special one. "I will be happy to give him your name," I said. He nodded and smiled, then stood up, waved goodbye and walked out of the room.

I let my head sink back onto the pillow and lay there thinking about what had just happened. It must have been a dream, I reasoned, because my grandparents and other relatives lived 3,000 miles away. But I was awake and he was there and he touched me and he talked to me.

At dawn the telephone rang. I wondered who would be calling me this early as I stumbled out of bed. My aunt's voice greeted me when I answered the phone.

"I have bad news," she said. I sucked in my breath and grasped the top of the kitchen chair. "Pop had a heart attack in his sleep and passed away."

I could feel the goose bumps rising on my arms as I slid onto the chair. "I know," I said.

My aunt gasped at my response. "How did you know, did someone else call you?" she asked.

I wanted to tell her about Pop's visit but I knew it would be impossible for her to understand, because I was still struggling to put what happened in perspective. "Yes, yes, the call woke me up so I don't remember who called," I said, knowing that was plausible since my relatives usually forgot about the three-hour time difference between the East and West Coast.

We talked for a few minutes and agreed it would be unwise for me to travel during the last trimester of my pregnancy, so I wasn't expected to attend the funeral. As was the custom in the family, she said she would send a copy of the obituary and one of the funeral cards to me.

I rested my head on the table, feeling a mixture of sadness at his passing and joy from his visit. Memories of my grandfather played through my mind for the next few days along with the reality of his visit. I knew it wasn't a dream. It was too real. I felt his presence.

When the copy of the obituary and the funeral card came in the mail I read the brief chronicle of my grandfather's life. He was born in Sicily, emigrated to America, married and fathered two daughters. He was a self-taught mandolin player, having learned to play by ear at an early age. His work history and retirement date and church affiliation were included.

At the end of the obituary was the cause and time of his death. I blinked and read the time listed once again. Pop's time of death was only minutes before I awoke to find him sitting on the side of my bed.

I gave birth to a boy two months later. His middle name is Sebastian in honor of my grandfather. And like his great-grandfather he is a self-taught musician of a similar stringed instrument, the guitar, which he learned to play by ear at an early age.

My loving memories of Pop will never die.

~L.A. Kennedy

She Stopped to Say Goodbye

Grandmas hold our tiny hands for just a little while, but our hearts forever.
~Author Unknown

Grandma was the center of my childhood world. My mother was often too tired to talk or do things with me when she got home from work, but Grandma had endless time to listen and talk, with a limitless supply of funny stories. I loved home and my mother, but life was more exciting with Grandma. The only downside to long afternoons or overnights at Grandma's was leaving. I especially hated to say goodbye. She knew that and when she died in November 1973, she made a special effort to reach out to me.

All of my friends were welcome at her home, but I most enjoyed spending time alone with her. While watching her knead bread or make soup, we talked. She shared tales of her own life, silly poems, and deliciously "naughty" stories about the exploits of my mom and her siblings. We fed the birds from her back porch. But whatever we were doing, we stopped to watch her soap opera, *The Guiding Light*, at noon.

On shopping forays into downtown Pittsburgh we haunted shops large and small. Lunch was my choice—chicken à la king at Kaufman's or barbecued chipped ham at Horne's. We rode the streetcar into downtown. If laden with packages, we often splurged on a cab to go home.

When I stayed overnight we stayed up late together, watching old movies from the perch of her bed on the tiny TV in her bedroom.

"We can eat cookies in bed if you want," she'd offer. We often did, and shook out the crumbs from the sheets in the morning. Then we'd eat cinnamon buns fresh from bakery home delivery.

Grandma took each grandchild, in turn, on a vacation with her. When I turned ten, Grandma and I waved goodbye to my parents as we boarded the train for a two-week trip to Atlantic City. My "turn" stretched into several years of vacations—Atlantic City before it was a gambling venue, a cruise to Nassau, a week in Miami, and more time in Atlantic City until my parents thought it too seedy for us to continue our trips there. The hardest part of any of these trips was returning home, bidding goodbye to Grandma and returning to regular life.

College took me away from Grandma and my parents for most of the year. While I was away, Grandma and I visited by phone almost as often as my parents and I did. After college I went to graduate school, using up all of my savings and taking out a loan for the first year. Grandma waved her magic wand and made my second year of graduate school possible by lending me part of my tuition. When I got a job and presented her with a repayment schedule, Grandma said, "Consider the money a gift."

After graduation in 1971, I moved to Washington, D.C. She visited once, with my mother. We talked about her visiting me alone. I wanted to take her to all of the new places I was discovering. Of course, we talked regularly by phone. She listened, as usual, never judging, but simply supporting and gently offering advice.

Late in 1972 she became very ill. For most of 1973 she was so ill that my mom and her siblings had to take turns staying with her. I took time off from my job that August to spend all of my leave with her. Alone again, we talked and laughed. She knew she was dying. When it was time for me to leave at the end of the weekend, neither one of us wanted to say goodbye. It seemed too final. When I left, Grandma simply hugged me. A few weeks after my visit, she took a turn for the worse and went into the hospital.

Mom and I spoke daily, not unusual in today's world of cell phones, but a difficult and expensive activity in the early 1970s. Each evening after hospital visiting hours ended, she gave me a report on Grandma's progress. On Sunday, November 11th, my mother told me I should fly back to Pittsburgh the following weekend.

"It might be your last chance to say goodbye," she said.

I didn't want to wait for the weekend. I decided that Monday morning I would ask my boss if I could leave on Tuesday.

Monday morning around 7:30, as I got ready for work, I rehearsed my request for leave. I had no roommate, so I wasn't disturbing anyone with my monologue. Suddenly, I "felt" someone in the dressing area with me. I was brushing my hair and my arm remained suspended in mid-air as I listened to a voice direct two words at me. Grandma's voice. She spoke what she had not wanted to say when I left her in August. Two simple words: "Goodbye, Joanie."

Filled with overwhelming sadness, I dropped the brush. I ran to my nightstand and picked up the phone. I dialed my mother. The phone rang and rang. When she answered, I blurted out, "How is Grandma?"

"As I told you last night, same, but growing weaker. Why did you call so early? I don't have any new information."

An hour later she called me at my office. "Grandma isn't fine. She went into a deep coma this morning about an hour ago. The nurse called to tell me not long after you called. This is the first chance I've had to get back to you."

On Tuesday I flew to Pittsburgh from Washington, D.C. and rushed to the hospital. Grandma's body was being kept alive. I sat with her until she was officially declared dead on November 15th. But I know that her spirit had left her body three days earlier on Monday when she slipped into the coma. I know, because on her way to heaven she stopped to say goodbye.

~Joan Leotta

A Stop on His Journey

*Grandchildren are the dots
that connect the lines from generation to generation.*
~Lois Wyse

Grandpa Macdonald arrived at my mother's house with a battered suitcase and little else. In his eighties, he stood barely five feet tall. My mother said he used to tell people he was 5'4" before he got old and shrunk, but that wasn't true—she said he'd always been about the same height.

He had a soft Scottish brogue that he denied he had. I found it enchanting. His strongest drink was tea, and he liked it well steeped. Cheese? He'd never tried it because he didn't like the way it smelled.

I liked him immediately.

My grandmother had died when I was about four, and until Grandpa came across the country from Seattle to live with my mother in Maryland he'd been only a faint shadow in my life. While I was growing up, my father was in the Foreign Service and we lived on the East Coast or overseas in India. Grandpa visited us once when I was ten; we went to the White House but then he left to go back home.

That was the story of my life. People came and went, but no one ever stayed. Friends I had overseas returned to their home countries, and I never saw them again. I went to nine different schools before I graduated high school. Nine times I adjusted and made friends, and nine times they were gone.

So I was happy when Grandpa Macdonald came to stay, even though by then I was in my thirties, married, and on my own. I finally had more than just my immediate family; I had a link to the past.

After a year with my mother, Grandpa was diagnosed with cancer. He had an operation. When I visited him in the hospital, he said he'd had "hallucinations." In one, he'd been back in the Scottish Highlands. In another I'd brought him fresh cookies I'd baked. I smiled, glad I was part of something pleasant.

When the hospital released him, he was temporarily sent to a nursing home for additional care. When I arrived for a visit, I hardly recognized him. He had aged years in just days. The bed engulfed his small body, and the wheelchair the nurse put him in barely held him up. We talked for a couple of minutes and then I pushed him into the social area, away from his institutional room.

"You can watch TV here with other people," I said as I set the brakes on the wheelchair and pointed to the others sitting quietly in wheelchairs.

He shook his head. "I don't want to watch TV. I'm getting too old for this. I don't want to be here."

I smiled, hoping I looked reassuring and cheerful. "It won't be for long. I'll be back tomorrow." I felt terrible for abandoning him, but fled nonetheless.

That night I woke up about 3:00 a.m. Grandpa Macdonald sat next to my bed.

"I'm leaving," he said.

For some reason, I knew what he meant immediately. "No. I don't want you to die."

"It's time. Life's too hard. I just can't do it anymore."

"Please…" I begged.

He shook his head. "I'm tired. It's what I want."

Somehow, somewhere deep down, I knew this was the way it was supposed to be.

I wanted to reach out, but I didn't. I just nodded, accepting that he would be gone. Before I knew it, I was asleep.

The next morning the phone rang. It was my mother. "The nursing home called. Grandpa died during the night."

Ordinarily I would have felt a terrible emptiness because yet again someone had left me. But while I was sad, I knew in my heart it was okay. Grandpa and I had discussed everything in the early morning hours, when he came to me to say goodbye.

~Michele Ivy Davis

My Prince's
White Horse

*Heaven is high and earth wide. If you ride three feet higher above the ground
than other men, you will know what that means.*
~Rudolf C. Binding

My husband Ben's health was quickly declining. He needed a liver transplant to survive. We spent weeks with him in the hospital, hoping to get on a transplant list, but hope was growing dim. He was losing his battle.

Ben was forty-three years old, once athletic, strong, and strikingly handsome with black hair and olive skin. He was always quick to volunteer, be a leader, and help others. He made it a priority to help kids play baseball by providing scholarships and coaching Little League teams. Now the man in the hospital bed looked more like a frail old man than my husband.

We celebrated our twenty-first wedding anniversary in the hospital. We sat close on Ben's hospital bed as friends served us a romantic Italian dinner, complete with a stereo to play love songs, transforming our room into a romantic Italian café.

"You're still my prince you know, so keep looking for that white horse," I said playfully to Ben. From the time we were dating I had called him my handsome prince, and teased him that he needed to find a white horse. I had always admired white horses. After all, the prince always arrives on the white horse to save the princess, and the knight on the black horse never stands a chance.

For my birthday years earlier Ben had surprised me with a beautiful white Arabian horse, and a dozen red roses hidden secretly in a brand new shiny horse trough. Over the years he continued to surprise me with more white horses in some form or another, usually the kind with an engine under the hood and four wheels. More than once he planned a night out for us in a chauffeured white limousine. "It has a team of white horses under the hood," he would say. I smiled now thinking of those sweet memories.

Our three children, Amanda, 15; Benjamin, 13; and Jordan, 12, visited their dad as often as they could, but it was difficult with the hospital located miles away in a different state. I wished they were with me now to say final goodbyes to their daddy.

A storm the night before had covered everything with a thick blanket of ice, completely shutting down the city. Even the freeways were closed. It was much too dangerous for friends to bring our children to the hospital to visit their dad.

Early that morning, Ben and I held hands as we watched the news on his TV. People driving looked more like they were playing bumper cars at a carnival. It was heartbreaking and scary to watch them helplessly skidding.

My sister Cheryl stayed with me and was my strong support. "I'm thankful we decided to stay the night at the hospital," I said. "We wouldn't have been able to come back today."

"I'm thankful too. You know, it's a blessing for you."

"Really? How's that?"

"Well you've had so many visitors, you haven't been able to have uninterrupted time with Ben. Now you can."

We held each other's gaze a few seconds as I comprehended the meaning in her words. I looked at Ben, who was intently watching me. Our eyes locked as we both understood what Cheryl meant. Ben wasn't able to talk, but his eyes were full of expression.

By 10:00 on that icy January night, Ben's condition took a bad turn. "We're losing him," Nurse Lisa said, checking Ben's oxygen levels. Tears flowed down her cheeks. She had been the main nurse in charge of helping Ben, and had come to love this man fighting so hard for his life.

"We have to help him!" I said, holding Ben's hand. "Please don't leave me, Ben. I need you!" I brushed the hair off his temples. Tears streamed uncontrollably down my cheeks as his breathing became shallow. "Dear Lord, please help him!" I cried out.

Suddenly a feeling of peace swept over me. I told Ben, "It's okay to let go and go home. God is waiting and has a beautiful place prepared for you. I love you, and when you get to Heaven, please find me a white horse."

Ben took in another deep breath. In a panic I looked to Nurse Lisa and waited as she checked for a heartbeat. "He's gone. I'm so sorry," she said through her tears.

I sobbed, barely able to catch my breath as I lay close to Ben, burying my face in his neck and wrapping my arms under his shoulders. I don't know how long we stayed like that, but at some point I opened my eyes and saw soft pink iridescent lights dancing around the room. They reminded me of floating bubbles, only they were teardrop shaped. It didn't register at first that anything odd was happening. I was mesmerized watching the dance of the lights around the room. Then I stopped crying and was filled with an unexplainable peace and calmness. I truly believe what I saw was the dance of angels in the room rejoicing with Ben. "Do you see that?" I whispered to Cheryl, with no answer.

Sitting up, I could see her through the windows in the hallway outside the room. She was already busy making phone calls. I lay back next to Ben and watched the dancing lights for a long time. Then, suddenly they took a turn out the window to dance on the rooftops, and were gone. Was it my imagination? Was I seeing things? I dismissed the questions as I basked in the peacefulness I felt.

The iridescent lights appeared again several days later at the end of the cemetery service for Ben. We had just released a bouquet of balloons to float up to Heaven when I noticed the large display of swirling lights coming closer. They were beautiful as they danced through the air.

"Do you see that?" I said with excitement to my mother-in-law JoAnn next to me, as I pointed to the edge of the cemetery.

"What do you see?" she asked.

"Little lights everywhere! I think they're angels dancing with Ben!"

"Oh I see them too!" she said. We both stood mesmerized. "Look, a white feather!" She bent down to pick up the feather. "That's a sign from Heaven that an angel has been here." She carefully placed the feather in her purse.

Six months after Ben passed away, I made a spontaneous decision on a beautiful warm sunny day to visit a nearby horse stable. All three kids had plans with friends that afternoon so I knew the house would feel extra empty and lonely.

I found comfort walking through the stables and petting the velvet soft noses of horses as they greeted me over their stall doors. The sweet smell of alfalfa hay wafted through the air, and the sounds of horses whinnying brought back fun childhood memories of horse shows with my dad. I liked hearing the clomp clomp sounds of horse hooves as they were led down the concrete center walkways. It refreshed my spirit to be near these magnificent animals. For a little while I could escape the deep pain in my heart.

I found solace sitting on a straw bale next to a stall in the quiet barn. "Dear Lord, thank you for the wonderful peace you have given me with the gift of spending time at the horse stables. I miss being around horses. Is there any work I can do here at the stable?"

I had no more finished my prayer when a beautiful lady with long blond hair came walking around the corner. After brief introductions I learned she was the manager of the stables. "Know of anyone that would like help with their horses?" I asked hopefully.

"Funny you should ask. I just told my sister an hour ago that we need to find someone to exercise Freckles," she said.

"Freckles?"

"She is our old barn mare and really needs someone to ride her. Do you have experience riding?"

"Oh yes!" I said, jumping up off the straw bale. "I used to be a rodeo queen, and I barrel raced and showed horses for years!"

"Well then, you're welcome to ride Freckles any time you want."

"That would be great! I would love to ride her!" I exclaimed.

"Well let's go take a look at Freckles."

My heart jumped for joy when I saw the manager lead a white mare out of her stall. Freckles was beautiful, with a long flowing white mane. Tiny speckles of red dotted her sleek coat.

"Oh, I see why they call her Freckles," I said.

My last words spoken to Ben kept running through my mind: "When you get to Heaven find me a white horse."

"Shall we go saddle her up and you can take her for a ride now?"

"That would be great!" That was the beginning of my relationship with Freckles, my beautiful white horse, a gift from Ben.

On one of our rides a month later, with the warm July breeze on my face, Freckles and I headed to the middle of a meadow covered with yellow and white daisies and surrounded by green horse pastures with white rail fences. Snow-capped Mt. Hood looked majestic in the distance with clear blue skies as the perfect backdrop. The beauty was amazing. The saddle leather creaked as I shifted my weight to look around. "Come on girl, let's go."

Freckles stopped in her tracks, her gaze fixed on something ahead. Ears forward, nose lifted to the air to catch a scent. "What is it, girl?" I said, patting the side of her neck, my heart pounding in my chest. Suddenly hundreds of swirling iridescent lights resembling bubbles appeared in front of us. Mesmerized, I watched as a calm peacefulness settled over me. I felt arms wrap around me in a hug, but there was no one else there. Freckles sensed something too; she appeared to watch the lights move. "Angels," I whispered to Freckles. "We're watching the dance of angels."

The silvery pink lights danced around us for several minutes; neither of us moved a muscle. Then, just as quickly as they appeared, they were gone. Freckles took in a big sighing breath, and started walking again.

Freckles and I covered a lot of ground that summer, but I didn't see the dance of the angels again, although I felt their presence many times. I'm thankful for my summer with my beautiful white horse, and the dance of the angels, my special gifts from Ben.

"I saw Heaven standing open and there before me was a white horse, whose rider is called Faithful and True and the armies of Heaven were following him, riding on white horses and dressed in fine linen, white and clean."
~Revelation 19; 11, 14

~Patricia Ann Gallegos

A Touch Goodbye

No matter how hard death tries it can't separate people from love. It can't take away our memories either. In the end, life is stronger than death.
~*Author Unknown*

Some of my first memories are of trying to get my dad's attention. He was always busy; he spent long hours at work and I didn't see him much during the week. He often seemed distracted when he was home, perhaps because he was tired, but that didn't stop me from trying my best to get him to notice me.

He had a powerful sense of responsibility in caring for the family and living up to the expectations society placed on him. He left the home life to my mom, but his was the business world. "It's my job to support this family," he told me often. "It's Mom's job to take care of the kids."

In central Canada, where we grew up, the winters were snowy and cold but we still bundled up and went outside to play. One winter Dad flooded the back yard so my older sister and I could ice skate, and in the front yard, he cheered us on while we built a snow fort.

We didn't have a religious household, though we did go to the synagogue on occasion. When I wanted to explore other religions, my mom was horrified, but my dad encouraged me. "Go," he said. "Learn. Knowledge is a wonderful thing."

He was the one who patiently taught me how to tell time and ride a bike, although I wasn't too happy with him when I fell into the prickle bush. He picked me up and put me right back on the seat. "Now's not the time to stop," he said, so I kept practicing.

My teen years were a trial for us both. He often said, "I just don't understand why you're so irrational." And I'd respond from my overly emotional adolescence with, "And Mr. Spock, I don't understand why you think logic is the only thing that matters."

As the years passed, I began to see that there was a lot more going on under the surface than there appeared to be. He kept his emotions under tight rein, but they were definitely there. He spoke often in an intellectual way, using big words and abstract ideas, and when I was younger I couldn't understand him and would irritate him by saying, "Could you translate that into English, please?" In later years, I realized that was his way of hiding emotions.

Yet, the complications of our relationship were what bound us together. He grew up in the 1920s and 1930s, and was a definite product of his time and culture; yet he struggled to grow and change with the times, including what he continued to call "women's lib."

After my mother died in 1983, I went to Canada to stay with him for a while. We became closer, able to talk about a lot of things not previously discussed. He was at odds and ends without someone to take care of him, so I was actually happy when, exactly a year later, he married his longtime secretary.

For many years we stuck to weekly phone calls and my annual visits. He never told me he loved me until one day on the phone when I got brave enough to say it first. There was a split second's pause and then a surprised, "Oh, I love you too, dear." After that, he was often the first to say it.

When he got sick, I convinced myself he would be well again, even though he was eighty-seven. After all, he was my daddy, so nothing bad could ever happen to him, right?

He was ill for a while, from a spreading melanoma that wreaked all kinds of havoc with his body. I had managed to spend a few weeks with him when he was visiting California during the winter, and that had been wonderful.

On days when he was feeling stronger, I was able to talk with him on the phone. In spite of the many problems he and I had in the past, I was able to feel and express the overwhelming love I had for him.

During the spring and summer, he worsened. Because of the new passport regulations and the time involved, I was unable to visit him before he died.

"Please, Dad," I whispered to him across the miles each day. "Don't leave without saying goodbye to me."

I received daily updates from my stepmother and my brother and sister who spent some time with him. At first, he wouldn't let them see him lying in bed, but had to get up and sit in a chair to receive them.

Early one August morning, I awakened while it was still dark to something flitting past my cheek. At first, I thought it was a butterfly, but even in my sleepy state, I realized there were no butterflies in my bedroom. The touch had been gentle and soft, a slight caress almost. As I thought about this mysterious caress, I recalled something I hadn't thought of in years.

My dad had a sweet gesture he used only with me. He would reach over and touch the back of his hand to my cheek, lightly touching his index and middle fingers together to caress my cheek. That perfectly described the butterfly kiss that had awakened me. It was my dad speaking to me in some way, perhaps with a kiss goodbye.

Several hours later, still mystified by my early morning dream, I received an e-mail from my stepmother telling me my father had died early that morning.

At that moment, I knew my father had heard my fervent wishes across the miles and had stopped by to say goodbye before he left.

Since then, I have wondered about a love that transcends death, about how much my father loved me, and if he knew how much I loved him. I felt so lost without him.

Raising kids has made me realize what a good dad he really was. He wasn't perfect, but he always tried his best.

The other night I had a dream that we were together again. I got the chance to throw my arms around his neck and tell him how much I love him. "I hope you know that," I added. He said nothing, but I knew that he did. It was a peaceful feeling, to have the chance to say goodbye.

~Roberta Carly Redford

Twin Pop

A sister is God's way of proving He doesn't want us to walk alone.
~Author Unknown

My twin sister Sue and I loved the first days of spring. As children we looked forward to those warm afternoons when we could shed our coats at recess and look forward to playing outside when school was over.

We could not wait to leap off the school bus, grab a basketball, bike or tennis racket and head outside to play. Sometimes we played at the park. Other times we grabbed some of our allowance and walked to the 7-Eleven for a cola Slurpee.

With the days getting longer, we finished dinner and homework as quickly as possible, then ran outside to play kickball or hide and go seek. We tried to squeeze in as much playtime as possible before dark.

Our time together was precious. As twin sisters we had a special bond. We even had a special nickname for one another: Twin Pop!

As adults we continued to enjoy the beginning of spring. Sometimes Sue called me on the phone and happily exclaimed, "Hey Twin Pop, did you know it's going up to seventy degrees today? Let's meet for coffee."

"That sounds great!"

Quite often we picked up coffees and met at our local park just to sit on a bench, chat for a while and enjoy the beautiful weather while the kids were in school.

Other times we got our kids together. Sue and I would trail

behind them as they rode their Big Wheels and tricycles in one of our driveways. As they got older we watched while they took off down the street on their big bikes. We smiled at each other, remembering our own childhood and those first days of spring.

But on the first days of spring in 2003 everything suddenly changed. Sue called me one evening. "Hi Donna, do you want to get together for coffee in the morning?"

"Sure, I have a Bible study until ten. Let's meet afterwards."

The next morning my kids and I were leaving for the bus stop when the phone rang. My third grader Caroline answered it. By her voice and smile I knew who she was talking to. "It's Aunt Sue!" she said with joy, handing me the phone.

"Hi Donna, do you mind if I cancel coffee this morning? I have a headache. Can we get together tomorrow or later this week?" I assured her that was fine.

"I hope you feel better."

"Thanks! See ya later!"

Two hours later when I came home, I found many messages on my machine from loved ones urging me to call them immediately. I reached my friend Terry. She told me that Sue had dropped her son Billy off at school, gone to the local bank, and while she was waiting in the drive-through, had a stroke.

I was stunned and confused. What was she talking about? Sue was forty years old and in perfect health! How could she have a stroke?

I was in shock as my friend drove me to the hospital. When I saw Sue in the emergency room, it hit me hard. I could not process what had happened. It made no sense to me.

My energetic sister who I had just chatted with hours before was lying on a table hooked up to machines and not able to talk to me.

"Hi Sue," I spoke gently. "Don't worry. You are going to be okay." I babbled on about the plans our families had made to go to the shore that coming summer, "You'll be feeling great in time for our vacation!" I tried desperately to find the right words to give her hope.

A few agonizing hours later I learned Sue's stroke was massive.

Time would tell if she would have a future with us. Close friends and family began to arrive. We sat quietly in the waiting room, frozen in shock.

It had been a long day. Late into the evening there was still no improvement. I prayed for her healing. I prayed for my strength.

We headed home for the night.

The next morning, I received a phone call. Overnight Sue had slipped into a coma. We headed back to the hospital.

The lowest point of the morning was as I watched Sue's three young children, Stephanie, Kristen and Billy, turn to us and smile, their faces filled with hope, as they walked through the critical care doors with their dad to see their mom. I went in to be with them a few minutes later. As the children stood courageously around their mom, even in a coma, from Sue's eyes one single tear trickled down her cheek. I wiped it away.

A little after noon my husband Marc took me home to rest a bit. As I tried to drift into sleep, I knew. Sue had just passed.

Moments later Marc came into our bedroom. He gently spoke to me. "Hon, we should go back to the hospital now." Later I would learn he had received a phone call at the time I received my message that Sue had passed. Neither of us said a word in the car ride over. We both wanted to believe a little longer.

But as we arrived at the hospital ten minutes later and were getting into the elevator, Marc turned to me with a heartbroken look on his face.

"Hon," he started.

I stopped him and said, "I know."

I went in to see Sue for the last time. Her oldest, Stephanie, had been sitting by her side for hours just holding her hand. I came up behind Stephanie, leaned over and spoke softly in Sue's ear. I wanted to reassure her. I tried to be strong.

"Hey Sue," my voice was shaky. "You know I love you. Please don't worry about your kids. I love them so much and I will treat them as my own. I will always be there for them." I felt empty and alone as I was speaking to her. How would I live without my twin sister, my Twin Pop!

My heart broke for her family. I wrapped my arms around Stephanie and hugged her tight. Just then an amazingly warm hug filled with love wrapped around me and Stephanie. I recognized that warmth and love. It was a mother's love, a sister's love. It was a beautiful feeling of comfort and peace. Like the warmth of the sun on those first days of spring.

I turned my head but knew no one would be there, at least no one I could see. I believe it was a gift from God, a hug from Sue to remind us that a special bond never dies.

See ya later, Twin Pop.

~Donna Teti

Final Connection

When you are sorrowful look again in your heart, and you shall see that in truth you are weeping for that which has been your delight.
~Kahlil Gibran

've always been close to my mom. Not that we didn't fight; we fought like cats and dogs. But the fighting was part of our connection. My mother was very outspoken. She didn't care who you were—if she had something to say, she said it. I tend to be the same way, so the two of us butted heads quite a bit. However, we were also best friends, always in each other's corner. If I needed her, she was there. If she needed me, I was there. We supported one another; we loved one another. We shared many fights, but many more laughs. We laughed all the time, sometimes until our stomachs hurt and tears streamed down our faces.

About ten years ago I noticed the laughter slowly subsiding, and Mom seemed constantly preoccupied. Something felt wrong; she could not remember where she put anything and she seemed to be mad at me all the time. When she couldn't remember certain things, I figured we all have bad days. Maybe she was just having many bad days. But the problems were consistent, and what started off as every now and then became more frequent. Then the laughter seemed to stop. I asked my husband one night, "When was the last time you heard Mom laugh?" He said he couldn't remember. Slowly the connection between mother and daughter fell away. At times I felt like I was talking to a stranger, taking care of a stranger.

It was obvious to me that something was seriously wrong with my mom. Mom and I shared the same doctor. I phoned our doctor and relayed all of my fears and concerns about Mom. The doctor said she would talk to Mom the next time she was in, but that my fears and concerns were nothing to worry about. She said that she had seen Mom recently and felt she was fine. I kept telling her that Mom was not fine. My mother was the best actress around—she had everyone fooled. She learned little tricks, and manipulated everyone around her to the point that when I said something was wrong, people thought that I was being a negative daughter.

As time went on, I pleaded with my family and our doctor to do something. Finally my doctor saw that something was seriously wrong and we had Mom properly tested. Four years ago the medical community finally agreed with me that my mother had Alzheimer's. I wanted my mother to come live with me, but she accepted my brother's invitation instead. My brother lives across Canada in Niagara Falls. I couldn't understand why she would move all that way. To be honest, it hurt and was a blow to me. All I wanted to do was take care of my mom, as I hoped one of my sons would do for me.

My brother wanted to do the same thing. I voiced my concern about sending our sick mother across the country, but he insisted that he wanted to do this. So I stepped aside. I packed all of her things, shipped what she needed across the country, and put her apartment up for sale. I drove her to the airport and put her on a plane with a one-way ticket to Ontario. It was one of the worst days of my life. My husband couldn't be there that day, so I had my two boys with me. They were seven and five years old.

As I watched Mom walking with an attendant to the plane, she turned to me to wave goodbye and tears were streaming down her face. It took everything I had not to run up to her, grab her and tell her that she was coming home with me. I turned to my seven-year-old with tears streaming down my face and said, "I think I've made a mistake."

"Mom, Granny won't remember who we are next year," he said.

"It's time to let her go and be with the other part of her family, and you haven't made a mistake."

That stopped me in my tracks. My mother had two sons, one daughter and six grandchildren back East. My son was right, it was time for her to go home.

Due to work and everyday life, it was a full year before I saw my mother again. My son was right. We got off the plane in Toronto and drove straight to Niagara Falls to be with Mom. She walked into the room and I could see it in her eyes—she had no idea who I was, who my children were or who my husband was. The actress part came out of her again. She did her best to please everyone and pretend she knew who we were, but everyone in that room knew that Mom had no bloody clue who we were.

It was a weird two weeks, no connection to Mom at all. I tried, we all tried. We saw her every moment we could and it was like I was sitting with the woman down the street, a woman I hardly knew. The day we left Niagara Falls, I drove by myself to the home where my mother was living. It was just the two of us. I had left the children and my husband at my brother's house. I wanted the time alone. Three hours, and my mother and I hardly said a word to each other. We sat outside in the garden just being together, the connection still lost. On the flight home I tried to remember the mother I once had, the laughter, the arguments, all the connections we had. But I couldn't get the Alzheimer's Mom out of my head, the woman who didn't know her daughters, her sons, her grandchildren.

This past Christmas, my brother phoned to tell me our mother had taken a bad fall. She broke her ribs and one of the broken ribs punctured her lung. We didn't think she would make it, but sure enough she survived and the doctors thought she might get out of the hospital. One night my mother asked about me, my children and my husband. My brother called to tell me that she asked for us all by name. He said for the first time in a long time he felt like he was talking to Mom. My heart went cold because I knew that this was God's gift—the clarity, the recognition—because Mom hadn't remembered who I was for two years. My brother was so happy. I told him I was thrilled that she had some clarity; however I didn't think it was a good sign.

The very next day Mom fell into a coma, and no one knew why. The next forty-eight hours were a strange time, because I lived across the country and was not sure what to do. No one knew how long she would be in a coma. I was torn. Should I fly back east now or wait? That night I felt the connection of Mom come back. Mom came to me in my dreams as my mother, not the woman I hardly knew but my mother. I could almost smell her. She told me I needed to stay where I was. I woke up with peace in my heart and I told my husband I would wait to see what happened.

Twenty-four hours later, my husband and I took our children to a movie. On the way home afterward, I fell asleep. I'm not sure how to explain it, but it was as if this energy moved through me. The feeling was so abrupt that I woke up immediately. I said to my husband, "Mom is gone!" The connection was there and then it was gone.

When we got into the house I went to the phone expecting to see a message on the answering machine. There was no message, but I knew in my heart that Mom had moved on. Ten minutes later the phone rang, and it was my sister-in-law. She said Mom had passed away. I asked her at what time, and she told me what I already knew—about a half hour earlier, the precise time I felt the energy move through me. Mom had managed to reconnect with me after all.

~Johanne Fraser

Life on Soldier Creek

The past is behind us, love is in front and all around us.
~Terri Guillemets

Babies raising babies described us best. As newlywed teenagers, Jason and I had struggled for two years to raise our son, Aaron, when we got an offer we really couldn't refuse. Jason's father's boss was looking for a family to move into his mother's farmhouse. He asked for a small rent payment in exchange for taking care of Mrs. Lineberry's property while she resided in the long-term care unit of our local hospital.

"She had her roses and he had his hummingbirds," Jody's boss had said, remembering his now deceased father and ailing mother. To us, taking care of the things they loved seemed like a small price to pay.

On moving day, I saw the beautiful white house on the inside for the first time. I had been forewarned that it would remain slightly furnished and I was pleased to see a few antique pieces left behind. What I hadn't known was that there was one room inaccessible to us, packed with furniture and locked from the inside. Even from the outside, a thick curtain hung down over the window.

For the first few months, Jason worked nights. I felt like a frightened little girl, having never spent the night alone. "I'm a mother now," I told myself. When I turned off the television and lights at bedtime, I told myself that anybody would be a little suspicious in a house with a secret room.

It wasn't long before I felt at home and safe. The longer we were there, the more I imagined the couple who had lived there their whole life and had raised their children in the old house. Many times, while snipping the rose stems, I wondered about them, him sitting on the front porch watching his hummingbirds while she tended her roses. I wondered what it was like on the other side and if he was waiting for her. Would we be happy growing roses and feeding hummingbirds? Even though I had yet to see a single one, I would buy a hummingbird feeder.

That fall, I started going to Murray State and working two nights a week. Driving home from work at one o'clock in the morning, winding down our narrow curvy road was definitely out of my comfort zone. Fog often blanketed the road, sinking into the many dips and crevices. One night, the fog looked like dead bodies lying in the road. "I've got to get more rest," I said. I mentioned this to my mother, expecting she would just laugh and think I was crazy. Her reaction was something I never expected. "Do you know the story of Soldier Creek? It's only a few minutes from your house."

I did some searching. In 1945, a warplane carrying four officers and five soldiers had flown into a terrible storm. The plane crashed after it was struck by lightning, killing nine of the passengers. Only one man managed to activate his parachute and fall 8,000 feet to safety. He spent the night out in the fierce storm until neighbors took him in. Hundreds of onlookers came to the site, some out of curiosity, some to take a piece of the wreckage as a souvenir, and some to fan the flies away from the bodies.

Afterwards, I no longer felt quite so silly. Were Mr. and Mrs. Lineberry living in our old house at the time? Could they have been the couple who helped the survivor?

Little did I know there would be more strange occurrences taking place near Soldier Creek. One night, Aaron and I were home alone, sleeping soundly, while Jason was at work. A lightning storm woke me up. I lay there for a few minutes trying to fall back to sleep when I heard somebody walking through the kitchen. At first, I was scared. But as I heard the footsteps pace the kitchen, open cabinets, rattle pots and pans, and pull out the kitchen chairs, I was convinced it was Jason, although he wasn't due home for hours.

My husband had had trouble keeping jobs, having hit the responsibility of the world a little too quickly once I had accidentally become pregnant with the baby. But so far, he had proven successful in keeping his job as a security guard, working nights from ten till six. Now, I was suspicious. Maybe he had been fired again. I waited for him to come and tell me. After several minutes, I called out for him. "Jason!" But there was no reply. I got up and walked into the kitchen. The light was on, but no one was there. I picked up the phone and started to dial 911 when something told me to call Jason's work number instead. When he picked up the phone, I whispered desperately, "Somebody's in the house!" As soon as I said that a sucking sensation went through the room and the screen door behind the back door slammed hard. Aaron woke up and came running down the hallway screaming and crying.

"What was that?" Jason asked.

"I think somebody left out the back door."

"Take a quick look around and see. If you don't come back in two minutes, I'll call 911 on my red phone."

That sounded like a great idea, but when I tried to lay down the phone, I realized I was frozen. No matter how hard I tried, my right hand would not let go of the phone and my right arm would not pull away from my ear.

"Jason, I can't move," I replied.

"This couldn't be about Mrs. Lineberry, could it?"

"What do you mean?"

"She died this evening. I was waiting for the right time to tell you."

All fear vanished. "That's it!" I said with joy flooding my heart. "Let me go check the house real quick!"

"Okay, I'll be right here," Jason assured me.

With the house all clear, I came back to the phone. "There's no reason to call the police."

"Well, okay. But, if you hear one more thing, call 911."

I promised him that I would. I put Aaron in my bed with me and he immediately fell asleep. I longed for daylight, so I walked into the living room, raised the shades and sat by the window waiting for sunrise. Had I really experienced Mrs. Lineberry's ghost?

Then, a single hummingbird came and hovered in front of me at eye level. I watched as it dipped down and hovered over a rose as if it were kissing it. I knew beyond a doubt that it was a sign!

I couldn't wait to call my stepmother who worked at the hospital where Mrs. Lineberry had been.

"Gail, tell Mrs. Lineberry's nurses that she's okay."

"Really?" she asked. I could tell from her tone that she knew she had passed away.

"Yes, she came home last night," I said, without any fear of embarrassment.

She promised to pass the word along.

I went and cuddled up to my sleeping little boy and slept more soundly than ever since moving in the house. Peace had come to Soldier Creek.

~Melisa Kraft

Everett's Play Date

Grandfathers are just antique little boys.
~Author Unknown

One of my father-in-law's greatest joys was spending time with his infant great-grandson Everett whenever we could make a trip to California or have them visit us in Virginia. In his eighties, Dad spent countless hours singing to the little guy pressed gently against his chest or reading him great adventure stories.

Sadly, Dad was diagnosed with terminal cancer with only a few months to live. He spent his final days at home with his wife Flora where we kept him as comfortable as possible. Still, he missed his buddy Everett more than anything, looking forward to the nightly calls from California with updates on Everett's growth and development.

"He's smiling a lot more now, Grandpa. You'd get a kick out of the fact that he actually seems to recognize the songs you introduced him to," our daughter shared over the phone one evening.

Too weak to even hold the cell phone now, Dad nodded in reply as I held the phone to his ear.

My husband and I took turns spending the night at our in-laws' apartment. I slept between the two bedrooms where I could hear either adult in case they needed anything.

Around three o'clock on a cold February morning, the angels arrived, taking Dad home to heaven at last.

We telephoned family members the following morning, including our oldest daughter Autumn and family in California.

"Grandpa passed away," I heard a choked voice from somewhere inside say.

"I know," our daughter Autumn replied. "It was around three in the morning, right?"

"But I don't understand! How could you possibly know that?" I asked.

"At 3 a.m. I was awakened by your grandson giggling in his crib. I crept into his room, finding him smiling across the room at the chair in the corner where he and Grandpa used to share their play dates together. Prisms danced across the ceiling and around the room before disappearing. Everett was having a final play date with Grandpa, there's no doubt in my mind."

None in mine either…

Thanks for the memories, Dad. Everett won't ever forget you… and neither will we.

~Mary Z. Whitney

Miraculous
Messages from Heaven

Love that Doesn't Die

Conversations
with Dad

There's a bit of magic in everything, and some loss to even things out.
~Lou Reed, "Magic and Loss"

When I was two and a half years old my dad died in a car accident. I don't remember very much from that time, but the things I do remember are really vivid to me. Now I am thirteen years old, and my mom and I talk about my dad a lot. She helps me keep my memories alive.

Since I was so young when it happened, I really didn't understand the concept of death. I did not understand that my dad wasn't coming back, or that he was in heaven. I think I just thought he was on a business trip.

One day, about a week after my dad died, I was taking a bath in my mom's bathtub, and she heard me having a conversation with someone while she was picking up the clothes I had thrown on the floor. She was curious and asked who I was speaking to. I told her I was talking to my dad. Being that I wasn't even three, my mom figured that it was my way of dealing with the situation, so she asked me, "What did you talk about?" I told her that my dad came to see me and told me that he had been to visit his friend Kirk, who was his boss and also our neighbor about a mile down the road. He said that he had asked Kirk to come take me horseback riding. My mom gave me a hug and kiss while she dried me off and got me ready for bed.

As the days went by, there were people coming in and out of our home constantly. I remember getting lots and lots of presents and meeting all kinds of family members and friends of my dad's that I didn't know. They were all really nice to me, and our house was full of people all the time, for weeks. One afternoon, a few weeks after he died, on a beautiful sunny winter day, the crowd had thinned out a bit, and things were unusually quiet. There was a knock on the door and my mom answered it. I heard her speaking to someone, and then she called for me to come to the door.

There, in front of our house, was my dad's friend Kirk, who I had only met once or twice and looked vaguely familiar. He stood in our driveway, holding the reins of a tall, beautiful, dark brown horse. Kirk shook my hand and reminded me who he was. He told me that he had been my dad's boss and that my dad talked about me all the time. He asked if I wanted to go for a ride. My mom stood by, watching as I jumped up and down with excitement. It would be my first ever horseback riding adventure. She thanked Kirk for his kindness in coming over and told him how much she appreciated the gesture.

I remember hearing Kirk say, "Joelle, it was the weirdest thing—I was outside, standing in my front yard, and I swear I heard Eric's voice, asking me to stop by and take Jackson horseback riding." I stopped petting the horse and ran over. I said, "See Mom, I told you Daddy said he asked Kirk to come take me horseback riding, and here he is!"

From that day on, I knew my dad was around me and I knew that he was watching out for me. As I grew up, I stopped hearing my dad talk to me the way I did when I was little. But just knowing that it happened changed me. It makes me believe in angels and that the people we love are never really gone. I guess, as we get older, our lives get so busy and noisy that we can't hear them, but I know my dad is there.

~Jackson Jarvis

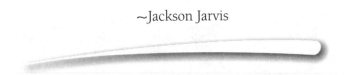

With Us Always

If you have a dog, you will most likely outlive it; to get a dog is to open yourself to profound joy and, prospectively, to equally profound sadness.
~Marjorie Garber

Our dog Johnathon was special. I purchased him for my husband as a Christmas gift, and we made the long trek over the snowy mountains to pick him up in Eastern Washington. A beautiful dark gray color, his eyes shone bright blue in the light, and his fur felt like velvet.

My husband decided to name him Johnathon since he had always liked that name. We called him Johnny for short. He was smart and learned tricks quickly. He always had a smile on his face and was infatuated with his tennis balls. He played with them for hours. When tired, he would hide his tennis balls under the couch so our other dog, Jasmyn, would not take them.

Water was Johnny's vice, and he would swim for hours, or open his mouth wide to be doused when we ran the hose. He was the king of making funny faces, and he loved nothing more than being fawned over and loved. He would even "dance" by chasing his tail when we played music. He especially loved the song by the Charlie Daniels Band, "The Devil Went Down to Georgia," because they sang his name in it.

One day, when he was about nineteen months old, he began having terrible seizures. Some would last five minutes; some would last more than forty-five minutes. It was terrifying to watch him have those episodes. We took him to see the veterinarian and they put him on an anti-seizure medication. This medication did not stop the seizures, so we took him to a veterinarian neurologist who diagnosed him with idiopathic epilepsy. They recommended that we start him on a custom compounded medication that we had to pick up from a special pharmacy. This combination of medications did nothing to help Johnny. They made him nauseous and he was unable to keep anything down, or in for that matter. He lost interest in his tennis balls and forgot his tricks. The doctors recommended that we restrict his activity, as they thought possibly too much stimulation was adding to his issue.

After being on the medications for close to three months, he still was having seizures, and even started to have more frequent tremors. We were unable to stop them, even with injectable anti-seizure medication. The specialist told us that Johnny most likely had a brain tumor, and he wanted to do a CT scan of his brain to make sure. Johnny was suffering and wasting away in front of our eyes, and it was unbearable. We made the heart-wrenching decision to euthanize him. We chose to do it on the Fourth of July because we felt that every year his life would be celebrated by the fireworks.

That morning, as we drove him to the veterinarian, he relished the wind on his handsome face. While spending our last moments with him, he kissed away our tears. It seemed like he was telling us not to be worried, that he would still be here for us. He loved us, and forgave us.

We were distraught for the next few weeks and our house seemed devoid of happiness. It seemed so unfair that Johnny had gotten sick so young and, worse, we had not been able to cure him. My husband was inconsolable.

One lonely evening, after sharing our favorite memories of Johnny once again, we headed upstairs to bed. Our other dog Jasmyn refused to climb the stairs behind us. As Christians, we believe wholeheartedly in life after death, so we asked aloud if Johnny was home. Suddenly, the phone rang! I looked at the caller ID, and it said it was my husband's cell phone calling. Confused, he pulled his phone out of his pocket and the screen showed that it was not actually calling. We let the call go to the answering machine. After our recorded greeting, four barks sounded from the speaker. The call hung up then, and it didn't save the message or the caller ID. Slow smiles crept across our faces as we realized Johnny had come back to let us know he was still around.

That night my husband had a dream that he visited Johnny in a large field with a pond, where Johnny was running around with other dogs, a huge smile on his face. We strongly feel that he is at the Rainbow Bridge waiting for us to join him. And because he was my husband's special friend, he was the privileged one to view him in that setting. Johnny now seems to come visit us when we miss him or need him the most. When my husband's knee was bothering him, he prayed to God to take away his pain. He woke up in the middle of that same night to find the bedroom bathed in bright light, and Johnny lying on that specific knee, licking it. He has never had discomfort in that knee again.

Though Johnny is no longer with us physically, we are grateful that he still visits us from time to time.

~Megan LeeAnn Waterman-Fouch

Turn the Page

Dad, your guiding hand on my shoulder will remain with me forever.
~Author Unknown

My father died young. He was only forty-two years old that November afternoon when his coworkers found him slumped over his desk. I was sixteen.

The memory is very clear. Mom and I were in the kitchen making spaghetti for supper. Italian sausage had been browned nicely and was simmering in a tomato sauce seasoned with basil, oregano, parsley, onions, and lots of garlic. I can still remember the garlic smell on my fingers as I lifted the phone receiver to my ear.

A deep male voice on the other end asked to speak to Arlene, my mother. I didn't recognize the voice, but I could hear the barely controlled panic and my stomach tightened into a knot of fear. That year had been full of unpleasant surprises for our family.

In May, Dad had been in California working and had been hospitalized with severe congestive heart failure. Doctors had not expected him to live, so Mom had flown from New Jersey to California to be with him. My two brothers, my sister, and I were left home with our aunt to oversee the household for a few weeks.

During Mom's absence our dog developed a fractured vertebra, which caused him severe pain and partial paralysis. The vet said there was nothing to be done, so we had him put down.

Mom was in California for over two weeks. The day she returned with Dad, all of us were speechless as they got out of the car. Dad had lost about forty pounds and was gray. He couldn't walk even a few steps without being out of breath and sweating profusely. The biggest surprise though was that Mom couldn't walk or raise her right arm.

Mom went into the hospital the next day. Ten days later the doctors gave us the diagnosis of multiple sclerosis. No one could tell us if she would regain the use of her right side. Our lives were changed forever. Four teenaged children were now responsible for the care of their two parents.

Dad stayed in New Jersey for a month to regain his strength and rest. He would have open-heart surgery at the end of November, but in the beginning of July he went back to California to resume working. We made plans for the rest of us to move to California as soon as possible. We had six weeks to get the entire household packed, and make arrangements for the moving company and our own journey across the country.

Since Mom wasn't in any condition to do much packing, it was left to us kids. We held a couple of garage sales to get rid of things we no longer needed. We sold one of the cars because there was no way for us to get two cars from New Jersey to California when the only person with a driver's license was Mom and she was in no condition to drive. We made arrangements to have a family friend drive us across the country in the remaining vehicle. Moving day arrived quickly and we set out on our journey.

On arrival in California we felt like visitors in a foreign land. Before school started in early September, the four of us kids had the house unpacked and things pretty well organized. Being a loner and a moody teenager, I took solace in my music. I played four instruments, but spent hours after school at the piano. When Dad came home in the evening he would listen to me play and ask me to play one piece for him over and over. This had been a pattern for years. I resented it. I didn't really like my dad. We seemed to constantly butt heads, and I was full of teenage angst and resentment toward him. I loved playing the piano, but I wanted to play the songs I chose, not be asked to play one song repeatedly for his pleasure.

On the afternoon he died I had practiced all of my favorite songs but I hadn't played his song, thinking I would have to play it for him at least four or five times when he got home. After my time at the piano I had gone in the kitchen to handle dinner preparations and that's why my hand smelled like garlic as I picked up the phone. Normally I would have let Mom answer it, but we had a wall phone in the kitchen and Mom couldn't get to it from her place at the table. So I answered.

With my stomach in knots, I could hear the words that my father was dead as the panicked man spoke to Mom. The next few days and weeks were a blur. There isn't much I remember, but I do remember feeling very compelled to play my dad's favorite song at his funeral.

The day of the funeral arrived. Even though I had the song memorized from playing it so many times over the years, I carried the sheet music into the chapel with me in case I got nervous or couldn't remember the notes. I can't tell you how the program unfolded or what was said. I remember that I became calm when a ray of sunshine came through the stained glass windows of the church, illuminating the piano and bench as I sat down.

I opened the sheet music to the page and started to play. It had been years since I had needed sheet music to play the song but I thought I would be nervous and might need to refer to it. Back when I had needed it, there were two places where I always had to stop and struggle to turn the page. The music was in a book so I couldn't just lay the sheets out flat and avoid a page turn. That day of my dad's funeral I sobbed uncontrollably as I played. I cried for all of the miscommunication between us over the years and how I had been so rebellious at times.

I played from memory through the tears, but was astonished when I reached the place in the music where a page turn would be necessary. I felt a hand on my shoulder and saw the pages of music turn without me lifting a hand. There was no visible person sitting next to me, but I could feel a presence and I could feel the weight of that hand on my shoulder as I saw those pages turn. As I finished the piece and reached to close the music, the tears were still streaming down my face. My hand was clasped tightly and I heard the voice of my father in my ear say, "Thank you. I love you. Goodbye."

I've played that piece thousands of times since his death thirty-eight years ago, but I have never again heard his voice or witnessed the pages turning on their own. On the other hand, I never play that piece without remembering his voice, his touch or his final words from the other side.

~Laura D. Hollingshead

A Voice from the River

You can't test courage cautiously.
~Annie Dillard

t was a chilly June day in the Austrian Alps as the Inn River rushed over rocks and boulders. I shuffled toward the bobbing raft. Fear of drowning had kept me away from deep water since I was a child. Now clad in a wetsuit and about to run dangerous Class IV rapids, I was terrified and had a stomachache.

Why was I forcing myself to maneuver around swirling holes and over high waves during spring runoff? My nine-year-old son Brian had drowned in a surge of high water on this river over three decades earlier. To say I was devastated doesn't come close to describing the pain. But in the days and months after the tragedy, I'd had to be a pillar of strength and comfort to my daughter, husband and friends, pushing aside my own need to mourn. Now I'd come back to Austria to finish grieving and find peace.

In the first years following the accident, I recalled with ease blond-haired Brian's special qualities. Wearing his trademark blue shirt and tan pants, he taught our cat Sunny to turn somersaults. While I cooked dinner, he'd whirl his fingers across the piano keys, blue eyes sparkling. If dinner was burned, his hand would touch mine and he'd smile. "It's okay, Mom."

My memories faded, but my longing for Brian grew. I finally realized I had to go back to Austria and I worked up the courage to embrace the biggest challenge of my life: go to the Inn River and find

Brian. I believed he'd be there and I'd be able to say goodbye and find closure.

Being in the Austrian Alps again almost felt like home. In Landeck, where I stayed, friends old and new buoyed my spirits. I immediately went to see Alois, the car mechanic whose shop still sits next to the accident site. He has become a dear friend and when we looked into each other's eyes, no words were necessary.

For several days, I walked the river paths, hoping to sense Brian's presence. Climbing down the bank, I put my feet in the rushing water. I called, "Brian?" Scanning the mountains, I listened for his voice. No response.

For three nights, I dreamed about being in that water and woke up yelling, "Help, I'm drowning!" The dreams stopped, but questions haunted me. Would I have to physically battle the raging river in order to find Brian? I couldn't even picture myself in a raft, having to paddle around rocks and crash through waves. What if the boat flipped and I was trapped under it? As a non-swimmer, that possibility horrified me. I trembled constantly, hardly eating or sleeping.

Those questions took me back to that tragic day on the river. My two children had gone to sit on dry rocks along the shore near Landeck. The river was a mere creek. With no warning, the dam miles above released millions of gallons of water. Brian was swept off the rock and away.

Still panicked after the dreams, I put off inquiring about available raft trips. But I was there to find Brian. The qualifications for rafting were: "capable swimmer, no fear of water, and experience paddling." I met zero of the three. My yearning to reconnect with my son won out and I booked a trip and signed the waiver.

The evening before, I walked the hills. I told myself I'd be okay. But would I find Brian? If so, how would he appear? Would he be the same nine-year-old wearing his blue shirt and tan pants?

At the boathouse the next morning, ten of us listened to the rafting guide repeat safety procedures. Then he handed out paddles. "This will be a fun trip, but the Inn River is serious white water. We've got to miss rocks and holes, and catch the current. The third rapid is huge and the most dangerous." I swallowed hard, but something kept me from giving up on the trip.

The water hurried by at the put-in site. I lunged for the raft three times before flopping into it. Huddled in the front, I gripped the safety rope, white knuckles and all. As the other rafters paddled to the middle of the channel, I clutched my oar and whispered, "Don't drown."

Our guide sat tall at the back. "Everyone, listen up. The first rapid is just beyond the bridge. There's a large rock on the left and big waves at the end. First we'll point right and paddle forward. Before the big waves, we'll paddle forward again and power through. Everybody, get ready."

Did I really have to paddle through big waves? Where was Brian?

"Paddle hard forward," the guide said to my side of the boat. I paddled until we got close to the rock. The boat bucked up and down. I screamed and slumped to the floor. Burying my head, I sobbed, "Take me back!"

A warm hand gripped my shoulder. Thinking it was a raft mate or the guide, I glanced back. Everyone was paddling. In front of me stood nine-year-old Brian in his favorite blue shirt and tan pants, cradling our beloved cat Sunny. I placed my hand on my heart and whispered, "Brian!"

His blue eyes sparkled. "It's okay, Mom, I'm here." He touched my face. "You can raft this river and do everything you decide to. I'll always be with you." His image faded.

Yes, I could raft this river. Having my precious son with me gave purpose to this journey. I paddled hard, then shrieked as we blasted through the powerful waves. Whoosh! Cold water splashed my tears away.

On peaceful water again, I whispered, "I couldn't save you last time, Brian, but we've found each other in a different way."

My raft mates and I punched through the second rapid with lightning speed, hammering the water below. Wow. I smiled to Brian.

"This third rapid needs your best skills," our guide said. "It has a very large, deep hole. If we get sucked into it, we could easily flip." My raft mates and I stroked as if our lives depended on it—they did. We missed the hole. At the bottom of the rapid, waves curled above my head, then crashed down, nearly knocking me over. But now I was having a great time. I cheered, "More, more!" By the time we returned to shore, a warm feeling of peace had settled over me.

Two days after the trip I left for home, continuing to bask in the experience. I'll always miss my son terribly, but that same peace gives me strength and comfort.

Brian has never appeared again in person or talked directly to me, but I talk to him. I tell him how much I enjoy his designer spaceship models and his lively drawings of Sunny the cat.

Most of all, I treasure his words. "You can do everything you decide to."

~Janice Jensen

25

The Strength of a Door

Be thou the rainbow in the storms of life. The evening beam that smiles the
clouds away, and tints tomorrow with prophetic ray.
~Lord Byron

D ad pounded hard enough on my hollow core front door to put his fist through it. "You're not staying here," he announced. "It's not safe."

Crossing my arms across my chest, I plopped down in the middle of the living room floor. This had been my home before I was married but during the last ten years renters had occupied and trashed it. Now that I was getting divorced, regardless of condition, I was moving back in. "This is my home, Dad. I'm not leaving."

Knowing I had inherited my stubborn streak from him, Dad gave me that special look that said even though he didn't agree with what I'd said, he respected my right to make my own decision. "Okay, sweetheart, but at least let me order a new door to replace the one I just destroyed."

No matter how upset my father got with me, whenever he called me "sweetheart" I knew everything was going to be all right. When I flunked a test in school, he'd reprimand me with, "You've got to try harder, sweetheart." When I got my driver's license and immediately smashed the car into a tree, his first question was, "Are you okay, sweetheart?" When I told him that my marriage was dissolving in divorce, he consoled me by saying, "You'll get through this, sweetheart."

My dad was not a demonstrative person. He didn't engage in public displays of affection, he seldom offered hugs and he never awarded sloppy kisses to those he loved. Instead, he showed his love by his actions and sometimes, as with me, one word. That was all I needed.

The new door turned out to be solid oak with a leaded, beveled glass window and a large polished bronze deadbolt. Even though I considered the deadbolt overkill, I never made a fuss about it because I knew it was just another of the many ways my dad expressed his love for me.

Since the door faced west, it only received sunlight late in the afternoon, but when the last sunbeams of the day penetrated the beveled glass window, my living room filled with an array of beautiful colors ranging all the way from violet to orange. It was like having my own private rainbow.

Sometimes, especially when I'd had a particularly bad day, I sat in the middle of the living room and let the colored beams of light wash over my body. They warmed my soul and always made me feel as if my father was in the room with me, saying, "It's okay, sweetheart, everything will be all right."

About a year after the door was installed, my dad was diagnosed with terminal lung cancer. Like so many others in similar circumstances, Dad went through chemo and radiation therapy. Nothing helped. Within three months, he was gone.

I had accepted the responsibility of delivering a eulogy at Dad's funeral. Although I felt as if my heart had been torn out, I followed my father's example and held back my emotions. Standing in front of the group gathered in the church, I held my head high and told them about the man who had been in my life every day since I was born. I compared him to Solomon, King of Israel, saying, "He was just and wise and although he made his share of mistakes, he loved God and repented of his ways. In the Song of Solomon, we read, 'Place me like a seal over your heart, like a seal on your arm; for love is as strong as death, its jealousy unyielding as the grave. It burns like blazing fire, like a mighty flame.' My father's love was stronger than death and it will forever burn within my heart."

As we accompanied my father's casket to the cemetery, storm clouds filled the sky and hid the sun, perfectly reflecting my mood and those of the people around me. Tears mixed with rain as my aunts, uncles, cousins and friends said their goodbyes. Gone was their brother, their uncle, their friend… the man who could make everything all right with just one word.

Throughout the luncheon that followed Dad's funeral, I accepted condolences, exchanged humorous stories and tried to smile, but my heart wasn't in it. Surrounded by well-intentioned people, I felt alone; I felt orphaned. I didn't want garden salad; I didn't want roasted chicken; I didn't want strawberry cheesecake. All I wanted to do was go home, crawl into my bed and pull the covers over my head. I wanted my father to call me sweetheart.

Sensing my distress, one of my cousins volunteered to drive me home. Pulling into my driveway, he asked if I wanted him to come in for a while.

"No," I replied. "I'll be fine. But thanks for asking."

"Okay," he said, "but remember. I'm only a phone call away."

It was still raining as I dashed into the house. The phone was ringing but I ignored it. The only person I wanted to talk to was gone and I'd never be able to talk to him again. Kicking off my shoes, I thought about heading for the bedroom. Instead, I plopped down in the middle of the living room, hung my head and sobbed.

I'm not sure how long I sat there—it could have been minutes; it could have been hours. When I finally felt cried out, I raised my head and saw that vibrant colors danced across the room. It was my rainbow. But how could that be? It was still raining and the sun was hidden by clouds. When I turned my attention to the front door, I realized the colors were not coming through the beveled glass window. But if the beautiful oranges, yellows, blues and reds filling the room were not coming from the door, where were they coming from?

I wiped my tears and smiled, knowing the answer. God had sent me a rainbow for the same reason He sent one to Noah—to tell him that he, and all of us, are loved and that He will always be with us.

The colors of my rainbow were the flames of my father's love and I knew that whenever I needed him, he would be there, calling me sweetheart and telling me everything would be all right.

It was his message from Heaven.

~Margaret Nava

26

Miracle on Clark Street

Sometimes being a brother is even better than being a superhero.
~Marc Brown

Explaining death to a young child is never easy. When my brother suffered a massive coronary while riding the Metro to work and died suddenly, I struggled with what to say to my young son about his Uncle Bobby. Spencer thought the sun rose and set around superheroes like Spider-Man till the day Uncle Bobby hoisted him up on his shoulders in one swoop and carried him through the streets of Washington, D.C., high above the crowd. That day, Uncle Bobby, not Spider-Man, was the strongest man in the universe. When I explained that Uncle Bobby's heart just stopped working, Spencer thought for a moment and then sighed, "Gee, I wish we could have gotten him a heart like Ironman's."

"Me too," I sighed, as I fought back tears and hugged Spencer. I kept the message in as simple terms as possible, and after our talk, Spencer said, "So Uncle Bobby is in Heaven?"

"Yes, and he'll still watch over all of us and take care of us just like always."

"Okay," Spencer said happily with a reassured smile as he hopped off the couch and went about his eight-year-old day.

At that moment I wished my own heart could have been as easily comforted. But I knew that my only brother was gone forever, and there were things I would never be able to tell him. Like how I measured every boy I dated against Bobby's character, or how, when he taught me to ride a bike, he also taught me how to pick myself up after I fell. I would never again hear his voice on my birthday when he would call me and, for that brief moment, make me feel like he had nothing more important to do than talk with his baby sister. How would he ever know now how much I loved and adored him? No, my sadness was not as quickly comforted with the simple knowledge that my brother was in Heaven.

A few weeks later we were in church, kneeling in silent prayer before mass, when Spencer started giggling. When I looked his way to give him the standard mom, stern "time-to-be-quiet-and-stop-playing-with-your-brother-look," I noticed he was staring up at a corner of the church. "What are you looking at?" I whispered.

"Uncle Bobby," he whispered back matter-of-factly, his gaze never leaving the spot. "He says to tell you 'Hi.'"

To say I was surprised or shocked by his response would not be true. Spencer has always been a "special" boy, and truthfully, this is not the first dead person with whom he's conversed. When he was three years old, he proudly announced at my niece's wedding that "Ra Ra" (a beloved family friend who had passed away a few months before), was standing next to the bride.

So on this day, I simply whispered back, "Tell Uncle Bobby Mom says 'Hi' and that we miss and love him."

"He said he knows that, Mom. He said to tell you he loves all of younz and it's pretty warm here."

The "pretty warm" comment was one thing, but the "younz" gave me the real pause. That's a Western Pennsylvania term that my family uses for "you all," but I quit using upon moving to Wisconsin fifteen years earlier.

"Oh," Spencer quickly added, "I mean it's pretty AND warm here."

I immediately smiled and shook my head. "Thanks for clarifying your location, Bob," I said to myself.

Spencer continued to giggle, and when I asked why he was

laughing, he whispered, "Mom, it's Uncle Bobby. You know he always makes me laugh."

I could not argue with that. Bobby's laughter was infectious. His trademark smirk was so permanently fixed on his face that even the funeral director could not make him look sad. This little exchange in church brought me back to my own youth and the many stern looks I got from my mom as a result of my brother's sense of humor, which was apparently still contagious, even in death.

"Did Uncle Bobby like comic books?" Spencer asked me one day as we drove to his favorite place in the world, Galaxy Comics on Clark Street.

"Yep! He liked Archie Comics and Mad Libs when he was a kid, and we watched the old *Batman* series on television every week."

"Cool," Spencer said, feeling his bond to his Uncle Bobby was still intact.

On December 26, 2012 the last book in the Spiderman comic book series (#700) was released. Galaxy is a block from my office, and I intended to go during my lunch hour to pick it up for Spencer, but work got in the way. It was after five when I finally arrived at the store. I looked on the shelf, but did not see anything with the number 700 on it. It was then that I learned from the laughing store clerk that they sold out within thirty minutes of opening the store. He told me to tell Spencer not to be too disappointed, as the new "Superior" series would be starting soon. I went back to the shelf intending to find something else to hold him over till then, when something with #700 on it caught my eye. I picked it up and asked the clerk, "Is this the one he wanted?"

Stunned, the clerk replied, "That's impossible! I know I sold the last one early this morning. I've been telling people all day we sold out. I have no idea where this came from!"

For a brief moment I thought I heard the distinct hearty chuckle of my brother behind me and then I smiled. "Don't worry," I said to the clerk, "I know where it came from." I whispered a grateful thank you to my brother.

I now have no doubt Bobby does look out for our happiness,

and my heart is a bit more consoled. Even though it was December 26th, in the eyes of a ten-year-old boy, it was a true Christmas miracle, confirming Uncle Bobby's status as a superhero in all our hearts.

~Jodi Iachini Severson

27

Left Behind

*Don't be dismayed at goodbyes. A farewell is necessary before
you can meet again. And meeting again, after moments or lifetime,
is certain for those who are friends.*
~Richard Bach

I stared at the wall in front of me, then turned to look out the
window at the people walking along the street. This was my
daily routine now, silently sitting in my husband's armchair, list-
lessly moving my eyes around the room, then going back to bed
to try to sleep away my despair.

A month ago, on an October morning, my husband Art, my best
friend, had suddenly passed away. We had often talked of growing
old together, but something had gone wrong and I was left behind.

Like a robot, I had arranged a memorial service. "Life will go on.
You will feel better soon," well-meaning friends tried to encourage
me. But I shrugged them off. How could they know the hopeless-
ness I was facing? I was alone. Alone with my grief, my pain, and
my agonizing thoughts. Art and I had just moved to this town three
months earlier. I had not yet had an opportunity to make friends. I
didn't even know my neighbors.

A few days after Art's death, I called one of our best friends.
Even though Gina and Ron lived an hour away, they came right over.
"Please, help me pack Art's stuff," I sobbed. "And would you take it
with you? Keep what you would like and give the rest away."

"Why don't you wait until you feel a bit better," Gina advised. "It's too soon to give his things away."

"No, No! I can't face looking at it. It hurts too much," I pleaded. There was no way I wanted to let them know that I also wanted to give my stuff away since my life was over too. After Gina and Ron left, I slumped into an armchair next to a side table where Art's photo was prominently displayed. Pain shot through my heart as I stared at it. Then, ever so slowly, I turned the picture over. I could not tolerate the pain of seeing his smiling face when I had no hope of ever seeing him alive again.

One day I decided that I should go down to the beach. At least I would see people instead of sitting alone at home. Slowly I trudged the ten minutes down the hill and began walking along the promenade. People passed me, arm in arm, hand in hand, talking, laughing, enjoying themselves. Everyone seemed to have someone. Everyone except me. So, with a wounded heart, I quickly fled back home.

Another day I went to the mall to buy some groceries. There my heart took another dive. The stores were decorated for Christmas and there were shoppers everywhere. How could I face Christmas without my beloved Art? Why even bother to put up a tree?

Then Ron and Gina invited me to spend Christmas Day with them. "Please," they urged. "We'd love to have you." I quickly declined. Joining in their Christmas festivities without Art would tear my heart apart even more. I would not tell them that I was slowly dying inside, and probably in a few weeks there would be another memorial service. Mine.

However, Christmas Day changed my life forever. That morning I awoke with a start. There stood my Art in the doorway of our bedroom: whole, healthy, alive. "Inga!" he called, looking at me tenderly. Overjoyed to see him again, I bolted upright, ready to jump into his arms. But at that precise moment, Art disappeared, leaving me wide-eyed in wonder and shock.

Was he real? Was it a vision? I sank back into the pillow in despair, my eyes filling with tears, dreading the new day. How I missed him! Just then a Bible verse I had read came to me. "I am the resurrection and the life. He who believes in me will live, even though he dies; and whoever lives and believes in me will never die" (John 11:25-26 NIV).

Suddenly it felt like a curtain was removed from my eyes. Art was alive in the beyond, waiting for me to join him when my time was up. A wave of hope washed over my anguished spirit, raising me from the grave of grief. I would see Art again in Heaven. Yet I sensed another message Art was bringing me. "Until we meet again, get involved in life," he seemed to say. Right away I sought activities I would enjoy. I joined the local walking club, a Bible study, and the widows' club that met weekly for lunch. Life became bearable again, especially when I made several new friends.

I savored the message of hope Art had brought me. God had not forsaken me. I was not alone. The Lord was with me even in the midst of tragedy. Yes, life would go on and I was left behind to fulfill God's purpose for me on earth. Today, I look forward to each new day's challenges and blessings because God sent Art to me, even though for only a second, to let me know He cared and that someday I would spend eternity with my beloved Art and with the Lord.

~Inga Dore

28

Pop In

He who has gone, so we but cherish his memory, abides with us,
more potent, nay, more present than the living man.
~Antoine de Saint-Exupéry

"How's the basement looking?" Pop asked. After moving in with his son Steve, I got used to these phone calls whenever a rainstorm hit. Our house stood next to a river, which sometimes overflowed and seeped into our basement. During one heavy storm we had at least a foot of water in the basement—I saw a small cooler float by—and the boys stayed up all night pumping out the water. From then on, Pop was on high alert whenever the forecast predicted rain.

So to assuage his worries, I took the phone with me as I went down the stairs to check. Again.

"Pretty much dry. Only a little water creeping in," I told him.

"Okay. Let me know if it gets worse and you guys need a hand."

That storm passed uneventfully. As did most since Steve put in a heavy-duty sump pump. But Pop still constantly fretted over it. And us.

Then it was our turn to fret over Pop. Over the course of a year, he went further and further into a dark, depressed place. Steve tried to help him. Mom tried. Friends tried. But on a Friday morning in May 2011, Pop took his own life. He was sixty-two.

Steve lost his father, his business partner, and his best friend. More than two years later, feelings of guilt, abandonment, and rejection still troubled him. And he missed Pop every single day. They had worked together, running their car repair business and gas station. When they weren't talking shop, they'd talk cars, motorcycles, music. We hung out with Pop and Mom most weekends—having dinner, seeing a show, going to a concert.

Steve learned to live without Pop, but there was still a void. While he didn't cry much, I think I did enough for the both of us. I cried over the good memories with Pop, and the memories he wouldn't be a part of—future Thanksgivings (his favorite holiday), Fourth of July picnics (his other favorite holiday), our wedding, our future children's lives. And I even got teary during storms, thinking about how he would always call.

Then something happened that made us realize Pop hadn't left us for good.

About a year and a half after Pop died, Hurricane Sandy hit our part of Connecticut with strong winds and heavy rain. We fared well, and only lost power for four days. During that time we fortunately had a diesel-powered generator to run a few important appliances—like the refrigerator and basement sump pump—as needed. (Thanks to an earlier purchase by Pop.)

We stored two extra containers of diesel in the sunroom. They stunk up the room. We kept the door closed so the smell wouldn't spread to the rest of the house. I had popped in and out of the sunroom once or twice, and the smell of fuel always hit me. One morning, Steve went into the sunroom to check something and called me over. Worried that something had spilled, leaked, or fallen, I dropped what I was doing and went to help him.

I saw Steve standing still in the middle of the room. And everything looked normal and in place.

"Smell that?" he asked.

I did. Standing right next to the containers, I smelled the familiar scent of British Sterling, not diesel. Stunned, I looked at Steve. He had a sad smile. I sniffed around more, just to be sure, and stated the obvious: "It's Pop's cologne."

The scent was distinct, crisp, and powerful. So much so that I looked around half-expecting to see Pop somewhere in the room.

The only sign of him, though, remained the cologne. Steve and I stood there, calm and silent.

"Hey Pop," I said eventually.

I stood a bit longer, absorbing the moment. Then I gave Steve a kiss on the cheek and went back to my morning routine, giving him some time alone. He hung back for a few more minutes, quiet. When he came into the kitchen he looked more at ease.

"Nice of him to come by and check on us," I said, half joking.

Steve smiled. And I realized it was true. Pop wasn't just "up there" as some kind of indeterminate spirit, as I always considered everyone who had passed. His spirit truly lived on, and it was paying attention! He had not abandoned us at all. In fact, when the "storm of the century" came along, he popped in to see how we were doing, and probably to make sure we were operating that diesel generator properly. I bet he checked the basement, too.

~Kristiana Glavin Pastir

29

The Sweet Smell of Success

Angels assist us in connecting with a powerful yet gentle force,
which encourages us to live life to its fullest.
~Denise Linn

I was a lively child with an inquisitive mind. I wasn't rebellious or bad—I just always wanted to know what was in this corner or around that bend, always asking questions, going where I wasn't supposed to go or doing what I wasn't supposed to do. I often incurred the disapproval of my father, who would probably have preferred a more sedate young daughter than the scratched and dirty tomboy I was.

At the same time, I was always eager to please. In school I was bright and motivated, my grades were good and, apart from remarks about talking too much, my reports were generally positive. My father, however, never seemed to notice these achievements. No matter how hard I tried and how much praise I received from teachers, my father's response to my academic success was minimal. On the other hand, my misdemeanors never went unnoticed.

By the time I was in my teens, my mischievous behavior had been replaced by stubborn opinions. My father and I clashed over everything from politics to what I should wear. In my egocentric sixteen-year-old brain, he was out of date and ill informed, old fashioned and stuck in middle-aged thinking. I still excelled at school. He continued to ignore my efforts.

As I grew into adulthood, I realized a few things. First, if I wanted success, particularly in higher learning, I was going to have to do it for my own satisfaction and not to please my father. The latter, I knew, was impossible. In addition, I began to understand that my father, who had to leave school to work in a factory at fourteen, was perhaps intimidated by my level of education and maybe even ashamed of his own shortcoming in that regard. This was a revelation to me. I never considered my father uneducated or beneath me. He was always able to hold his own in a good argument, political or otherwise, and I respected his views. Nevertheless, I could see how he might feel.

Years passed and although it took me almost three decades, I eventually got a college degree. My father seemed a tiny bit pleased. Perhaps I was making progress!

I went on to graduate school and received a master's degree. Again, there was a little bit of attention from him. I went on to study for a Ph.D.

Then my father died. He had been chronically ill for some years but his death was still sudden. A massive heart attack in the middle of the night saved him from the lingering death of the slow-moving cancer that had invaded his body a decade earlier.

My mother followed my father into the hereafter three years later, so neither of them was there the day I received my Ph.D., nor did they witness the successful career I carved out for myself. They were not aware either of the devastating skiing accident that interrupted that career, seriously injured my neck and left me with a closed-head brain injury that laid me low for several years. And, they certainly did not know how that event was a catalyst for me discovering my calling as an intuitive and energy worker and launching a new career in a very different world… or did they?

A few years after my accident, when I was tentatively stepping out of the metaphysical closet as a Reiki practitioner, offering to others the wonderful benefits of energy healing that I had discovered while recovering from my injuries, I rented my first office. It was in an old house that had been converted into a healing center. My office was small but perfect for me. I enjoyed moving my belongings in and arranging a calm and serene place for both my clients and me to work.

On one visit to the office to put the final touches on the decorating and arranging, I opened the door and was greeted by an overwhelming smell of cigarette smoke. I was shocked. I didn't smoke. No one in the building smoked. Smoking wasn't allowed. No one had been in the room since the previous time I was there. I aired out the room and, although mystified, I put the incident out of my mind.

The next time I visited, the same thing happened. I called the owner of the building, a healing professional herself. She couldn't explain the phenomenon. We even discussed what the house might have looked like before its conversion and what function my room had—it was the kitchen—in case that might help explain what was going on. Nothing, however, made sense.

It took a few days to dawn on me but then, I knew. My father was a smoker until about ten years before he died. He even worked for forty years in the tobacco industry. In my childhood memories he always had a cigarette in his hand. It was so obvious. My father approved of my new life and furthermore, he was letting me know! I finally had the recognition I had craved all those years before and I knew that not only did my father support my calling, he was encouraging me to keep on that path. I was moved and touched.

Since that time, on several occasions, as I have progressed with my career, added new modalities and taken fresh risks, my father has expressed his approval in the same way. The cigarette smoke smell always happens in places where no one smokes or is smoking and it is strong.

A few years ago, my son and I were walking our dogs. We were talking about my father. My son and he were very close, especially when my son was young. I mentioned to my son for the first time that I sometimes smelled cigarette smoke when no one was smoking and I knew that my father was around. My son, an army veteran and a welder by trade, with a down-to-earth approach to life and a sensible head on his shoulders, paused for just a brief moment and then responded in a matter-of-fact way. "Yes, so do I."

~Gillian Driscoll

Leave Now

The guardian angels of life fly so high as to be beyond our sight,
but they are always looking down upon us.
~Jean Paul Richter

I was the third child in my family. My older brother Bill was of course the boss. He was always ordering everyone around and in charge of keeping us out of harm's way. Looking back, I am amazed at how many times Bill stepped in and kept us safe.

I vividly remember the day when I was nine years old that our horse, Midnight, got his saddle horn caught in the clothesline. He was wild-eyed and frightened. Nothing could calm him or stop him. He charged at me, and Bill yelled, "Leave now. Jump in the pond." I was terrified of the horse but even more terrified of the pond. Bill had always told us to stay away from the pond, as it had no bottom and would swallow us up. I froze and to this day I don't know how Bill managed to beat the horse to me; he shoved me into the pond and jumped in with me to hold me up. Scared to death, I was trying to tread water and hoping the horse would stop before it got to the pond. Thankfully my dad showed up and got the horse under control. Bill and I emerged from the pond unscathed.

"Leave now" was his famous order and it always stuck with me. Bill was killed while serving in Vietnam, but I never forgot that advice from him.

One day I had a business meeting with a client who needed to sign up some new employees at his repair shop for group health insurance.

I always liked seeing Russ, the shop manager. He was a wonderful man and always cheerful and willing to help. The moment I arrived, Russ cleared his desk and told me to use it to sign up employees instead of trying to juggle my paperwork standing up. One by one, Russ sent in each new employee to be enrolled and brought me a cup of coffee just the way I liked it. "Strong and black." It was a standing joke between us that I would gladly adopt him if he promised to make my coffee every day. Russ was definitely a bright spot in an otherwise boring and routine stop that day.

Just as I was finishing with the last sign-up I distinctly heard my brother's voice from all those years ago say, "Leave now." It startled me so much I almost spilled my coffee, but it also gave me an uneasy feeling that I really needed to finish up quick and get out of there.

From there I continued my day as usual and returned home that night safe and sound. From time to time throughout the evening I thought of that strange moment in the day when I heard Bill's voice saying, "Leave now." As I got ready for bed I suddenly remembered it was the anniversary of Bill's death. How could I have forgotten? It was the first time in many years that the day did not send me into tears. I shrugged it off and decided Bill just wanted me to know he was still in charge and looking out for me. After drifting off to sleep, I was startled awake at midnight by the shrill ringing of the phone.

Half awake, I fumbled in the dark and answered the phone. My heart was in my throat as my father had been very ill and I was afraid something had happened to him. As soon as I said "hello," I heard the voice of Mitch, who owned the repair shop. Mitch blurted out, "Russ is dead. Someone came in the shop just after you left and shot him at his desk and fired at all the other employees. They managed to escape by the back door or dive into the repair bay pit." I was in complete shock and devastated at the loss of such a fine man.

Suddenly I knew my brother was with me as I had made my rounds that day. Bill knew the danger I was in, and that was why

I heard him say, "Leave now." Even from beyond the grave my big brother Bill was still watching over me.

~Christine Trollinger

Heaven Sent

In the Light

Wandering re-establishes the original harmony
which once existed between man and the universe.
~Anatole France

Screech! Steel wheels came to a halt in the Frankfurt rail station. We were on our way north from Switzerland. We had been traveling for six weeks bearing backpacks and sleeping in small inns and hostels in England, France, Spain, Italy and Greece. With our student Eurail Passes, we had unlimited use of any train on mainland Europe. Occasionally we saved on hotels by traveling overnight on the trains. This particular morning, Laura was not feeling well.

"We don't have any Deutschmarks," I said. "If we want food we won't have the right currency to buy it with. How about if you stay here with all our stuff and I go change some money?"

"Okay. Thanks, Raine," she said.

I left Laura in our compartment, slouched in a corner surrounded by our belongings. I walked through the station amidst the sounds of trains and people echoing in the girded, high-arched steel ceilings. I entered the terminal only to exit briefly onto a busy street where there was a bank. The teller was quick and efficient as I exchanged a few dollars. It took me only a matter of minutes, but when I returned to our track, the train and Laura were gone. I looked up at the rail number. It looked like the same one I had left behind. I looked through the station. Did I get it wrong? No, this was where I left the train and my friend. I was stunned, paralyzed. The track was empty. Laura was gone, as were my passport, address book, maps, guidebooks, clothes, toiletries and the rest of my travelers checks. We had no set itinerary. We traveled on a whim like nomads from one place to another. Cellphones were a thing of the future. How would we find each other?

I stood, wondering whether to take a train to the next destination on the schedule or to stay where I was. I was hoping Laura would either be waiting for me or come back for me. I was working all this out in my mind when I saw a train arriving on our track. As it loomed larger, I saw a small round head pushing its way out of the window—sun lighting its crop of short brown hair being rustled by the breeze. A hand reached out, eagerly waving. And then I saw that smile, a smile that could light up a room, and I beamed.

"Hi Raine," she called to me excitedly.

It was Laura. We were ecstatic to be reunited. We hugged. She explained that the train had been moved temporarily to add more cars, but she didn't know what was happening when it started moving and she was worried about having left me in Frankfurt.

Monday, June 14, 2004—thirty-four years later—I sat at my office desk remembering this story.

The previous evening, Laura's husband had telephoned. He told me of Laura's passing. After thirteen years, a recurrence of breast cancer spread throughout her body. Less than three months ago we had danced at her son's wedding—Mary, Alice, Pat, Laura and I—five college friends and our spouses. She looked radiant and brimming with vitality. We celebrated not only a marriage, but her life.

Now, I felt like I was waiting at that empty track.

As I sorted through my business mail, the scent of roses filled the air. "I wish they would stop sending fragrance through the mail. Perfume gives me an allergic headache," I thought. I sifted through the envelopes to find the source of the smell, but found nothing. I rifled through the magazines, but there were no scented inserts. I pulled my clothes, sniffing them. Perhaps they'd been stored with a sachet. But the fragrance was not coming from what I was wearing or what I was holding. I walked into our bookkeeper's office. There were no roses there. The scent became stronger. I thought, "What the heck! This is crazy."

I telephoned a friend who I knew was clairvoyant.

"Do you happen to know why I might be smelling roses this morning?"

"Yes, someone is by you. She is small with big eyes, intent. She has a short white top on with kinda flared sleeves, sort of like an angel, but not an angel. I don't know what they call those sleeves. And she has short pants, light pink pants on, short pants," he said, concentrating on the image.

"Capris?"

"Yes, and there is sun on her head. There is light around her... her feet, her feet are not on the earth. She is over, over the burden. And she is waving and smiling. Nice." I heard his smile. "Real nice. I—rene. I—rene."

"Irene? Who is Irene?"

"Oh, I am so bad with names," he said. "I—rene. She's waving."

"Laura?" I asked. "My friend's name is Laura."

"No, she is saying I—rene and waving. She is waving goodbye now. She said she won't be back for a while. She blew you a kiss. It is blue, very spiritual. There is spirituality coming from her fingertips. She is uplifted, light, smiling."

Then the scent of roses faded.

Who is Irene? I wanted to know. I looked up the name on the Internet. It means peace.

I thought about e-mailing the other girls. I was reluctant. They were grieving, too. They might think I was a weirdo. Still, I thought I should let them know.

It was Mary who simply replied, "Not I—rene. Hi Raine!"

Suddenly, I felt like I was in Frankfurt seeing a train arrive with a small round head pushing its way out of the window, sun lighting its crop of short brown hair being rustled by the breeze, a hand reaching out eagerly waving.

"Hi Raine!"

Whether I wait here, or "board the train" to the next destination, Laura let me know we will meet again.

~Lorraine Bruno Arsenault

32

The Miraculous Meaning in a Name

When you're a nurse you know that every day you will
touch a life or a life will touch yours.
~Author Unknown

I have served as the administrative director of the Johns Hopkins Breast Center since 1997 and have worked at Hopkins for more than thirty years. There have certainly been times that I have felt divine intervention must have occurred for patients to recover, or I have seen some other amazing occurrence that reaffirms for me that there is life after our time on this earth. One specific incident however, with one particular patient, confirmed for me that I was meant to survive breast cancer twice (diagnosed in my thirties and again at age forty) so that I could do the work I do now, which truly is a calling for me.

I commonly answer my own phone. Always have. Probably always will. On this specific day back in 1998 I answered the phone with my usual greeting of, "This is Lillie Shockney, how many I help you?" The voice on the other end was a very distressed young woman saying, "Who is there? Where am I calling?" I responded with my name and told her that she had reached the Johns Hopkins Breast Center. She then said, sounding upset, "Oh my goodness, can you help me?" I told her yes and asked her what the problem was. I wasn't even sure if this woman needed help within our breast center, but no matter what I was going to get her to the right person.

She told me that she just had a baby girl three days before, and had a C-section. During her pregnancy (her first), she noticed at her five-month mark that her left breast had turned red. She showed it to her OB, who told her she had mastitis and put her on antibiotics. She returned a month later and the breast looked worse, with enlarged pores, redder, and firmed. He told her to stay on the antibiotics for another month.

She next returned at her seven-month pregnancy checkup and told him she had severe back and rib pain. He told her it was "all part of pregnancy." At eight months, she could barely walk because of bone pain, and the breast looked no better. Her doctor put her on a different antibiotic, and told her that he didn't remember ever having a young mother (she was thirty-three) complain like she did during an "uneventful pregnancy."

After the C-section the baby was healthy and doing fine. However, this young mother told me that she had severe rib pain. She had reported it to her obstetrician and he told her that he thought she would have stopped complaining by now, given that the baby was born. The anesthesiologist, however, listened to her when she said that her ribs hurt more than her C-section incision. He ordered a chest X-ray.

Lo and behold, she had metastatic breast cancer throughout her bones (including ribs and the other areas she had complained about) as well as in her liver. The red breast was not mastitis but inflammatory breast cancer. She immediately went to a medical oncologist. The doctors told her that the cancer was too far along to attempt to save her, and they would send her home with pain medications. They estimated she would live about a month, and she should focus on her time with her newborn baby.

After telling me this appalling story, she then asked me again, "So can you help me?"

"Yes," I said. "Come here tomorrow."

I gathered members of our breast center faculty to see her the next day—breast surgical oncology, medical oncology and radiation oncology. When she arrived she walked like a woman in her nineties, assisted by her terrified husband. Her mother was home with the baby. I walked over to her and gently put my arms around her, being careful not to squeeze her. I introduced myself to her husband, who responded in an unusual way. He looked at my face, then said loudly while pointing at my ID badge, "Is that your name?" I calmly told him yes, and we proceeded into the examination room.

The consult took two hours. We decided to get scans, insert a port and immediately start chemotherapy with the goal of buying her some time. Her husband asked me three additional times if the name on my ID badge was in fact my name. I assured him it was and further told him that everyone calls me Lillie, however my legal name is the name on my ID badge—Lillian. At that moment his wife said, "Honey, I told you that I got connected to this nurse here yesterday." He still looked perplexed.

Chemo started. I discussed short-term goals with the patient and her husband. She told me that she wanted to live long enough for her daughter to remember her. I thought this baby would need to be three or four years old to achieve that goal. So I expressed to her that it might be best to focus on shorter goals, like seeing the baby sit up at six months. She was adamant, however, about wanting the treatments to provide her three to four more years.

Her treatments went better than we anticipated and the tumor responded well to these drugs. The response was so good that the liver metastases cleared completely and more than half of the bone lesions resolved. The breast again looked healthy and a mastectomy was performed. And she reached her personal goal. This woman lived for three and half more years before succumbing to this disease. She enjoyed every moment she could with her daughter and husband.

A few weeks after she died, her husband called me. He said that he owed me an apology from when he had met me at the breast center nearly four years ago. I did not recall any issue that warranted an apology. He reminded me that he kept quizzing me about my name on my ID badge. I told him it didn't require an apology, and I knew he was very stressed, having become a new daddy one day and the following day learning his wife was going to die of breast cancer.

He said he wanted to tell me why he was so focused on my name badge. All his life his grandmother had lived with him and his parents. He felt closer to her than anyone, to the degree that even after he married, he continued to swing by his parents' home to see her each evening after work before going home to his own wife. His grandmother was wheelchair-bound for all of his life too. He explained that two days before the baby was born his grandmother died. He was at her side when she passed. She held his hand and said, "I wish I could have held on long enough to see this brand new baby come into this world but I simply can't. I will return to the three of you however as your guardian angel and you won't know me by my face; you will know me by my name."

He then said, "Lillie, her name was Lillian."

After I took in a deep breath I said, "Well, no wonder you were so focused on my name badge."

"Well, there is more," he said. "When my wife reached you on your private phone at Johns Hopkins she wasn't even calling you; she was calling her mother in another city, different area code and totally different phone number, but instead was somehow connected to you."

"Then you have confirmed for me and yourself that your grand-mother fulfilled her promise to the three of you. What a blessing."

So, if ever I had a doubt in my mind that I was destined for the field of work I am dedicated to 24/7, that profound experience iced it for me.

~Lillie D. Shockney

33

A Look Back in Time

Death is not extinguishing the light;
it is putting out the lamp because dawn has come.
~Rabindranath Tagore

Our pickup labored over jumbled boulders and squeezed through an opening cut by a recent flash flood in a narrow desert canyon. Once through that newly formed crack in the rock wall, my desert wandering friend Muskrat John and I looked up on a ledge and saw a magically pristine cabin. Around it were the signs of a long abandoned mine.

John and I had discovered a perfect ghost cabin, mislaid and forgotten for decades in a maze of Mojave Desert canyons. We climbed steps that led onto a comfortable front porch. This stairway was not thrown together with scrap lumber—each step was cut and laid at precise angles, built strong and solid. An old rocking chair sat in one corner of the porch. The front door was the work of a skilled carpenter. The windows were caked with decades of desert dust, but it was obvious they had been installed with a craftsman's skills. How did the builder get the wood and glass up to this remote spot?

The door swung open easily and noiselessly to reveal a cozy one-room cabin. A small cot in one corner, a large table in the center, and some work tables placed along the walls completed the furnishings. Shelves along the walls were full of cookware and canned goods. We puzzled over the unfamiliar brand names of the canned food. They belonged to a different time. The sharp footprints we left in the fine dust on the floor were additional evidence that no other visitors had come, perhaps since the cabin was abandoned.

The mine diggings showed the same capable workmanship. A long horizontal tunnel had been blasted deep into the back of the canyon. Rails for a hand-pushed ore cart had been skillfully installed along the length of this tunnel. John and I saw the vein of silver ore the miner was working. Everything was in such perfect condition we could have filled his old ore cart and started up the mine right then. This one-man enterprise had been created by a master builder, and our admiration grew with each discovery.

He had dug a second tunnel, much shorter and wider, to serve as a workshop. A small bed sat in the corner—this may also have been his summer bedroom when the desert heat became unbearable. The shelves were still stocked with rock drills, sledgehammers, pickaxes, and other tools of the miner's trade. I picked up the smooth worn handle of a still useful pickaxe and swung it. I felt a surge of extra power—was that the old miner swinging it with me? An image of a strong, white-haired old man flashed into my mind, a proud face smiled at me. The memories clung powerfully to this place, and even more strongly to these old tools.

Muskrat John and I explored the old miner's works so exhaustively we developed a strong appetite. We headed back to the truck and broke out some lunch. The shaded porch made a perfect lunchroom, and we sprawled on the solid planks in comfort, eating our food directly from the cans, just like the old miner likely did for his meals.

As we ate and talked, we discovered that back in the workshop the fleeting image of a white-haired, strong, smiling old man had appeared to both of us at about the same time. We talked about his life at this cabin, and wondered what had happened to him. Finishing lunch, the sun still high in the sky, we stretched out and lit our pipes, watching the smoke rise lazily upwards. In the heat of the slumbering afternoon the air was almost perfectly still. There was not even the sound of a bird or an insect to mar the silence. It was so calm and quiet, that life seemed to have stopped.

Slowly we became aware of a soft, steady sound—a slight

creaking, a shadow of movement. It was coming from the corner of the porch. We turned. The hairs on the back of our necks stood up. I felt chills racing up and down my body. The rocking chair was rocking. Steadily, back and forth, the chair was doing what a rocking chair is supposed to do. When a person is sitting in it!

The Muskrat and I stared at the rocking, yet empty, chair. We were scared at first but the steady creaking on the porch floor was reassuring. In a short time we felt at home sharing the porch with the old miner sitting comfortably in his rocker. We sensed that he was happy to be with us, pleased to visit with folks that finally came by to appreciate his life's work. There was no threat, just welcome. We sat for a long time with the invisible old gentleman, enjoying the afternoon, and the company, and smoking our pipes. Our pipe smoke continued to rise straight up in the still air as the chair rocked away. We talked about how well this mining operation was built, and how much we wished we could have been here when it was operating. No replies came from the chair, just the gentle rocking, and a feeling of gratitude and contentment.

Our pipes went out, the shadows were getting long. It was time to leave. Regretfully and respectfully we said goodbye. I remember feeling sadness coming from the chair, as if the old fellow did not want us to go. We packed up the truck, took a long final look at the cabin, and with the chair still rocking, more slowly now, we headed down canyon.

In my mind that old cabin was never found again by anyone. It still perches, in its perfection, on the ledge over the streambed in that lost canyon. From time to time, on warm afternoons, the occupant of the rocking chair remembers our visit. And the chair rocks again, peacefully.

Goodbye old-timer. Thanks for the memories. And thanks for coming by to visit with us…

~William Halderson

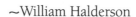

34

Good Company to Keep

Good company in a journey makes the way seem shorter.
~Izaak Walton

My grandmother loved cardinals and had them all over her apartment. There were pictures of cardinals, glass cardinal ornaments, cardinal knick-knacks, even pillows with cardinals embroidered on them. She loved their bright red plumage. She said seeing a cardinal always cheered her up and kept her from feeling alone. A cardinal, she once told me, was always good company.

When she passed away at the age of eighty-seven, I thought about what she had said about cardinals as I picked out her outfit for her funeral. I made sure that her little cardinal pin was affixed to the lapel of her dress suit.

"There," I said out loud. "This will keep you company."

Several years later, I received a promotion at work. I wished I could share the good news with my grandmother. She, too, had worked in an office and had shared a lot of her experiences with me. My new office seemed huge to me, with two glass walls, one of which looked out onto a beautiful courtyard. I was thrilled at the move and the additional responsibility, but I found myself struggling with doubts the day I began moving in my belongings.

The IT guy was working on setting up my computer and printer as I unpacked my boxes. I had worked with Jeff several times in the past on various IT issues, so we chatted comfortably as we worked to ready my new office.

"I'll be honest with you, Jeff," I said as I shared some of my concerns. "I'm really kind of nervous about this move. I mean, I know I can do the work, but this office... Well, it's just so big! And it's so far from the rest of the crew that I've been working with. I'm already feeling a little isolated, and I haven't even finished unpacking!"

"I see what you mean," Jeff answered, looking around at the space. "But they wouldn't have promoted you if they didn't think you were up to the job. Yeah, this office is a lot bigger, but it's really not far from the center of the office. You'll get used to it."

I nodded and continued unpacking, storing things in the new desk as we chatted. As I stocked items in the desk drawers, I said out loud what I had been worrying about the most: "It just seems so lonely back here. I'm used to being in the middle of things in the office, with lots of people around. I'm just feeling a little out of place, that's all."

"Well, well—there's somebody to keep you company," said Jeff.

I looked up to see him nod toward the courtyard. "Looks almost as if they've been waiting for you," he commented.

I caught my breath as I looked into the courtyard. There sitting on top of the bushes right at the window were a couple of cardinals—a bright red male and a more conservatively colored female. They both tilted their heads a couple of times, as if in acknowledgement of their new neighbor. The male tapped his beak once against the window; then they both took off and flew out of the courtyard.

"I think they just welcomed you to the neighborhood!"

During the years that I occupied that office, with its beautiful courtyard view, the cardinal couple returned each winter, visiting for a few minutes at a time, brightening the view and reminding me each time that I wasn't really alone after all. My grandmother saw to it that I had good company.

~Ginny Dubose

The Voice

Put your ear down close to your soul and listen hard.
~Anne Sexton

Coloradoans are so accustomed to unpredictable wind currents sweeping over the Rocky Mountains, bringing rain, snow or sunshine, that we often joke to visitors, "If you don't like the weather, just stick around for ten minutes and watch it change."

Happy to reside in our beautiful state, I drank in the beauty of the Rocky Mountains silhouetted against a cloudless blue sky as I drove to a nearby shopping mall. During breakfast, my husband Jim mentioned that since it was such a nice day he might clean leaves from our roof gutters and check the chimney bricks while I was gone.

I reached the mall and went inside. After browsing through stores and making some purchases, I was surprised when I heard a masculine voice say, "Sally, go home."

Startled, I looked around, but saw no man near me. It was still too early for the morning rush so there wasn't a large throng of shoppers. Puzzled, I left that store and entered another shop. Soon I heard the same voice repeat that same message. Thinking a friend might be hiding and playing a practical joke I searched the area nearby, but there were no men in sight.

Unnerved, I took a deep breath and told myself that healthy people do not hear voices. Do they? Was it possible that the voice I heard was in reality my subconscious mind warning me that some predator lurked in the mall seeking an easy prey to rob?

When I heard, "Sally, go home," for the third time, I remembered a Jewish friend telling me that "angel" and "messenger" were the same word in the Hebrew language. Whether that voice belonged to an angel or my subconscious didn't seem as important as the message. I hurried toward the parking lot saying a silent prayer: "Dear God, thank you for surrounding me with your white protective shield of love so my heart, mind, body and soul are attuned to your positive forces."

I looked around as I hurried to my car to make sure no one was stalking me, unlocked the door, shoved my packages on the passenger seat, and scooted inside. After locking the door, I drove away, constantly checking my rear view mirror to make sure I wasn't being followed.

As I drove toward home, leaden clouds and gusty winds replaced the cerulean blue sky I had admired only an hour earlier. Since I was accustomed to these short wind bursts, I adjusted my speed and arrived back in my neighborhood safely.

All the way home, I wondered about that message. But as soon as I turned the corner to my street and saw Jim clinging to the chimney and his ladder lying on the ground, I realized why the voice urged me to return home.

"Thank God, you're back," Jim called.

I parked the car, picked up the ladder, leaned it against the house and steadied it while he climbed down.

Smiling, I looked toward heaven and thanked the voice.

~Sally Kelly-Engeman

A Change in Perspective

Millions of spiritual creatures walk the earth
Unseen, both when we wake and when we sleep.
~John Milton, Paradise Lost

"Christ! It's hotter than hell down here. Not good for a party, that's for sure." And with those words from my grandfather, our family cookout began.

My grandmother had died five months earlier, so my cousin Jeff and I took over her role and hosted a cookout at my grandparents' cottage on Plum Island. We had high hopes of honoring Gram by pulling off her magic hostess abilities. I imagined my family all together, sitting on the porch above the beach, eating strawberry shortcake like she used to make, and reminiscing about her life. I imagined everyone hugging, toasting Gram, and vowing to carry on this new tradition.

Instead, people sat and complained.

"The tide's too low. Too bad we didn't come on a different day."

"Who the hell mashed these strawberries? They've got lumps."

"Nobody put out the cushions on the glider? Humph. I woulda."

My grandfather ranted about the state of an air conditioner that he couldn't part with after twenty years. My uncle fidgeted in his chair, brow furrowed, clearly looking for something else to gripe about. Jeff and I met up in the kitchen, where I swore to him that I would never host again. "Seriously," I muttered, "who could be miserable here? Sea air? Kids playing? Sun. Sand. And who complains about strawberry shortcake anyway?"

Jeff shook his head. "I know. It's ridiculous."

We took our kids to the beach and left the other adults back in the house. As we watched the kids catch minnows and crabs, I started to relax. But, by the time my husband and I returned to our house, I felt like crying. I missed my grandmother more than ever. Why couldn't Jeff and I keep Gram's peace? Why couldn't everybody get along? And why couldn't we imitate her strawberry shortcake? Nobody whined about lumps when she was alive.

Gram was the quintessential Mrs. Claus in looks and spirit, the one who held the workshop and the elves together. She was a soft-spoken matriarch in an eyelet apron. Even die-hard curmudgeons rose to their best behavior around Gram. Whereas my grandfather has always been the town icon of confrontational ways, Gram was never anything but warm and welcoming. Many, including her minister, called her a saint for the way she dealt with the abrasiveness of others.

She kept things running smoothly, which was no small feat in her household. When my grandfather was about town on his own, trouble ensued. He checked up on his tenants by popping in when they weren't home. He frequented the auto body shop, oil company, and lumber yard, haggling for a lower price. He stopped by construction sites to oversee the workmanship and made it known when he thought it was shoddy. With her by his side, however, people could ignore his criticism because of her sweetness.

She'd open the door to visitors and exclaim, "Well, I am tickled pink to see you!" giving kisses that smelled like Ivory soap. In the morning, she wore a skirt, heels, and nylons as she prepared, canned, blanched, pared, and husked her way through the vegetables she grew on the family farm. Wearing heels, she appeared the ultimate city lady, and yet she had fingers stained pink by berries. In the afternoons, she donned her sunhat and knelt in the dusty soil to pick vegetables for the next day's preparations.

When she died suddenly, I grieved for her, but I also mourned an era that I feared had ended. For thirty-five years, I knew everything would be okay because she was there to mediate and uplift. Now, without her, I saw how much we needed her to function as a family.

When I drove to the grocery store later that day, I thought about the cookout. What could I have done differently to make the day better? I couldn't have changed the tide or the heat. I could have mashed the strawberries longer. I could have taken out the cushions for the glider... I started to drive myself crazy with "what if's," becoming more and more frustrated. But then a mile down the road, I was distracted by a turtle plodding its way across the street. Because I can't pass any creature in distress, I stopped to pick it up and carry it to its destination. The turtle actually seemed to appreciate the help, and the encounter made me smile. I returned home, grinning, as I told my husband about helping my friend cross the road. The turtle had snapped me out of my funk.

Early the next morning, my husband opened the front door and said, "You've got to come here." I walked over and peered over his shoulder to see a turtle sitting at the bottom of the steps, looking us straight in the eyes. It looked like she'd been there for a while. Had she been waiting for us? I rested my chin on my husband's shoulder as I looked down with astonishment at our morning visitor.

"Do you think it could be the same turtle?" I asked hesitantly.

"Of course it's the same turtle," he whispered, as the turtle continued to stare straight at me with unblinking eyes.

I crept down the steps and bent to pick her up. She made no motion to go into her shell. Instead, she kept her neck out, still looking me in the eyes. I carried her into our backyard, through some woods to a brook. I had to prod her to walk away, as she kept turning back to look at me. I felt sad when I could no longer see her. She had seemed to want to stay.

At work that day, one of my colleagues asked about my weekend. I started to explain my disappointment with the cookout, but I then stopped to tell the anecdote of the turtle. As I was speaking, I saw my friend's eyes widen, and I suddenly felt the two parts of my weekend connect. The connection clicked for good when she said, "You know the turtle is one of the most spiritual symbols in Asia? It's a vessel for spirits before they pass on. It's also a sign of good fortune and longevity."

These thoughts stayed with me for the rest of the day. I didn't usually believe in spiritual signs, or in messages from turtles, but this couldn't be ignored. Gram knew I needed a blatant message. Perhaps Gram had come to remind me not to take things, including family gatherings, so seriously. I thought back to other holidays when she was there and remembered them honestly this time. People had complained even then. Actually, they'd complained a lot. The difference was that Gram had helped me to overlook the negative just by her presence. She had chosen to focus on the positive, being "tickled pink" by any moment, and so could I.

When I got home, I said to my husband, "You know, I've been thinking…"

And my banker, MBA, extremely logical husband, without prompting, completed my sentence, "that the turtle was Gram? … Me, too."

~Amy Rodriguez

I'll See You

Love is something eternal; the aspect may change, but not the essence.
~Vincent van Gogh

Grant was tall and lean, with dark bangs that hung in his dark blue eyes. He was the kind of guy other guys like to hang out with, and girls crushed on. He had a goofy smile. He was the boy I loved in high school.

The outstanding thing about Grant was his kindness. His answer to queries about career plans was always, "The Catcher in the Rye. I want to stop children from falling over the edge." Though he was no pushover, you could tell Grant anything. Your darkest secret would be met with understanding and a hug.

I knew we'd eventually marry. To me, the group of girls he dated were no obstacle. I knew he'd realize how sincere my love was. I was a cutie too, and wasn't spending all my weekends dateless. I was a romantic but pragmatic teen. I figured we were both just "sowing our wild oats."

Grant was always there for me. When I became very ill, he was my sole visitor. He held my hand and spoke comfortingly, when even my best girlfriends abandoned my unpleasant symptoms.

Grant and I continued seeing each other after high school, growing even closer. We had a special routine. We both loved roaming our rural community on warm nights. So as not to awaken my mother, Grant would gently tap on my bedroom window. I'd climb out and join him. We walked and talked. We lay down in the soft, fragrant dirt between rows of green hay grass.

Given Grant's incredible care for people, how he met his death isn't surprising. In his early twenties, he fell victim to a fire while trying to rescue friends. They got out. Grant was found curled up just past the fire stairs. He'd sacrificed his life, a thwarted version of Catcher in the Rye.

At his funeral, a group of his old friends (including myself), questioned the new friends who'd survived. We were further devastated when it became clear they'd simply left him behind to die.

I was inconsolable. At his funeral, I couldn't stop my ragged sobbing. I dropped two roses into Grant's grave. A red one for passion and a white one for true love.

The wake was held at his sister's farm. My friends found me climbing into a shallow grave I'd dug for myself in a plowed field. I didn't exactly want to die; I just wanted to be where Grant was. If he was in the dirt, I'd be in the dirt. I do believe I temporarily lost my mind.

Three days later, I was no closer to peace. I cried myself hoarse. All day and into the night, I was gripped with sadness that felt as if it would never end. My belly and chest hurt; my throat was raw. The third night, I finally fell into a fitful sleep. Around 3 a.m. I awoke with a start. The dogs were growling by my bedroom window, the fur raised along their spines.

I heard a gentle tap tap tap. It sounded exactly like Grant's fingers. I sat up, frozen in my bed. As it was a hot night, my window was slightly raised. "Who-o-o is it?" I asked, my voice quavering.

A soft, emerald green mist floated in through the opening. The dogs continued to growl as the mist enveloped me. I felt warmth and love.

I heard Grant's voice. Clearly and firmly, his voice was in my ear. He said, "I'll see you."

That was all. "I'll see you."

My desperate pain ceased. I felt a glow in my heart, and fell easily back to sleep. My dreams were gentle.

Though my peaceful feelings lingered, the next morning, I thought, "It was a dream."

Then my mother asked, "What was all the commotion in your room last night? I've never heard the dogs like that in the house."

~Reisa Stone

Buckets of Pennies

When love is lost, do not bow your head in sadness;
instead keep your head up high and gaze into heaven
for that is where your broken heart has been sent to heal.
~Author Unknown

"Bette, how can I go on?" I said, pleading for an easy answer.

"Sallie, you just keep putting one foot in front of the other every day. It is not a destination but a journey," she counseled me.

My mind drifted back to that ugly day when this journey had begun. Paul, my husband of forty-six years, had died suddenly at the age of sixty-nine. I was set adrift in a sea of grief. My days were filled with sadness and crying. I longed for his touch, his laugh and his presence. My children had grown up and had families of their own; they were scattered in far off cities.

I also missed the way we ran our household as a couple. Paul took care of the outside and all the maintenance on our home while I took care of the inside. I missed this stability in my life. Broken sprinklers, dying dishwashers, big purchases such as garage doors and home repairs were foreign to me. I was swimming as fast as I could to cope with not only my loss, but also my new duties as head of the house.

Everything was upside down in my world and my spiritual side was shaken too. How could a just and loving God take my sweet husband from me? We had known each other since high school. He was my rock. We were supposed to be together into old age and beyond. I wanted him back and longed for him every day.

In desperation I turned to an eighty-year-old friend and spiritually wise woman named Bette. I asked her if I could drop by for some tea and sympathy and words of wisdom. She had lost her grown daughter years before so she understood my grief. I was begging for some reassurance that Paul was still around me, just outside my realm and reach.

Bette's words brought me back from my reverie.

"Sallie, are you listening to me?"

"I'm sorry Bette. I was just remembering. I know it's a journey. Even though I know it isn't possible to get Paul back, I want to know he is with me. I want some sign that he hears me, loves me and watches over me from the other side," I said, tears starting to flow.

"I know sweetie," she said, giving me a hug. "This is what I want you to do. Every time you go out, ask Paul for a sign he is with you, and I'm sure you will get an answer."

I followed Bette's advice and the strangest thing happened. I started to find pennies everywhere I went. There were pennies in the apple bin at my health food store, pennies under the clothes rack at the boutique, pennies when I walked the dog, pennies in the garden. Pennies, pennies, pennies. I doubted they were from Paul. I mean, really, everyone finds pennies.

I called Bette.

"Bette, I keep finding pennies all over the place. It's so simple but could it be a sign from Paul?"

"Of course," Bette replied. "I find pennies from my daughter all the time. They are pennies from heaven letting you know your loved one is with you."

I continued to doubt, but I guess Paul wanted to be sure I understood the message. I am a cynic sometimes, so he delivered the message loud and clear.

That following week I stopped at my local pharmacy. I was in a hurry to get home because I was expecting a package delivery. As I stepped from my car I looked down to make sure that in my haste I had parked between the lines. When I returned to my car no more than five minutes later, it looked like someone had emptied a piggy bank in front of my door. I stared in awe at the piles of pennies. I opened my car door and crumpled onto the seat sobbing. How could I have doubted that Paul wasn't nearby?

I gathered all the pennies and went home to call Bette.

"Bette, it's true! Paul is with me! I just found a bucket of pennies in front of my car," I sputtered out excitedly.

"I know, Sallie," she said laughing. "I know. Isn't it grand?"

The pennies keep coming and I talk to Paul every day.

"Thanks honey. I know you're there as my special angel. I'll love you forever."

I have an earthenware jar that I put my pennies from heaven in. Someday soon I will buy a tree to plant in Paul's garden to honor our love. And at the base with be a plaque in his memory. At the rate I'm finding pennies it won't be long now.

~Sallie A. Rodman

39

Petunia

Count the garden by the flowers, never by the leaves that fall.
Count your life with smiles and not the tears that roll.
~Author Unknown

Every year, my partner Mel and I plant flowers in our yard
to honor our deceased loved ones. A few years ago, we
couldn't get around to it. The reasons were many that
year, including me getting laid off and Mel being injured
at work.

One day, we rushed out of the house to Mel's physical therapy.
On the way to the car, Mel paused and smiled. "Hey honey, look." He
pointed to a flowerpot near our front gate. "Your mom says, 'hello.'"

I looked at the flowerpot, and my jaw dropped. A single, white
petunia grew among the many weeds. It should've been choked out,
but it flourished anyway. Because petunias are annuals, there was no
explanation for the single flower. It had to be a miracle.

Warmth flooded through me, and tears filled my eyes.

Every year, Mel and I planted petunias in a variety of vibrant
colors in different pots around the yard, but never white ones. The
flowers honored my mom, who had always called me "Tunie." When
I was a little girl, she'd chase me through the house, saying, "Kissy,
kissy, Tunie." I'd giggle as she scooped me up into her arms, kissing
me. Our ritual ended when I became a teenager and too big to be
called such a childish name. When my mom died ten days after my
nineteenth birthday, that declaration didn't matter as much. I missed

being called Tunie. Since my nickname was short for petunia, we declared it my mom's memorial flower in our yard.

Staring at the single, white flower, I knew my mom was letting me know she was still there for me. Nothing could keep her away from me, not even death. Suddenly, all the trials life threw at us weren't as bad as I had thought.

That single flower reminded us to slow down and enjoy the simple things in life, not get caught up in the temporary, short-term trials.

As I cried, Mel placed his hand on my shoulder. "She must have known we needed her," Mel said. He caressed me as he spoke.

I nodded and said, "Thank you, Mom."

~Ellen Tevault

40

The Bookmark

Fiction reveals truths that reality obscures.

~Jessamyn West

I hadn't meant to read anything in the book, let alone pick it up, but it was early morning and I couldn't get back to sleep. I was bored scrolling through the news on my cell phone. My fiancée was still sleeping, so there was no hope for conversation. Staring at her in her deep sleep, I hoped she was in a relaxed world, if only to make up for the real one that we had been in for the past week. We had had quite the day, standing on our feet for hours greeting grieving relatives and friends before returning to my future mother-in-law's house.

I had packed light: two suits, two dress shirts, one pair of black shoes and my darkest, most somber tie. I had neglected to bring any of the books I was currently working through. I decided to peruse the contents of a bookshelf I spotted in the corner of the room. The novels were old and dusty, forgotten years ago for the conveniences of a Kindle I suspect. My sleepy eyes found a pair of books standing side by side. One, *Seven Short Novel Masterpieces* (edited by Leo Hamalian & Edmond L. Volpe), was quickly passed over for the other, *Short Story Masterpieces* (edited by Robert Penn Warren & Albert Erskine).

Feeling half awake and in an early morning daze, I picked up the book. Once on the bed, I realized I had picked up the wrong one. Too lazy to get back up for the intended book, I decided it might be fun to revisit the adventures of Voltaire's *Candide*, which happened to be quoted on the back cover. I lay back and opened the book, finding the pages crisp and brown with age. A small business card fell onto my face. What seemed like an ancient relic was a thirty-year-old business card of my fiancée's grandfather, the man whose life had just ended and whom we had spent the last few days mourning.

Each wake had been packed with lively people chatting, laughing, weeping, and more than anything, remembering. Among them were his immediate family: four children, ten grandchildren, and one great-granddaughter, all of whom were wondering if they might "hear" from him in one way or another. The family frequently spoke about his wife, who had passed away years before, and how she turned on lights just to say "hello." Many family members wondered: Where was he now and how would he let them know that he was watching over them?

I knew that I had a choice. I could brush off the mysterious card as coincidence or I could view it as something else entirely. I also had the choice of whether or not to tell the rest of the family, and feared they might wonder why he had not contacted one of them directly, if a contact was what it was.

I thought about it; if all we have to rely upon are memories of the past, our reimagined versions of a person will become stale and that person will never surprise us again. We want to believe that those who have passed on can still show us something new, as they did when they were alive. Letting the family know would surely widen their eyes and allow them to feel surprised by him once more. It would also make them feel as though their loved one was sending them signals.

Later in the morning, I read the passage that the card had marked in the book. Then I knew what to do. I walked downstairs to find my fiancée and her mother drinking coffee. I walked up to her mother and handed her the business card. I told her it fell on my face. I told her I thought she might like to read the paragraph that the business card marked. It was the last page of "Master and Man," a short story by Leo Tolstoy. The final passage read:

"Whether he is better off, or worse off, there, in the place where he awoke in that real death, whether he was disappointed or found things there just as he expected, is what we shall all of us soon learn."

~Robert Rome

Thank You, Sue

A friend is a hand that is always holding yours, no matter how close or far apart you may be. A friend is a feeling of forever in the heart.
~Author Unknown

n February of 2005, my husband's youngest sister, Sue, passed away after a long and courageous battle with cancer. Hers was an exceptionally hard loss to accept. First of all, she was only forty-five. Secondly, she was the third person in my husband's immediate family to succumb to cancer in eight years. Thirdly, and most painful to my heart, was the fact that she wasn't only my sister-in-law but also a loyal and special friend.

Sue and I were close in age and we had a lot in common. We spent a lot of time together raising our children. We had fun during those years; she was great to be around, and she had a vivacious personality. She also had a big heart, always ready to lend a helping hand to a friend or stranger in need. We went through some rough times together as well, but always had each other for support. Then there were the misadventures that we shared, and there were several of those. They were the kind of adventures that memories are made from.

One of those adventures was when we tried to move a not-so-small tree after hauling it in the back of a pickup truck. The man who had loaded it for us had set it to one side of the truck bed instead of in the middle, resulting in the two of us driving down a major highway in a truck leaning so far to one side that the two passenger side tires almost lifted off the ground.

Then there was the time that, while on a family trip to Louisiana, Sue and I were chased and surrounded by a large group of goats at her cousin's ranch. We had started off going for a walk down the old country road that led to the rear of the property. Her cousin had jokingly warned us to watch out for a few of his goats that were roaming loose in a wooded area.

Our stroll was pleasant. The air was warm, and there's nothing like the fragrant smell of the South in the morning. We'd been walking, or rather hiking, for about half an hour when we stopped to rest. We were sitting on a fallen tree and drinking the sodas we brought when suddenly we felt we were being watched.

Looking around us, we noticed little faces within the bushes. All at once, they emerged from their hiding places. We were about to encounter the few goats that we had been warned about. First we counted five, then ten, then twenty-five, and the number kept growing as they made their way out of the bushes and closer to us. I think we stopped counting when we reached eighty-five.

Goats are nosy creatures, and they're always hungry. They will eat just about anything. As they closed in around us, we started to get a little nervous. A few goats would have not been a problem, but this was too large a crowd for either Sue or me. Slowly we began to walk away from them, only to be followed. So we gave them all of the leftover soda in our cans, and then we began to run, laughing hysterically all the way. It seemed like the faster we ran, the louder the hooves following us became.

After a while the goats gave up and went back to their stomping grounds, while Sue and I made our way back to the gate that would safely separate us from the annoying, smelly, but awfully cute creatures. When we reached the house, looking all the worse for wear, my husband and his cousin were waiting for us. My husband's cousin asked us if we'd met his goats, knowing full well that we had. The joke was on us that day, and we were reminded of it at family gatherings for years to come.

I loved Sue like a sister, and after her death I thought of her constantly. Most often she made contact in the warm months, by sending me butterflies. Sue always loved the delicate winged creatures, and I knew that she was sharing her admiration for them with me. As the years passed, I didn't think about her quite as often, but then one chilly October morning, as I was getting ready for work, she suddenly came to mind. I thought that it was strange, because just moments before I had been thinking of something else entirely. Even stranger was that I could not get her image out of my head. As I drove to work in the early morning darkness, I continued to think about her.

As I approached an intersection that I go through every day, I saw that I had the green light. I was almost into the intersection when suddenly something or someone tapped me on the right shoulder. As a natural response, I looked to my right. That is when I saw the truck. It seemed to come out of nowhere, and was moving at about sixty miles an hour. I swerved to avoid a collision. The driver barreled through his red light, only missing me by inches.

I was in a state of mild shock, but I continued on my way. I was only about a mile from the hospital where I work when I began to shake, and then tears started to trickle down my face. I thought about my husband, children, and grandchildren. I had almost left them all.

When I reached the parking lot and parked my car, I became overwhelmed with emotion. I thanked God, and all the loved ones who have passed on in my life. When I spoke Sue's name, I felt wrapped in warmth. I pulled myself together and went into the building. I spent the day trying to forget what had happened.

Later on, at quitting time, the weather had warmed up enough to drive with the windows down. As I was buckling my seatbelt for my journey home, a beautiful butterfly fluttered in through my driver's side window. It hovered in front of my face for a second before fluttering back out through the other side. All at once, it made sense to me. Sue had tapped me, and Sue had hugged me in the parking lot, and now she was sending me a butterfly to let me know that she had been with me.

I believe my friend saved me that day. I think she knew that it wasn't my time.

I'll never stop looking for butterflies. I know she will continue to send them. And every time I see one, I will remember Sue, and I will thank her for sharing their grace and beauty with me.

~R.W. Bryant

Miraculous
Messages from Heaven

Heavenly Comfort

Still Neighbors

Peace is not the absence of affliction, but the presence of God.
~Author Unknown

Our thirteen-year-old son, Nick, who had been battling cancer for several years, had a seizure on Thanksgiving Day of 2008. I feared that I would never hear his voice again as I sat on the floor next to him holding his hand.

At the very same time, our neighbor Sandra's elderly mother Myrna was nearly two hours away under the care of hospice. Sandra and her husband were spending Thanksgiving with her and did not know how sick Nick had become. They had not discussed his condition with Myrna, Sandra's mom, in over six months because Nick's illness upset her deeply. She had once lived in our town and had watched Nick grow from a cute little baby into a handsome, sweet young teenager.

Hospice workers had given Sandra a book to read that instructed family members to listen to every word their dying relatives spoke, because many times they were sharing deep and meaningful messages. The book shared how it was not unusual for dying loved ones to have supernatural experiences in their last months as they visited with those who had gone home before them in audible conversations. In many ways what they recounted was often a "last gift" for the family. Little did Sandra know that Myrna was leaving a "last gift" for our family too.

As Tim and I were facing terrifying moments within our own home, Sandra was sitting at her mom's bedside over 100 miles away listening closely in case her mom said anything significant. Myrna would often speak of seeing her husband, and this always made Sandra smile. However, on the evening Nick had his seizure, Sandra, who had no idea what was happening at our house, was not expecting to hear any words from her mom, as she had become much worse. Imagine Sandra's surprise when her mom reached out, after days of silence, and grabbed her arm. Myrna looked straight into Sandra's eyes, and said, "Tell Tammy not to be scared. I've got Nick."

Nick passed away forty-eight hours later.

Sandra shared this story with me for the first time two months later as we stood in the church sanctuary at her mom's visitation. She had been afraid to tell me the story when it happened, because she did not want to upset me. Hearing these words brought me incredible peace and even a sense of joy as I reflected on the fear I had felt during those last days of Nick's life. I suddenly realized that while Nick seemed to be alone in his sleep, he was not. Myrna, and I am sure many others, were right there with him. They were taking care of him, cheering him on, and welcoming him Home. Hebrews 12:1-2 became more than words on a page to me as I envisioned the cloud of witnesses who were certainly present with Nick as he passed from this life to the next.

I do not know what I would do today if it were not for those supernatural words from Myrna. God allowed her to bring a message of hope and peace to me even as she was dying. Unaware of our situation, her words reaffirmed the closeness of Heaven and continue to give me strength to face my past as well as my future.

~Tammy A. Nischan

The Epilogue

There's a story behind everything… but behind all your stories is always your mother's story…because hers is where yours begins.
~Mitch Albom, For One More Day

An early flight allowed me to get home ahead of schedule from a business trip. Mom had arrived in my absence for a visit, and she would be the only one home at this time of day. I looked forward to walking in and surprising her. However, she did not respond to my greeting at the front door. I called up to the guest room, but did not get an answer. Just then, I heard sounds in our garage. Hurried footsteps, objects bumping and falling. Worried, I rushed to open the door to the garage. The smell of cigarette smoke overwhelmed me. I cried out, "Mom? Are you out here?" Silence. Then, good heavens, my dear old mom appeared sheepishly from behind some shelves, caught smoking in the garage by her son!

After four strokes and three heart attacks, Mom, a brilliant and intense person, had finally quit smoking. But, having found some cigarettes smuggled into the house by my mother-in-law, who was also not supposed to smoke, Mom had given into temptation. It somehow figured that I, her oldest son, would be the one to catch her. Mom and I had been on the same page for as long as I could remember. We read each other like an open book.

Speaking of books, Mom and I used to raid the library in our little town, walking home with shopping bags full of books. I learned to read at an early age, and Mom and I bonded strongly through our shared love of books. We read voraciously. Those bags of books lasted just a few days. We were like addicts; we would hide favorite titles in secret places to be able to read them first. To the end of her life, Mom remained curious and wondering, devouring books with an insatiable appetite. I always stocked the guest room with fresh books for her visits.

Back in the garage, we stared at each other. I smiled, remembering Mom, my protector a lifetime ago on blueberry-covered islands, as she and a four-year-old me picked our buckets full, with bears eating right beside us. Then I saw a Mom who listened patiently as I explained life and all there was to know when I was fifteen and knew it all. And finally, a Mom who gave me wise advice in my twenties when I stumbled and learned I didn't know it all. Now, here was Mom in her seventies, feeling awkward about a bad decision. I remembered what she always did for me, and I walked over and gave her a big hug.

I got the call just a few months after the smoking episode. Dad said Mom had suffered another stroke. I needed to get to the hospital quickly. It was a long drive, to a city in a nearby state. I had time to think. Mom had fought back from prior strokes and heart attacks. Our family now knew that my younger brother would pass away soon from an unfixable heart problem. I felt that Mom would not wish to live this time, only to watch one of her children die.

Certain that Mom would wait for me, I was not surprised to be greeted with words of bravado about recovery. But as we looked into each other's eyes we saw the truth that words can avoid. We knew this was goodbye, so we made the visit last, holding hands and sharing stories of our life together.

It was goodbye—but it was not our final goodbye.

The next evening, back at my home, I was exhausted and retired early. In the dark of the night I awoke with a start. Someone was talking to me. "What is going to happen now? What is going to happen now?" I sat up on the edge of the bed. This question kept repeating and repeating, urgent and insistent. I felt compelled to answer. Looking, I saw my wife sleeping soundly next to me.

The question was clearly spoken by my mom—but her voice was in my mind. From Mom and Dad's guest room next door arose an unsettled rustling, as of pages in books turning rapidly. Then, louder, and more distinctly, I heard the unique yet unmistakable clapping sounds produced when opened books are decisively closed. The noise of books slamming shut increased until one final clap announced that the last book in that room was closed and finished. In my mind echoed one last "What is going to happen now?" Then silence.

Instantly in the stillness, serenity replaced all the anxiety in my heart and soul. Peace, love, and joyfulness swept through me. For a moment, a world beyond flashed open to me, and then was gone. Mom was home, her question answered. And I was granted that briefest sense of what she had found.

I looked at the clock. It was 2:31. I lay back in bed, and my wife asked if everything was all right. I said it was. I slept soundly then, until the phone rang early in the morning. It was the hospital reporting that she had died peacefully, at 2:31 a.m. I knew that.

So close in life, we were close at the end. Mom had come by for our final goodbye. She gave me a lifetime gift of the peace that she had found. Until we meet again Mom…

~William Halderson

44

The Dragonfly

In the night of death, hope sees a star,
and listening love can hear the rustle of a wing.
~Robert Ingersol

I swatted at what I thought was a fly, but it flitted away and landed gently next to my right hand. I sat on the railing of the wooden bridge where Henry and I were passing the time this comfortable August morning. The sun beat down on my face, but a nearby tree protected four-year-old Henry's fair skin and blond hair from the rays. At his age, he had little patience for things that did not fascinate him, but between digging for worms and this new activity of throwing rocks off the bridge into the waterfall, he was thoroughly content. If lunchtime didn't come, he'd probably continue this all day. But at that moment, all I could focus on was the glittering dragonfly. Even when my eyes returned to the giggly boy, I couldn't help but notice that the dragonfly did not leave.

The rest of that Thursday continued as a normal afternoon would between two babysitting jobs and an evening relaxing with my parents. In just a few weeks, I'd be returning to Syracuse University for my senior year. I had started turning my phone off when I went to bed, because I still battled sleeping issues since my former boyfriend passed away eleven months before. I had just begun to feel like my old self again, but that changed when I woke up the following morning.

My alarm rang for my 6:30 a.m. spin class, but as soon as I shut it off, my phone continued to buzz and chirp. Multiple voice mails, too many missed calls to count, and an unusual number of text messages lit up the screen. One text caught my eye because it came from someone I hadn't spoken with in a while. When I opened it, I immediately regretted my choice:

"I'm sure you already know this, but Hannah Smith died in a car accident last night."

Tears filled my eyes, and I bolted from my bed to my parents' bedroom. All I could do was sob. I didn't understand. Why Hannah? Why was I going through this again?

My mom explained that my best friend had found out last night and called the house, but they chose not to wake me up because they knew it would be a while before I slept again. But as soon as she finished, something in me hardened. I stopped crying and said, "I'm going to spin class. I've been through this before; I can do it again."

So I went about my day. After spin class, I got ready to spend my morning with Henry again. I would have cancelled, but spending time with him would put me in better spirits. He wanted to go back to the bridge to play, and it wasn't until I had settled on my same perch that a shimmer caught my eye. I followed it down to my right hand, and there rested a dragonfly. Not just any dragonfly, but the same beautiful, purple one from the day before. It couldn't be. But after further inspection, I confirmed it was the same dragonfly. I started to wonder what this bug meant to me, but Henry's request to leave put it out of mind.

The next few days continued in a blur. Sunday became a double-dreaded day because it was my former boyfriend's gravestone unveiling in addition to Hannah's wake. So down to Philadelphia my father and I went, only to drive back immediately to see Hannah's family for the first time since the accident. All I could think about was how good it was that I already had a "funeral" dress. After the wake, I met up with friends and reminisced over drinks. It felt good to be around the people who knew and loved Hannah too.

On Monday morning, the pews were filled by the time my mom and I arrived at the funeral, so we stood along the wall. I watched friends weep as I cried for Hannah, who we all knew really lived her life. Afterwards, I rekindled high school friendships and tried to keep busy before heading back to school in the next few weeks. I stuffed my pain back inside me. "I've done this before; I can handle this," I'd repeat to myself as the tears would threaten to fall.

But one afternoon, on a routine run to clear my head, my legs took me to the graveyard, where I found a flower-covered gravesite showered in sunlight. It was only appropriate that no tree would ever block the sun near where she lay. Hannah was a sun child who would sunbathe from dawn 'til dusk whenever she could. As I sat down on the grass and turned my iPod off, the pent-up tears came.

All the pain, suffering, and longing to just hug her again came boiling to the surface and flooded out. At one point, I cried so hard I found myself curled up in the grass lying next to her asking why. Why her? Why again? Why now?

Unsure of how much time was passing, I calmed down and lay on my back, staring at the almost cloudless sky. I rolled to my left to lean on my side before getting up, and it appeared: a dragonfly. Blinking away the remaining tears, I couldn't believe my eyes. Was I really seeing a dragonfly? This time sitting on Hannah's grave marker? It couldn't be.

I reached out my hand towards the dragonfly. Instead of flying away, it flew closer to me and landed on the grass. I sat up, mesmerized by this beautiful creature. I bent my knees to hug them to my chest and tears began to creep up again. But before I could really cry, the dragonfly flew up and landed on my knee. That's when I started to laugh. This was no coincidence. I knew it was Hannah, visiting to comfort me.

I left the graveyard after the dragonfly caught a breeze and flew away. Even though my pain and ache for Hannah will never quite go away, I always keep an eye out for dragonflies because I know she's with me. It's only appropriate that she appeared as a dragonfly because she was as beautiful, vivacious, and gracious as one.

~Amanda Romaniello

45

Tom, Are You There?

*You block your dream when you allow your fear to grow bigger
than your faith.*

~Mary Manin Morrissey

"I know it has been over twenty years. Please Tom, if you are there, can you give me a sign?" I hesitantly asked my long departed brother. I nervously looked around my living room. I half expected to see an indent in a chair, a cushion flying at me, or maybe lights flickering on and off like in the movies. But there was nothing.

Well, what did I expect? All I did notice was the dust floating through the sunlight that was streaming into the room. This reminded me that I needed to do my weekly dusting. Feeling deflated, I got up and walked into the kitchen. I temporarily abandoned the thought of communicating with my deceased brother. Instead I decided to focus on what to prepare for supper.

As I threw myself into creating a scrumptious meal, I began to chastise myself.

"What are you doing?" I asked myself.

"You've really gone over the deep end this time," I scolded myself.

I had recently read a very popular book that dealt with the death of a loved one. In it, the author showed the departed person looking down from heaven as she waited to hear from a loved one. The years went by and eventually someone did talk to her. She contacted her loved ones through different signs, perhaps by leaving feathers and coins along their paths. I had always been quite frightened by death but reading this book made me want to reach out to Tom. His birthday would be in a couple of weeks. It was time to put my fear aside.

A week went by since I tried to contact Tom in my living room and there was still no sign. On the Monday of the following week, as I was preparing for work, I noticed on my rather long bathroom counter something small and shiny. As I approached the object, I realized that it was one of my favourite earrings. I ignored it, as I was late for work, and would look at it later.

Well, this went on for a week and I just kept forgetting about it.

While at work, I kept asking myself, "When and why did you take the earring out of the jewelry box?"

During the summer I had lost its match in our pool. I was upset because my husband had given it to me on our Alaskan cruise a few years back.

On Thursday, one day before Tom's birthday, I finally took the time to go into the bathroom to look for that specific earring. You can't imagine my surprise when I opened my jewelry box to put away the earring and realized the earring in my hand was in fact the one I had lost. Not only was it the match, but both had their gold backings attached as well.

I felt like ice water had been poured down my spine. I knew then and there that this was from Tom. I was thrilled! You see, Tom loved jewelry. Up until his death, he was always drawing different styles of rings or necklaces. Tom would then bring his ideas to a jeweler and have them made into beautiful unique pieces. This message from him was not threatening or frightening in any way. If anything I drew great comfort from it!

I quickly found my husband, Greg, and related everything to him. If he was skeptical about it, he did not show it. He was just as baffled as I was about the found earring.

I contacted my mother as well. I knew how she missed her eldest child. She was a little in shock but I think she was secretly happy to hear anything from Tom. It made sense for him to use this type of connection. While he was alive, we all found it unusual for a man to enjoy jewelry as much as he did!

From that point on, I would easily find missing jewelry or lost earring backings. Necklaces would unclip from my neck and fall into my lap while driving or sitting. One time I lost my necklace while on vacation, but when we got home, there was my necklace on the ground by the passenger's side of the car!

Someone up there was helping me find my lost jewelry.

In less than a year, my father passed away. As soon as I got the news, my husband and I drove the five hours to be with my mother. When we arrived she had us sit down. I made myself comfortable beside her small hexagonal table where the phone sat.

My mother seemed especially agitated. She kept pacing and talking about having lost the last of the backings to her earrings. This made my ears perk up. Something caught my eye; I looked down at her table. There, sitting on one of the corners, was the backing to an earring.

I picked it up and looked at Greg. As we made eye contact, we both had a look of disbelief on our faces. I knew it was Tom trying to contact us. Upon hearing of my father's death, we had been in mourning and in shock. Now I actually felt elation from what I had just witnessed! I knew what Tom was telling us.

I called to my mother who was still in the hallway. "Mom, I found the backing to an earring right on your small table!"

She replied, "What? How can that be? I know I lost it over here on the floor in the hallway."

I explained to her as carefully as possible. "Remember that story I told you about how Tom contacted me? How he finds my jewelry and the backings to my earrings when they are lost?"

"Yes I do, but what does this have to do with anything?" she asked.

"This is a message from Tom. Dad is with him and he is letting us know that everything is okay!" I told her confidently.

She was so surprised she did not know what to say, but I sensed she knew it was true.

Later that night, as I stood on my mother's balcony looking up to the heavens, I whispered sadly to Tom, "You know that you were Dad's best friend and he missed you so much for these past twenty years. It's your turn to have him. Goodbye, Dad! Big Brother, thanks for the sign that you are helping him adjust to his new home. Love you both and until we all meet again!"

~S.G. Desrochers

46

A Gift from the Sky

In thee my soul shall own combined the sister and the friend.
~Catherine Killigrew

The year my sister Amanda died was undoubtedly the worst year of my life. While I tried to make some sense of what had happened, I often found myself on the receiving end of others' stories.

People felt compelled to tell me that Amanda had visited them in their dreams. She told them that she was okay and that we were going to be okay also. "That's nice," I usually said, and then went about my business. I really didn't believe them.

Other people told me that Amanda had sent them rainbows, butterflies, and feathers. "They are signs that she's okay," people explained. "Don't you get it?"

I didn't.

I didn't get why Amanda would choose to visit these people instead of me. Why would she send signs to her boyfriend's mother, ladies at church, and distant cousins, but not to me? Why would she leave out her sister who needed more reassurance than anybody?

After a while, these stories made me furious. I felt more alone with each one I heard. And eventually, people stopped telling me.

Amanda died almost ten years ago. And in those ten years, I had married, welcomed my first child, and said goodbye to my first dog, Tyson, affectionately called Tysee. I had experienced a great amount of joy in the past decade, but I had not made peace with my sister's death, until one day when I was playing outside with my son, Evan. Not quite two, he had a great vocabulary, incredible comprehension, and was quite logical. So, I wasn't too surprised when he struck up a conversation with me.

"Sky Mommy," he said as he pointed up.

"I see," I told him. "It's pretty, isn't it?"

"Yes," Evan said, with a quick nod of his head.

"What do you see in the sky?" I asked him.

Evan looked up and around.

"Birds. Tweet tweet."

"Very good," I told him. "What else?"

I'm not sure what I was expecting him to say next. I thought he might be able to point to some clouds, the sun, or an airplane. He had noticed those things on previous occasions. But I was definitely not expecting his next response.

"I see Manda Tysee," he told me.

Completely shaken, I asked him to say it again. It sounded like he was saying the names of my sister and my dog.

"Who do you see, sweetie?" I asked.

"I see Manda Tysee," he repeated.

"In the sky?"

"Yes," he confirmed. "Manda Tysee in the sky."

"Okay," I told him. "Let me know if you see them again."

Then I left it alone. I didn't want to upset him by continuing to ask for more information about something he was probably unable to explain to me. So, I waited for him to start playing again and then I called my parents.

I asked them if they had ever mentioned Amanda around Evan. They said they had told him her name when he pointed to a photograph and asked who she was. But they had never said Amanda was in heaven or made a reference to the sky. And neither had I. How do you explain the concept of death to a toddler? It's hard enough for a thirty-three-year-old to understand.

I was completely thrilled. It was amazing that Evan was telling me that he could see my sister. And it was even more amazing that he saw Amanda and Tyson in the same place. It was something we had never discussed. How could he possibly know this? Unless it was true...

I have heard stories of children and the spiritual world before. I know that children are pure and are closer to God than most adults. So, it would make sense that my sweet Evan was experiencing something that was impossible for me to see. He was giving me my sign, my own personal gift. And the fact that he was completely unaware of it made it even more special.

We have not had another experience since that day. And though I would love to learn more, I have been given exactly what I need for now. My conversation with Evan gave me the sense of peace I had needed for ten years. It allowed me to let go of past anger, hold on tighter to present joy, and open my heart and mind to a future of eternal life and a grand reunion with the loved ones I have lost.

Thank you, Evan. What a beautiful, priceless gift.

~Melissa Face

Everlasting Life

A little faith will bring your soul to heaven,
but a lot of faith will bring heaven to your soul.
~Author Unknown

No one but another parent who has lost a child can understand how the anguish can send one to the edge of sanity. When my son died, I wanted to die too. I wanted to escape the pain and be with my child. This had become my constant prayer after my little boy died from a stroke—until I heard my deceased father's voice.

"Don't be sad," my father said, nodding next to him where my little boy stood, holding onto his grandpa's hand. He looked at me, wide-eyed and worried. They were there right in front of me, albeit transparent, ethereal forms. I sat up a little straighter and wiped my tears. Then, they were gone.

It had been a bad year. My grandmother, my father and my little boy died within twelve months. My grandmother and father often visited me in dreams but when my son died, the grief was so terrible that my doctor prescribed sleep aids so my mind could shut down, and my sleep was dreamless.

I tried; honestly, I tried not to feel sad for my little boy's sake. I knew he didn't want to see his mommy cry. But I missed him and wanted to be with him so badly. My prayers, my appeals to God continued. Then, one day, as I sat in my chair crying as usual, I smelled a noxious odor. A burning smell mixed with sickening chemical fumes.

"Live or die. The choice is yours," a gentle voice said. "But know this: Alex is safe and happy where he is while your other children will still be on this perilous earth. If you go, you will not be able to help them on their journey." I was conflicted but in the end my faith won out. I believed that Alex was in a better, safer place. Like a loving, eternal daycare tended by angels. So, I elected to stay. With a curious calm, I went to the garage and got a clean rag, bunched it up and returned to the growing flames where I rubbed out the fire at its base. It snuffed out immediately. Later I often wondered how I knew to kill a fire like that when on any other occasion I would run around the room in a panic and then call 911.

I chose to live to tend to my surviving children. People say that it must be hard to lose a child, but it is not as hard as having to show your surviving children how to move on with the grief they'll have to carry for the rest of their lives. When you lose a child, you have faith that everything you learned about God and heaven is true so goodbye is not forever. When you lose a child, you allow yourself those days when all you can do is lie in bed and hug your memories. But when you have to teach your surviving children how to keep going, to go through the motions of everyday life, brush their teeth, go to school, plan for their future… it forces you to move beyond your own grief, to show them by example how to do so.

One day as I held a photo of Alex grinning, I wailed aloud, "I'll never be happy again!" Then out of nowhere, I heard Alex exclaim, "Oh, Mommy! Wait 'til you see what's coming!" A fresh breeze of hope whooshed into the room and blew away my sorrow.

That night, Alex appeared in my dreams. We stood in a lush, green meadow rimmed with glorious flowers in Technicolor hues. He held my hand and pulled me from bush to bush just to point out the different colors that couldn't be seen on earth. Indeed, some of the blooms were a rainbow of colors all at once!

The next day and all the days thereafter, my sorrow was not the same. The debilitating pain was replaced with happy anticipation.

I've taught my children how to make the most of their lives through example. I went back to school for my master's degree, started a new business, began to learn new languages, and wrote the stories that were inside me all these years. I can live again now that I know what death truly holds for our loved ones and for ourselves when we are reunited. Life and death hold beautiful surprises for us all. And I can't wait to see what's coming.

~Lori Phillips

Comfort Food

No matter what else they're doing, women are also always nurturing.
~Cokie Roberts

M y oldest sister, Joyce, was diagnosed with cancer on her sixty-fifth birthday and died three months later. In her final days, family gathered around to say final goodbyes. With each of us she would ask, "Are you okay with this? Is there anything I can do to help you find peace with my dying?" That's the kind of person she was—thinking of others when it should have been the other way around.

Before Joyce went into her deep sleep, she lay in her sick bed discussing favorite foods with me and another sister, Vina. Seafood was a favorite for Joyce; Mexican was my and Vina's favorite, with seafood a close second for both of us. Vina asked Joyce, "Have you ever eaten coconut shrimp?"

"I've always loved fried shrimp, grilled shrimp, shrimp scampi… any way it's cooked I love it. I haven't ever tried coconut shrimp though," Joyce replied with a wistful sigh.

My eyes met with Vina's in a silent agreement. Joyce would have a chance to try it this very day. We went on discussing favorites. My favorite Mexican food is chile rellenos. It happens to be Vina's favorite as well.

"You're looking tired, Joyce." Vina stood and motioned for me to come with her. "We will let you get a little rest but we'll be back in after you sleep."

Vina and I found a nearby seafood restaurant in the phonebook and called in an order of coconut shrimp. "You stay here, Chris, and I will go pick it up and bring it here."

Vina returned shortly and Joyce was awake. We took the food into her bedroom and got her fixed up with a bed tray. "You two didn't have to do this, but thanks." As she thanked us she bowed quickly to bless her food, then picked up a shrimp and quickly put it down again on her tray. Her voice was weak and fragile as she said, "I will have to try it in a little while, I guess. I need to close my eyes for a few moments."

We quickly took the tray and made our exit. "Don't worry, we'll save it for you," we promised. I placed it in the refrigerator, along with the casseroles and sweets. It was the very last food discarded. Perhaps both Vina and I hoped she would miraculously awaken and want it.

Joyce never came out of that sleep. She had spoken her last words and then went into a coma. We called in friends and family who had not had a chance to say goodbye and we waited. Taking turns we each sat by her side and held her hand. She lingered in this state for three more days.

We had a kitchen full of fried chicken, casseroles, and desserts that people had brought and left for us to eat. The house was over-filled with people now. My brother, sister and I decided we needed to leave for a short while and could use some food other than chicken or casseroles. We decided on a nearby Mexican restaurant. My nieces and nephews joined us, and we munched on chips and salsa with hardly a word spoken between us. Vina and I had both ordered chile relleno platters. Just as the waitress had delivered everyone's plates, and before anyone even took a bite, our cell phones began to ring. We knew before the words were spoken that my sister had died while we were all absent. Silently, we all stood, left our food untouched, paid the check and returned to Joyce's house.

The next few hours and days were spent in a fog. We all did what had to be done. However, Vina and I both shared a deep regret that we had not been there when Joyce took her last breath. It was almost like we felt we had deserted her for the sake of a tasty meal. Neither of us voiced this sentiment but it was there nevertheless. Guilt is such a senseless enemy.

For many years afterward I could not eat a chile relleno. I somehow associated this food with my failure to be there in the end for my sister.

Recently, my husband ordered for me while I was in the ladies' room. He had done this often before. He knew what I liked. "I ordered you a chile relleno. Is that all right?" he asked upon my return.

My pulse quickened, and a lump formed in my throat. "Yes, thank you," I replied.

How could I enjoy this meal? How could I even manage to take the first bite? My heart filled with sorrow and guilt. I picked up my fork but just could not make myself eat. Then I saw it. Right there on my plate, beside the rice and beans, a lone shrimp... a coconut shrimp... in a Mexican restaurant! "Did you order this shrimp for me?" I asked my husband.

"I didn't know they even serve shrimp here. Guess it comes as a food garnish or appetizer," he answered. "If you don't want it, I'll have it!"

My eyes filled with tears even as a smile covered my face. "No, I think it was Heaven sent... just for me!" I replied. My heart swelled with joy and peace.

I was able to eat my meal that day and have eaten many chile rellenos since. Although we discovered that coconut shrimp was indeed on the menu, our waitress assured us that it was not their policy to put them on a Mexican dish. How one single coconut shrimp ended up on my plate was a mystery. But I knew.

My sister managed to send me a message that only Vina or I would understand. Though Vina had let go of her sense of guilt, I never had. I am convinced that's why the shrimp was on my plate!

~Christine Smith

Affirmation

Friendship isn't a big thing — it's a million little things.
~Author Unknown

Marianne was my best friend and she was dying. I had been blessed to be her caregiver. Cleaning up vomit, talking about death, and going to chemo or radiation, or to this test or that appointment every single day for three years had been a joy and never a burden. Marianne and I had prayed, laughed, and cried together every day of those three years and my life was forever changed by the experience.

One night, after presiding over a big, joyous dinner with seven very loud people, of whom I was the loudest, Marianne went to bed and fell into a coma. Hospice was called.

Thirty-three hours later, about nine o'clock on a Saturday night, I went to the bed where my friend lay on her side, struggling to breathe. Overcome with grief, I was at a loss as to what to do. Could she hear me? Could she feel my touch? Uncertain of anything, I went to my friend, who was curled in a fetal position. Ever so solemnly, I placed one hand on Marianne's thigh and the other on her pillow. Then I slowly leaned down and kissed her cheek.

To my great surprise, Marianne opened her eyes, awakening from this coma just to talk to me. "Oh, you finally came," she said with a smile, as though she was the one who had been waiting and not I.

I sat beside my friend on the bed and we talked. "You have been the best possible friend I could have ever asked for," Marianne said. "I want you to know that I will always love you."

"I'll always love you, too, Marianne," I said as I tried not to cry. "I think you got the short end of the stick on this whole friendship business, though." I tried to laugh, as if I was joking, but Marianne would have none of it.

"Did you hear me?" She squeezed my hand with a strength that amazed me. "I could not have handpicked a better friend." Marianne had written this sentiment in countless cards and letters over the years, but to hear it now was a true blessing. We talked another minute or so and Marianne went back to sleep.

Our brief conversation was to be Marianne's last conversation ever. She never woke up again. Her husband called me several hours later to tell me Marianne had died.

I got through the funeral better than I'd expected, but as soon as I was alone, I crumbled. I cried as I walked my dogs. I cried while I did laundry. I cried in the shower and I cried in my sleep.

Three nights after Marianne's funeral, I went to bed defeated. Not crying, but exhausted by grief and certain I'd never feel okay again. I went to bed early, around eight o'clock. I fell asleep right away.

I woke up to the touch of a warm hand on my thigh. I don't know why, but I had no fear. The clock said 9:14. As I had done to Marianne the night before she died, I lay in stunned silence while my gone-and-buried friend leaned over and kissed my cheek. "I can't stay," Marianne said. "I just wanted you to know I meant what I said: I will always love you. And I could not have picked a better friend to see me through my three years of illness."

I couldn't speak, but I didn't need to. "Marla," she said. "I don't want you to grieve. I just want you to know I meant what I said. And Marla," she went on, "Heaven is beautiful! It's so much more than we imagined! I'm going back now, but I wanted to tell you that I'll be waiting for you. One day, we will be great friends again. So sleep, and don't cry. You'll make your dogs sad." I heard Marianne's sweet laughter and then I was so, so tired I couldn't keep my eyes open anymore and I was asleep again in seconds.

When my alarm went off the next morning, I remembered every detail of what had happened the night before. Had I dreamed the entire thing? Or had Marianne really visited me from Heaven?

The only proof I had that this event had truly taken place was the way my dogs acted afterwards. For days my beloved pups sniffed and investigated the place on my bed where Marianne had sat while talking to me. They were obsessed with that corner of the bed. Even changing the linens didn't stop their curiosity about that spot.

The message got me through. I stopped grieving and started celebrating the life of my dear friend. I celebrated my own life, too, and the lives of my dogs. No way was I going to let my dogs be sad when Marianne specifically mentioned avoiding that!

I still miss Marianne, but all my memories of our time together are happy ones. I'm certain my two final conversations with my best friend — one just before she died and one just after — had everything to do with turning my grief into joy. To this day, if I ever get down on myself, I remember the things Marianne told me, and I remember that she came back briefly from Heaven to say them once more.

~Marla H. Thurman

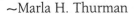

Free Bird

*The bitterest tears shed over graves are for words left unsaid
and for deeds left undone.*
~Harriet Beecher Stowe

grew up in Chicago, where I lived with my dad and his wife. My
dad and I were really close, but I didn't get along so well with
his wife. After a big blowout, I dropped out of high school and
moved in with a buddy. He lived in a home where rules and
supervision were nonexistent. I was making $6 an hour, so I thought
I had it made.

Before long I realized somebody in the house was selling drugs,
dangerous drugs, and I realized I had put myself in a bad situation. A
couple of nights later I was cruising around with my buddies when
somebody took a shot at us. I had a real bullet hole in my car! It's not
at all like TV. It scared me silly, even more than the drugs. A slightly
different angle and it might have come all the way through and hit
somebody. A fraction of a second later it might have hit the gas tank
and blown us all to bits. Nobody had any reason to shoot at me. It
had to be completely random or it was a message to somebody else
in the house. I didn't think it was random, so I had to think it was
related to the drugs. I knew I had to get out.

I went to my dad. He was in an impossible situation, stuck in
the middle between his only child and saving his marriage. If I came
back, she would leave. Even then I knew he'd say yes if I asked. But
since I was more than a little concerned about who was shooting

at my car, I instead asked him to buy me a plane ticket to the West Coast to go stay with my mom. Turns out $6 an hour didn't go as far as I had expected.

The Oregon coast is beautiful, and I was happy to see my mom, but I no longer had any idea where my life was headed. The guys I had known all my life were now 2,000 miles away. I felt isolated and alone, wondering how this had happened. Then a guy my age who worked with my mom asked me if I wanted to shoot some hoops.

Ronnie and I became instant friends. We worked together and even shared a house for a while. He was a genuinely kind person with a smile that lit up a room and a crazy sense of humor. Whenever we met we picked up right where we left off, no matter how much time had passed.

Several years later he went down to California for a while. He called me when he got back. I remember that phone call. I'll never forget it. Something was off, but I couldn't put my finger on it. It was a brief conversation and I thought about it often over the next few days. I couldn't get over thinking something was wrong and I needed to call him. Working in construction, I was tired by the time I got home and kept telling myself "I'll call tomorrow." But "tomorrow" didn't come in time.

I also remember the next call. I was stunned. Ronnie had killed himself. Nobody knew why. He just got up, walked outside and they heard a gunshot.

At the wake I stared at the million-dollar smile in his photo, the smile that I would never see again. "Free Bird" was playing in the background. I felt overwhelmed with guilt. What could have possibly happened? Why didn't I call? Maybe I could have helped. I would have done anything for this guy. Had anybody else noticed? As I wandered among our mutual friends, I found nobody else had noticed anything amiss. In fact, most hadn't heard from him since his return. Me. He called me. The guilt became palpable. My shoulders slumped as if I was carrying a physical load.

A couple of years passed. I thought of Ronnie often and never got over the guilt, but I learned to live with it. One day at work I came down off the roof for a break. I sat down in my truck, opened a soda and turned on the radio just as "Free Bird" started to play. I would never hear that song again without thinking of my friend and feeling I had let him down. As I sat there, a little bird landed on my windshield wiper. It cocked its head and stared at me.

"Is that you, man?" I asked.

The little bird hopped over to the mirror on my door.

"I'm so sorry," I said, as tears streamed down my face. "I knew something was wrong. I should have called. I'm so sorry. Please forgive me."

I sat in my truck sobbing until the song ended. But then, instead of the usual DJ chatter, there was dead air.

"It's okay. You couldn't have changed anything."

My head snapped up and I looked around. I had heard that voice as clearly as if Ronnie was sitting in the truck with me. I looked back at the bird. It winked at me, and as it flew away the radio came back on.

I looked at the can in my hand to make sure it was just soda I was drinking. It was then that I noticed a feather on the seat of my truck. I couldn't explain how it came to be there since I always kept my truck locked. I wasn't sure what had happened, but I felt different, lighter somehow, as if I had been relieved of a heavy load.

In the weeks that followed I found that when I thought of Ronnie I remembered the good times we had together. In place of the sense of loss and the guilt I had carried with me since his death were memories that warmed my heart and made me smile. I discovered many feathers, but they were in strange places like in my boot or in the shower. Not places one would typically find a stray feather, but they were places somebody with my friend's wacky sense of humor would leave them.

I believe Ronnie and I were both granted a rare gift that day. He must have felt guilty that I was feeling guilty. He wanted to make sure that I knew that I hadn't let him down. So he found a way to let me know he was okay and that I needed to let it go.

I still find an occasional feather. Not surprisingly, it often coincides with my hearing the song "Free Bird."

~Bill Young

My Husband's Last Gift

In faith there is enough light for those who want to believe
and enough shadows to blind those who don't.
~Blaise Pascal

Mike and I met on Labor Day 1968. We dated for a short while and then broke up. However, we got back together around Christmas 1968, and were married in February of 1969. He was twenty-two and I was twenty.

Mike was a career Air Force man, so for the next eighteen years we moved around extensively, living in eleven states in eighteen years. During that time we had a son and a daughter.

When Mike retired, we re-settled in Las Vegas, where we had met and married. Our children graduated from high school, then went onto college and careers.

I won't say our marriage was perfect, but Mike and I always had a special connection. He and I were part of each other, and our love deepened as we got older and led our lives as empty nesters.

My husband had been troubled by a shaking hand for quite some time. His mother had this condition, as did several of his siblings. Finally, in 2000 I talked him into going to a neurologist who had been highly recommended.

This neurologist thought that Mike had familial tremor, which is a hereditary condition. To be on the safe side, he decided to do a CT scan to make sure Mike hadn't suffered from a series of small strokes. It showed that Mike had a very large brain aneurysm that needed to be taken care of as soon as possible. If left untreated the aneurysm could rupture and cause severe impairment or death.

We saw a neurosurgeon in Las Vegas, but we were both unhappy about the surgery he wanted to perform. We then decided to go to a clinic in Santa Barbara that my coworkers had highly recommended. The neurosurgeon took one look at the MRI that had been ordered and told us that surgery was too dangerous. He recommended that we go to UCLA and meet with a specialist who would "coil" the aneurysm. This involved putting coils in the aneurysm through an artery, which would harden the aneurysm so that it would not burst.

The neurosurgeon told us the aneurysm had a troubling aspect: there was an area that was pushed out. But doctors would pay special attention to that spot. The doctor was confident the operation would be a success and Mike would be fine. In fact, he said that Mike could go home the next day. We were overjoyed that we had finally found a doctor who could help him.

We went home and prepared ourselves for this surgery, which was to take place in a week. On the day of surgery, we drove back to UCLA and Mike was admitted. I stayed with him in the pre-op room and he joked with the technician who was giving him a shot. The last thing I said to him was "I love you."

I was instructed to wait on the first floor. Someone would come and get me when the operation was over. I waited and waited, but no one came. Finally, I asked the receptionist if she could find out what was happening. I was told Mike was being transferred to the fourth floor. I waited and waited on the fourth floor, but he never came. I finally discovered he was in an ICU wing in the basement.

I stayed all day at the hospital, and was able to see Mike for just a few minutes at a time. When I did see him, he was disoriented and could not speak clearly. I assumed this was a result of his operation, and no one told me otherwise. Finally, at about 8 p.m., I went back to my hotel, assured he would receive morphine for the pain.

About twenty minutes after I returned to the hotel, the hospital called, asking me to return. When I got near Mike's bed, the neurosurgeon told me Mike had bled throughout his brain and was brain dead.

I called our children and told them what happened. At the time, my daughter was living in Washington State, and my son was living in Germany. I would have to make the decision to take my husband off life support, but I knew I could not make that decision until my children came to say goodbye. So I sat through the night at Mike's bedside, holding his hand and praying to God that he would perform a miracle and let Mike live.

Sometime during that long, dark night, Mike gave me his last gift, a symbol of his love for me.

I saw a figure come from above, a diaphanous figure with arms, or wings, covered in a soft cloth. The figure came to receive Mike's spirit or soul. But before they left, their spirits passed through my body. The feeling of peace I received was so profound that I knew I would never experience it again here on earth. Then they were gone.

I also knew that Mike had asked the spirit to let them pass through me, to let me know that he was all right and at peace. That was my husband's last loving gift to me.

In the years since Mike's death, I have missed him so much at times that my heart actually hurts. But then I remember his journey with this angel up to where God received him with love, and I know that my soul mate and I will be together again. Mike's gift showed me that.

~Susan Simmons

Chapter 6

Miraculous
Messages from Heaven

Miracles of Love

Miracle of the Green Tide

When you open your mind to the impossible, sometimes you find the truth.

~From the television show Fringe

'm a nurse. I always believed in science, not miracles. That is, until I experienced one of my own.

It happened one August day, walking the shoreline from Red Rock in Swampscott, Massachusetts, to the Tides, a restaurant in nearby Nahant. I had done this nearly every day that summer. But that day, dismal and gray, was different, sadder, for it marked the tenth anniversary of Dad's fatal stroke. With each step, I relived that pain.

Back then, I'd just returned home from errands and casually hit the answering machine. "Your dad has been rushed to Springfield Hospital. We found him on the floor." It was a neighbor of his. "I think he had a stroke."

I grabbed some things for the two-and-a-half-hour drive. Mom was away visiting family in Charleston, South Carolina. My brother lived in Texas, my sister in Myrtle Beach.

Dad, a vibrant seventy-eight-year-old, walked and played golf almost daily. He did all his household chores and was repairing the porch roof. Months earlier, he had cheered as I graduated as a nurse practitioner.

When I saw Dad, I knew it was not good. He had suffered a

massive stroke, his entire right side paralyzed. He could not sit, speak, nor swallow. But he was alive and his eyes showed relief — his daughter, his nurse, had arrived.

Luckily, he understood me. "Daddy, you're going to be okay," I repeated, trying to hide the fear in my eyes. I phoned my mother and siblings. That night, and for most of the next fourteen, I stayed by his side.

Dad could not tell me what he wanted or needed, frustrating us both. Then, I gave him a pad and put a pen in his left hand. He scratched out a few words. Dad was still there.

Dad was so ill that he could not make his own health care decisions. The doctor explained that he needed a "health care proxy," to authorize someone to make health care decisions. "Dad, who should this be?" Slowly but clearly, he wrote, "Bonnie (my childhood nickname) is in charge."

Over the next few days, Dad seemed to improve, and that weekend, he rallied. With support, he sat up to enjoy time with his wife, children, and grandchildren. As we were leaving for dinner, he teasingly wrote, "Make sure Dick (my brother) picks up the check!" Dad always had a fondness for greenbacks. Surely he must be getting better, I thought, if he's thinking about money!

Dad still could neither eat nor swallow. A tube in his nose was giving him liquid nutrition, but it was only temporary. Now we had to decide if a permanent tube should be put in his stomach. Would Dad want that? I recalled our talks about his wishes. I carefully weighed the benefits and risks of such a procedure. My mom, brother, and I were uneasy about it. But my sister in Myrtle Beach insisted, "You just can't starve him to death!"

In the end, Dad went to the OR. After many long hours, he was rolled back on a stretcher, a permanent feeding tube in this abdomen. I looked at his face, the pain visible. His eyes spoke, "Why did you let them do this to me?" I was shaken. Had I let Dad down?

The next day, his condition worsened. He was burning with fever and was not responding to my voice. He could not sit, write, or communicate in any way. The antibiotics were ineffective. A brain scan confirmed that he'd suffered another, more severe stroke, with irreversible brain herniation causing all basic life functions to quickly fail. There was nothing more that could be done, the doctor said.

I thought about my grandmother. Dad had found her collapsed from a stroke. She died within weeks. Dad said it was "for the best;" she wouldn't have wanted to live "like that" completely dependent on others. Neither would he, he said.

I recalled our talks about the difficult end-of-life decisions made by my patients and their families. He'd listened, then had nonchalantly said, "When my time comes, you'll know best what to do for me." Nothing was ever written. It was understood then. It was understood now.

Being a devout Catholic, Mom consulted the priest, then calmly said, "We can't let Dad continue to suffer. We have to let him go in peace."

Dad's care now changed from curing to care, comfort, and dignity. The antibiotics and tube feedings, no longer helpful, were stopped. His only medications were for comfort. This decision was too excruciating for my sister in Myrtle Beach, who shrieked, "Who do you think you are, Dr. Kevorkian?"

But Dad was our focus. In his final journey, we chose the path of least suffering. He'd been there for me at my birth and I would be with him in his death.

We all had our final goodbyes. In the end, he left on his terms, in a brief peaceful moment, with Mom, his love, at his side.

Now, ten years later, I walked the shoreline recalling my sister's words and the anguish in Dad's face when he returned from the OR. Had I let Dad down? I softly sobbed.

All that summer, I'd walked the beach finding treasures: starfish, shells, sand dollars, a green bottle, an unopened green can of beer, and green sea glass. I even found a denture with inlaid gold initials, but never any money. So, being my father's daughter, I thought, Dad, if I did the right thing, please send me a sign? Let me find some real money!

Just then, sloshing through the area called the Red Tide (really harmless red algae) I looked down—a green one-dollar bill! "Wow!" I chuckled. "But gee Dad, couldn't you do better? More like a $100?"

No sooner had I giggled, there it was, another green bill! I reached down; it was a $100 bill! Oh my God! This couldn't be real! Was it a fluke or was it the sign that I'd been seeking?

I shook my head in disbelief. Could a ship have sunk in the harbor? Not feasible. Could someone have lost his wallet in the surf? Not likely. Could someone have been robbed? Nothing about it in the paper.

I need to find one more dollar to prove this was real. I had to prove this was not just some strange coincidence. So I searched, turning over red algae; not another dollar appeared. I drove home stunned. Who finds $100 on the beach?

The next day, I walked the same shoreline, puzzled and uncertain. Then, as I passed through that red algae, there it was—another dollar!

This was no coincidence, I knew then. The red tide had turned to green money, a sign from Dad that I had not let him down. From that moment, I felt at peace.

I still believe in science. I'm still skeptical about many things. I still think of my father and miss him. But now I am a nurse who believes in miracles.

~Barbara A. Poremba

A Simple Answer

Angels descending, bring from above,
Echoes of mercy, whispers of love.
~Fanny J. Crosby

walk the beach, the moist sand feeling rubbery on my feet. Occasionally I must stop to wipe away a small pebble stuck on a toe or heel. A small reminder my physical body feels pain also.

It is the in-between season now, not summer with the swimmers and the families on the beach. Not yet winter, when the cold wind from Lake Michigan makes this walk almost impossible. My body is bundled, but my toes are bare in the sand.

My life for so long was an in-between. Some days wanting to stay with him, some days frustration making me consider leaving. Thirty-eight years of marriage is a long, long time, like old ruts in a dirt road you drive on. Bumpy with age and worn in spots, making part of the drive miserable, but part of it smooth, a pleasure. Worn old patterns we fell into, him first, then me. Maybe it was the other way around. Hard to know, and I tell myself it doesn't truly matter anymore who's angry and who's not.

Not that I can't go to anger, because I can. It takes a second to send me back to one of our memories, a fight or more likely a non-fight, words never said, never truly expressed. I say them now, "Why couldn't you? Why didn't you?"

Can you fight with a ghost? Are all our old words now irrelevant? Unresolved? Like taking a sword and jabbing at a windmill. What sense does anger make in grief?

No in-between for him and me anymore. Now it is just me—me with my future, with my decisions—me alone. The long debate: am I happy, am I not? Do we work, do we not? It is gone from my will. Off the table more quickly than I could ever have believed possible. Taken and shelved away. I try to focus my eyes forward, looking only for me. Hoping and praying the good parts of life remain for him in spirit, for me on earth.

It is my birthday today. For him, my birthday was always simple, a card that said love with a $100 bill inside for me to spend. My daughters and grandchildren over for a dinner I would make, wine to drink, small noses to play with, the little ones on my lap. Life we created and made, the two of us, then the four of us, extending now beyond our nucleus. Afterwards I would gripe to myself about the mess to clean up as all of them scattered back to their lives, leaving me once more to be the mistress of the kitchen.

This birthday feels so different, as they all will from now on. I'm at my sister's house celebrating a new way, in an old form.

"Like when we were kids," she told me when she called to offer the stay. "Been a while since we've done this," she had added, trying to put cheer in her voice. Millions of years back I think, a different time, a different family. And so I came to try on the new, forcing myself forward in my new role as widow on my birthday.

"Guide me," I request of him, my newly departed husband, as I continue my walk. "Protect me when you can, send me hints of where to go, who to trust." Would he do that for me? But such a thought goes away quickly. I know the answer. Even in life I would know this answer.

"Of course," he would say, dismissing the question, turning his attention back to his book, his evening football or baseball game. It would be a given for him, even without the request.

I pick up stones from the beach and cast them out in the water. I would love to skip rocks, but the water is too rough, and I have to settle for trying to hit a white cap before it disappears. A freighter passes by, chugging along the horizon, moving quickly into my life and then out. I watch it disappear on the water line, hazy at first and then gone.

I search for more things of interest using my toes as a tool to shift through the sand. They fumble along feeling something foreign, something not of the beach. I look down to discover a greenish paper. A dollar I think. Excited, I reach for it and clear the beach sand away, getting small damp grains on my fingers. Pulling the money free I brush away the remainder of the sand, ready to push the bill down into the front pocket of my jeans. I stop; I stare. The president isn't right for a dollar. I bring the bill to eye level. Tears well up in my eyes, blurring the picture, the numbers. But I've seen it; I know what it is.

"How'd you do that?" I ask, lifting my eyes to the sky, laughing and crying. I hold the hundred-dollar bill to my heart, pressing it close with both of my hands. I stand alone on the quiet beach, me and the gift, amazed and grateful.

"Come on, come on," I hear my sister's voice in the distance. "Time to start celebrating your birthday!"

I see her jogging towards me, her hands in the air calling me back, now doing the silly jumping thing she did when we were kids.

"Time to start..." I repeat, gazing once more to the sky. I move the bill into my front pocket and smile. For him it was always that simple.

~Diana Creel Elarde

54

Listening to Our Angels

If you can't hear the angels, try quieting the static of worry.
~Terri Guillemets

D riving home after a long day of teaching computer class to a group of people, my mind whirled with ideas for the next class. The car was on "auto pilot" as I drove the familiar route home. With the windows slightly open, I could feel the warm breeze on my face and I enjoyed the sweet smell of springtime air. The large knobby tires of my Jeep Cherokee hummed along the pavement as country music played on the radio. The sound was almost hypnotic and I continued my thoughts on fine-tuning the Office 2003 class. As a new instructor, I wanted to make sure to teach people the essentials to make their work easier, without overwhelming them and putting them into a computer coma. Teaching was not easy for me. I felt uncomfortable in front of the class, even though I knew the material in depth. The major benefit was that it allowed me to work part-time so I could be there for my kids. They were, and still are, my main priority in life.

As the yellow lines of the Veterans Expressway streaked by, my mind wandered from the computer class to what I needed to get from the grocery store. What would be quick and easy to prepare? The girls had karate, so it couldn't be too heavy. I continued making the mental list as I slowed to the stoplight.

Grocery store, dinner, karate, homework… why was I still sitting at this red light? It seemed awfully long. Anxiously waiting for the light to turn, my foot was ready to release the brake and press the gas at the first sign of green.

The light turned green and my thoughts were suddenly interrupted by the appearance of my grandmother sitting in the passenger seat next to me. She said very clearly, "Wait, just wait." I remember her holding up her left hand telling me to stop. "Don't go. Don't release that brake."

The only car in sight was a silver car behind me. I still saw my grandmother's hand telling me to wait. My foot was frozen on the brake. My mind was trying to process what was happening when a car speeding down the road in front of me ran the red light.

If I had pressed the gas when the light first turned green, as I would normally do, that car would have crashed into the driver's side door of my car. At the high rate of speed that person was driving, there is no doubt in my mind that I would not be here today if I hadn't listened to my grandmother. I glanced in my rear view mirror as if to ask, "Did you see that?" The driver behind me had wide eyes as he nodded his head, confirming that he saw the car run the light, too. I don't know if he saw my grandmother next to me, but he knew what would have happened to me, and perhaps him too, if I had pressed the gas pedal when our light turned green.

The Bible is full of stories of angels appearing. In Psalm 91:11 "For He will order His angels to protect you wherever you go." In Hebrews 1:14 "Therefore, angels are only servants—spirits sent to care for people who will inherit salvation." When it actually happens, it is hard to comprehend. My hands were shaking as I gripped the steering wheel. I cried all the way home, my mind whirling with "what ifs" and trying to understand how my grandmother came to me. Needless to say, I didn't make it to the grocery store.

I didn't tell anyone about the experience for a long time. I had to process what happened before I could share it with anyone. I remember the first time telling my family. We were in the Outer Banks of North Carolina, sitting on the porch talking and the subject of angels came up. "Grandma Wilson is my angel," I said. My heart was racing as I told them what happened. I don't know if they believed me or not. Someone made a joke and we changed the subject. Later that evening, my sister-in-law shared a story with me about her own incident with an angel. I felt such relief in knowing I wasn't the only one who had been through this. Over the years, I have shared this experience, and each time, I learn of similar encounters.

My grandmother had passed away in 1989, a year before my first daughter was born. This event occurred thirteen years later. I find comfort in knowing that she is still with us and able to see all three of my children.

I am so thankful for many things that occurred that day—to God for sending my grandmother to me, my grandmother for saving my life, and to myself for actually listening and not ignoring the warning. Our daily lives can get so hectic that we ignore the messages we receive.

~Karen McBride

55

Dancing in Heaven

Dancing faces you towards Heaven, whichever direction you turn.
~Terri Guillemets

Shortly after crossing the state line from Georgia into Alabama, I saw a handsome young man right outside my front windshield. I blinked a couple of times to focus, trying not to get too distracted from the highway I was negotiating at eighty miles per hour. But sure enough, there was Daddy, who had died twelve years earlier, his arms outstretched, grinning from ear to ear, looking off in the distance, eyes twinkling. He was thin like I remembered him when I was a little girl. Gone were the bags under his eyes and the slightly protruding abdomen. No longer was there any gray to be found on his full head of hair.

Out of the clouds on the left side of my view, a beautiful young woman came running toward him, her long wavy dark hair flowing all around her. He wrapped his arms around her.

"Oh, Huck, you are so beautiful," he whispered softly in her ear as they embraced. "Oh, David, you too," she whispered back, snuggling comfortably into his strong arms. "I've missed you so much."

"Come on, I have a lot to show you," he said, excitement in his voice. He twirled her around as if in a dance. She hesitated. "But what about the children?" she asked. In a reassuring yet insistent voice, he said, "Don't worry, they'll be fine. Janie will be there soon; they have each other. They'll be fine."

They danced off into the puffy clouds hand in hand. I wanted to remember all the details of this incredible image so I could describe it to Mama and my sisters and brother when I reached Tuscaloosa. They'd get a big kick out of it.

Just moments before this vision, I had given up trying to find something interesting to listen to on the radio. I figured I'd just think about something else to occupy myself on the long drive from Macon, Georgia, to Tuscaloosa. As I was sorting through my brain for what I wanted to think about, Daddy had appeared.

The ringing cell phone startled me.

"Janie, pull over a minute. I want to talk to you about your mama." Why was my sister's friend calling me? How did he get my number and how did he know I was in the car? That was the only time I ever used this old-fashioned bag phone. I had yet to join the modern world of the smaller, handheld cell phones. Waiting for me to stop the car, he asked where I was and how the trip was going. I wondered why he cared. By the time I pulled off Interstate 20 onto the shoulder a few miles west of the Oxford/Anniston exit, it hit me. Something must have happened to Mama.

Shortly before I left Macon a couple of hours earlier, I told my sister, who was in the hospital room with Mama, to call me if anything changed. I was on my way to help hold a bedside vigil until Mama returned to consciousness. She had been unresponsive for nearly thirty hours. But she wasn't supposed to die. Since her heart attack six months earlier and her stroke a few days later, we had almost lost her several times. But her strong will to live always kicked in (with a lot of help from activated prayer chains), and she came back from those near-death experiences stronger and more determined than ever to get her life back.

Not this time.

The friend on the phone described the last few minutes that he and my sister held Mama's hands from each side of her bed, reciting the twenty-third Psalm—"Yea, though I walk through the valley of the shadow of death, I will fear no evil..."—and whispered comforting words to her. I closed my eyes, feeling like my own heart would stop. I pictured the monitor over her bed showing the ever-increasing space between her heartbeats, until there was nothing but silence. I could hardly breathe.

"She quietly slipped away at 3:48," he said. I glanced at the clock on the dash. Oh my gosh. That was the exact time I watched my parents embrace. I smiled through my tears, and said a quiet "thank you" to them for that gift.

I quickly got back on the road as soon as we hung up. I still had more than 100 miles to go and wanted to see Mama before the hospital staff removed her body. My sister promised to do what she could to keep Mama there, but was concerned about me driving. She didn't have to worry.

Mama kept me company, painting a gorgeous canvas for the entire world to see. I drove into the most magnificent sunset I've ever seen. And it stayed with me the entire trip, getting more dazzling every time I crested a hill. There were a few times I thought I saw Mama dancing through the clouds, splashing a little more pink here, a dab of gold there, a brilliant blue in between.

I later discovered that a few days earlier, just hours before Mama was transported for her last time from the nursing home where she was recovering to the same hospital where I was born nearly fifty-two years before, she told my other sister that she wanted to dance. At that time, we still thought that she was getting better. She had a little bit of movement in her left hand, which had been paralyzed since her stroke, and it was just a matter of time before she was coming home.

My sister picked up her limp arm and Mama started moving her good hand to the music. Of course, she was too weak to actually get of the bed and make any movements. But she was dancing with her hand. Her spirits were high—she seemed so free and wanting to just dance and play. A few hours after that, Mama took a turn for the worse and announced that she was dying—the first time she had said that in the months she had been bedbound, despite the many crises and close calls she had survived.

She slipped into a deep coma from the morphine the nurses gave her to relieve the pains in her chest and never woke up. My brother called me that Tuesday morning and said Mama had not come out from under the morphine yet, although it was well past time for her to come around. I was driving over from Macon to help keep her bedside vigil until she woke up, which we were sure would be any minute.

But instead of waking up, she slipped away from us that afternoon and went off dancing with Daddy in the clouds, leaving her broken body behind for good. She finally got her wish to dance once more. This time, she was again in the arms of her husband of forty-two years and the father of their four children, just like the night they met.

~Jane Self

Unexpected Help

I sought my soul, but my soul I could not see. I sought my God,
but my God eluded me. I sought my brother and I found all three.
~Author Unknown

sped down the interstate, my heart pounding in my chest, tears threatening to blur my vision. The call from Saint Elizabeth's, the assisted living center where my parents lived, had sent me into a panic.

"Your dad isn't doing too well. He has slumped to one side and isn't talking or eating. We'd like to send him to the hospital," said the kind voice on the other end of the line.

One thing my dad had been very clear about after his recent bout with pneumonia was that he did not want to go back to the hospital again. He was still under hospice care, although he had made a remarkable recovery, beyond what anyone expected.

"No, please don't send him to the hospital. He is on hospice and has requested not to go the hospital. Please. I am coming. I will be there as soon as I can," I pleaded.

It was nearly an hour drive from my home in rural Boulder County to the heart of Denver where my parents lived, where I had been raised, and my parents before me. We were so glad to have found a well-kept, caring place for my parents when my mother's Alzheimer's became too much for my father to care for at home. Once in a place where my mother was taken care of, the toll of caregiving on my father became more evident. After the pneumonia, he was diagnosed with vascular dementia, caused by a series of mini strokes that left him more disoriented and debilitated each time.

"I'm coming, Daddy, please don't die, please don't die. I'm coming as fast as I can." I wished for someone else to be able to get there to help my father. My thoughts moved to my brother, who had lived closer. My brother who had been there to help me take care of my parents in previous times of need. My brother who had overdosed on drugs last month. "How could you leave me like that? Where the hell are you now, when I need you so much? When Dad needs you?"

I heard a deep, gentle and so familiar voice speak in my heart. "I am right here with you. And honey, you really need to slow down. You are driving way too fast. He isn't going to die today. Please, please slow down."

I looked at my speedometer and was shocked to see it was over ninety. I let off the gas, but my anger did not abate. "Well, why aren't you with Dad? He needs you more than I do right now. Please go to him!"

The answer was swift. "I am with him. And he is going to be okay. I can be with both of you. Pretty cool, huh?"

Tears were fully running down my face now as the brother who I missed so much, despite my anger with him, gently supported me as I dealt with my loss.

"I don't understand. Where are you, Matt? Why did you go? What happened?"

"That's a lot of questions and I think you better focus on your driving right now. Just know that you are not alone. I'm here and I'm helping you take care of Mom and Dad."

"You are not alone," echoed in my mind and I felt calmer. I drove safely to Saint Elizabeth's where my dad was already doing much better, sitting up and talking, though still disoriented. I kissed the top of his head and held his hand, grateful to be able to be there with him when he needed me. "He is not going to die today," Matt had said. And he didn't. My head was full of questions and doubt about what happened while I was driving. But my heart was full of love, for both the father beside me and the brother who had protected us that day.

~Lisa Shearer Cooper

The Very Long Distance Call

The most beautiful thing we can experience is the mysterious.
~Albert Einstein

loved my cousin Morgan. He was, during my youth, more like an older brother to me. My love of sports, entertainment, music, etc. was heavily influenced by him. We remained extremely close into adulthood. Morgan was someone who had an almost supernatural "life force" about him. When you were in his company, you felt his vibrancy, his positivity and his goodness. I don't know how else to describe it, but anyone who met him would know what I mean. That's why it was especially devastating and shocking beyond belief that a life force like Morgan's could be extinguished, at age sixty-two, by pancreatic cancer.

There are certain people who I find it hard to believe are no longer with us. It's a strange and eclectic list, I know. It's celebrities like Dana Reeve (Christopher Reeve's wife), Tim Russert, Phil Rizzuto, Michael Jackson, Merv Griffin, Bobby Murcer, Elizabeth Edwards... just that life force thing, I guess. Morgan was in that category.

One day, about a year or so after his passing, my wife Dana and I got home early on a Saturday evening to hear a message on our answering machine. It was from Morgan's son, Adam, telling us to make sure we watched psychic John Edward's television show that evening. The program was about to start. We turned on the TV and there was Morgan's wife, Jennifer, along with their two adult children, Adam and Alana, having a psychic reading by Edward regarding Morgan's attempt to communicate with them from the great beyond. It was pretty intense and incredible stuff. Normally I would be highly skeptical, but the ultimate shocker for Dana and I came when Edward stated that Morgan was communicating about "a certain song from the Broadway musical *Wicked*." Jennifer, Adam and Alana shook their heads, not immediately recalling any particular association between Morgan and a song from *Wicked*. But Dana and I sure knew of one.

The previous year, when it had become clear that Morgan had no more than a few days left to live, Dana handpicked a song that she felt best expressed her feelings about him. She recorded her version of the song "For Good" from the show *Wicked*, and overnighted a CD to the hospice where Morgan spent his final days. Jennifer played the song for Morgan that next evening. According to Jennifer, a very weakened Morgan smiled and cried at the recording's conclusion. And the very next morning, he passed away.

So you can only imagine how stunned Dana and I were to hear Edward mention, of all things, "a certain song from the Broadway musical *Wicked*. Nobody outside of me, Dana, and Morgan's immediate family would even know that it was the final song Morgan had listened to before he passed!

As Dana and I struggled to keep it together during the fascinating and chillingly on-target reading, the telephone rang. I hurriedly picked up the phone. There was no voice on the other end, just a loud, piercing, electronic screeching sound. Very strange, I thought, and hung up. Again the phone rang. Again that screeching sound. I don't ever remember hearing a noise quite like that coming through a phone. I hung up once more.

Even more bizarre, when I picked up the phone again I couldn't get a dial tone—just that strange electronic piercing noise, louder than ever! I checked all the connections. Everything was fine. But no matter what I tried to do, I could not get rid of that noise. Then literally within seconds of Edward's segment with Morgan's family ending, the screeching sound stopped and the dial tone mysteriously returned!

I have since been told by people who have studied the field of parapsychology that departed family members often use modern electronics to communicate from the great beyond, and that the telephone is the tool most frequently employed. No one would have found that kind of stuff more absurd than I, trust me. But Morgan, I truly believe with all my heart that it was you trying to reach us that Saturday night. And you sure did, Cuz. You sure did.

~Gary Stein

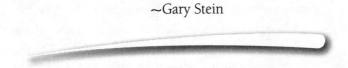

Lilacs and Roses

Flowers seem intended for the solace of ordinary humanity.
~John Ruskin

Grandma Ellen was dying. I knew it. Cancer was winning the battle. I was devastated that I couldn't see her, even for a few minutes, but my grandfather insisted that he wanted all the grandchildren to remember Grandma healthy and happy.

I was ten at the time and very close to Grandma. She babysat me often, so we spent a lot of time together. The hours would seem like minutes. I have many memories of us working together in the garden or the house, taking bike rides, visiting people, running errands, making meals, playing card and board games, and even napping together. I loved how she'd rub my back while we took turns spelling words aloud until one or both of us dozed off.

One night I drifted off to sleep and dreamed of Grandma. I was in the big orange seat on the back of her bike — one that I had been on frequently as a small child. She pedaled us down the paved country road to the enormous stand of lilac trees a short distance from her house. It was a place that we visited every spring when the blossoms opened. I loved how the scent of flowers intensified as we got closer, luring us forward. The sun felt so warm. The hum of bees was audible even before we got off the bike to smell, touch, and pick a big bouquet of lilacs. I woke up before we could take the bouquet back to her house. Several times that night, I had the very same dream, waking each time at that same point. Over and over it happened. I just couldn't fall into a peaceful, dreamless sleep.

Then, during one of the awake moments, I sensed someone enter my room. Lying on my stomach, I turned sleepy eyes to the closed door. Suddenly, I smelled lilacs. My bed creaked and lowered like someone was sitting down on the edge. I felt a hand upon my back, rubbing it just like Grandma always did when we napped together. In no time, I dropped into a deep, dreamless sleep.

My alarm clock woke me. A peculiar emptiness ached in my gut. I lingered in bed, remembering what had happened, clinging to those precious moments with Grandma. Something in me sensed she was gone. Eventually, I forced myself out of bed and went upstairs. My teary-eyed mother met me at the door. She gave me a long hug and in a strangled voice told me Grandma had passed away early that morning.

The news confirmed what I instinctively knew. "I know," I admitted, tears spilling while I explained that Grandma had come by to tell me goodbye since I hadn't been able to go to her.

The scent of flowers touched me one more time shortly after Grandma's death. It happened on one of the visits my mom and I made to her grave.

It was a temperate, late spring day. I knelt down on the sun-warmed earth and with my finger traced the roses engraved on her headstone.

I wondered why the stone didn't have lilacs engraved on it so I asked Mom, "Why did all of you pick roses for the stone?"

"Roses were her favorite flowers," she answered. "Grandma loved roses of all kinds. They're my favorite too."

"I thought she liked lilacs," I said. "We always picked lilacs together."

"She did like them, but roses were her favorite. She knew you preferred lilacs though. That's why she would take you to the big grove to pick them."

My throat tightened. Lilacs were my preferred flower. Grandma must have chosen that scent for me the night she said goodbye.

After a few minutes of silence, we walked back to the car. We got in and Mom started the engine. The strong scent of roses suddenly filled the vehicle. In disbelief, I turned to Mom. She looked as stunned as I felt.

"Do you smell roses?" I asked in a choked voice.

She nodded, her eyes wide and damp.

"They were her favorite, and yours?" I asked for confirmation.

Mom nodded again and smiled. It was a sad, yet joyful smile.

The intense fragrance lasted most of the way home as we cried, laughed, and shared precious memories of Grandma Ellen. Perhaps the scents were a gift from her, or perhaps, they were simply a hint of the sweet perfume of heaven.

~Jennifer Taylor

The Miracle Lady

Reason is our soul's left hand, Faith her right.
~John Donne

My mother and I always had a close relationship, but we saw life differently—until she was seventy-nine years old. Her faith was deep, but based on strict rules. A first-generation Italian-American, she was a creative first grade teacher with a zest for life. Used to dealing with six-year-olds, she enjoyed being in charge. My parents had a happy marriage because her fun-loving bossiness balanced perfectly with my father's kind and gentle Pennsylvania Dutch personality.

I was an idealistic child of the New Age, writing poetry and fascinated with yoga. I knew my mother loved me and was proud of my accomplishments, but she didn't share my belief that there is more to life than what we can see and hear.

My beloved father, a high school teacher and professional musician, who said he felt closer to God in his garden than in church, died before my twenty-first birthday. At the age of fifty-four, my tough, strong mother was suddenly vulnerable and frightened. Eventually she regained her courage and returned to teaching full-time.

At age thirty-nine, living with my husband and working in Manhattan, I was hit with the news that I had breast cancer. After a diagnosis of cancer, life is never the same. Fortunately, the cancer hadn't spread, but I needed surgery and radiation. Mom insisted on taking the bus to New York to visit me after my operation. When I saw her from my hospital window, striding down the street in her red coat, I knew everything would be fine.

Cancer caused me to reflect on my life and feelings even more deeply. I joined a dream-sharing class and discussed a dream about my father. I was at our summer house in Avalon, in the garden he loved. Mom was inside. Suddenly, my father appeared to me in a radiant glow. He told me that I would recover from cancer, and to try to get along with mother—even though we were so different. Then he turned into a beautiful monarch butterfly and flew away. The butterfly is the archetypal symbol of eternal life in many cultures.

Mom retired at sixty-five and lived year-round at Avalon. She enjoyed getting together with family and friends, church, civic groups, crafts, gardening and travel. Her cerebral aneurysm at the age of seventy-nine changed everything.

She lapsed into a coma following emergency surgery. The doctors were pessimistic about her recovery. Standing at Mom's bedside in the critical care unit, thinking she was dying and remembering stories of the comforting white light many people saw in that limbo world between life and death, I tried to help my mother by shouting, "Mom, can you see the light? Go toward the light!"

Mom remained in a coma for several weeks. We didn't know whether to pray for her to live or die, because the doctors said that if she came out of the coma, she might be severely brain damaged. One day, a good friend was praying over her and said loudly, "Jo, wake up and come back to us." Mom suddenly opened her eyes and gave him a big smile! She looked around the room, saw a rose in a vase by her bed, and said "beautiful"—her first word since going into the coma. The doctors called her "The Miracle Lady" and we were thrilled.

Soon, however, a CT scan revealed fluid buildup in her brain, which could cause her death. The only hope was a risky operation to help the flow of fluid from the brain and through the body. She might die during surgery, but we knew Mom would want to take the chance.

"We almost lost her," the surgeon said after the operation. My husband and I were there when Mom opened her eyes.

Looking directly at me, she asked, "Where is my mother?"

"Grandmom died a long time ago," I replied, feeling dismayed.

"But she was standing here at the foot of my bed, with her arm out toward me and a beautiful garden behind her. She wanted me to go with her."

I was stunned that my usually skeptical mother had just had a near-death experience. "What did you say to her?" I asked.

"I told her I didn't want to go with her yet—that I wanted to return to life—that she could come back for me when it was my time."

Her recovery was swift, amazing the doctors. She returned to her own home with a new belief in miracles. Not only did she heal in body, but in spirit. Mom and I became closer than ever, with a new sense of connection. I felt that my father's request in the dream had been fulfilled.

It was a special day when she took my arm and walked to the altar of her church and read a prayer she had written, thanking the people for their visits and prayers, ending with the words: "May I be a constant reminder to everyone that God still performs miracles."

In her seven remaining years, Mom was blessed by the birth of two great-grandchildren. She also enjoyed the "little things" in life more than ever—watching the birds at her window feeder, gazing in wonder at the sunset, and connecting with God and nature on a deeper level. Sometimes we just sat together quietly, holding hands and looking at the ocean.

One night, on the evening of the full moon, I tried to call Mom at our usual time, but there was no answer. I tried again when I got to the YMCA to teach my yoga class. Still no answer. I phoned my husband and asked him to call to be sure she was all right.

At the end of each yoga class, there is a period of meditation. As my students and I sat in our circle, I prayed for Mom. Suddenly, I felt her spirit within me—joyfully letting me know that she was passing on to that other place! I drove home in a daze. I knew what had happened.

My husband met me at the door. "Honey, I'm so sorry, but we

lost her. I called twice and finally got her on the phone. She had fallen and was too weak to get up. I told her to hang up and that I'd call the rescue squad right away. She wasn't in pain and didn't sound frightened. The police called a few minutes later and told me that they were talking to her as they came in the door, and then she just stopped responding. When they reached her, she was gone. She died at 7:45."

That was exactly the time I was praying and felt her spirit move through me. I know in my heart that as the rescue team came through Mom's front door, my grandmother appeared to her again. This time, Mom decided to take my grandmother's hand and go with her.

~Linda Texter Hall

Dad's Quarters

All that is in heaven... is also on earth.
~Plotinus

My dad always collected quarters. He was delighted when the new U.S. state quarters were announced. He would go to his longtime neighborhood banker and make sure they put at least twenty rolls of each new quarter aside for him. It was a special treat and a family tradition to get your quarters from Grandpa. He gave them to his children, to his grandchildren and closest friends. He loved the whole process of collecting—carefully placing one of each state quarter in the special collectors edition portfolio as they were issued.

When my dad passed, I felt such a sense of emptiness. My father and I had been so close, I was lost without his guidance, support and wisdom. I wondered if I would ever feel my dad around me again. I wished I could have some kind of reassurance that he was there, watching over me. It was right after Hurricane Katrina and I was doing a motivational seminar for about three hundred volunteers. At the end of the event, everyone was in a circle and as I looked at the faces of these generous, committed individuals—I felt so grateful and appreciative. I again wished my dad were there to see me with these amazing people. I looked down in the center of the circle. To my astonishment, I saw nothing on the floor except for one state quarter, from North Carolina, the state in which my dad was born and raised.

Then, two months later, I went back to North Carolina to visit my mom. While I was there, I went to the bank to cash a check. The bank manager, who had known me since I was a little girl, called me into her office. The quarters for all the states my dad had ordered were in the corner of the office. She didn't know why, but she felt she needed to hold them for me.

Ever since that time, throughout the years, I have found quarters at the most extraordinary times, when I needed support the most. When I needed the strength to pull my son's tooth (a job that my dad used to be responsible for), a quarter miraculously appeared. When I need emotional support during a tough time, a quarter will show up in a strange place.

It has now become a tradition in our house and family. Every time a quarter appears, one of my kids says, "Oh, it's Grandpa!" At the most unbelievable times—even in foreign countries—a quarter appears. I found an American quarter in Fiji! Even in my brand new car—when I picked it up from the dealership, I found a quarter under the mat.

My daughter, my two sons, my mom, my friends, and I all feel a sense of peace and comfort every time a lone quarter turns up in an unexpected place. We have all accepted it as a message of love, guidance and support from my dad—and every new quarter we find makes us smile.

~Loren Slocum

A Great Grandma Forever

A grandmother is a little bit parent, a little bit teacher,
and a little bit best friend.
~Author Unknown

There was nothing better than spending the night with my Great-Grandma Mead on New Year's Eve. I'm not sure who was more excited about the annual sleepover. Even though she was in her eighties, Grandma loved being around kids. My brother and I stayed up later than usual, playing card games for hours after we had eaten homemade fried chicken, mashed potatoes with milk gravy, bowls of fruit, and gingersnap cookies that Grandma stored in the cupboard behind her tiny kitchen table. She never allowed us to drink soda because she didn't want our teeth to decay. She was my great-grandma, but I always referred to her as Grandma.

Our eyes were wide as saucers when she told us the story of The Three Little Pigs. We begged her to tell the tale, and I loved hearing her say, "Not by the hair on my chinny chin chin." She loved to watch repeats of *The Lawrence Welk Show* on PBS, and she did so as she instructed us to take a shower or at the very least, wash our feet. We ate grapefruit (we never had this at our house) and toast the next morning before my mom came to pick us up. It was the best way to start the New Year. After each visit she hugged us goodbye and said, "God bless you." Then tears welled up in her eyes.

Grandma had endured tremendous loss during her life: her oldest child died in a tragic fire, her left hand was amputated after it became infected, and her husband died at an early age. She never made excuses. She raised four children by herself, including one with significant hearing loss, during the Great Depression. She earned money by cleaning houses and helping others with their children. She was proud and never received financial assistance.

A plaque hanging in her kitchen said, "Today is the day the Lord has made; let us rejoice and be glad in it." She never shared how much she leaned on her faith or how she made the conscious choice to be positive each day. Grandma fed the birds and admired the red poppies in her yard. When she gave thanks for God's gifts, she said, "Wonderful, wonderful." Her response was the same when we told her about our accomplishments. She said the same thing when she looked at a sunset or when family appeared at her door.

She passed away a few days after my husband and I returned from our honeymoon. I felt as though she had been waiting for us. At ninety-nine years old, she had her positive attitude, her mind, and her teeth. (She was proud of having her own teeth. She wanted us to have our own teeth, too, which is why she didn't allow us to drink soda.) It was hard to believe she was gone.

After Grandma's passing, my parents' doorbell began ringing at odd times. On more than one occasion, my mom sprang out of bed in a panic, wondering who might be at the door. Nobody was ever there. We decided it was Grandma saying hello.

The day my husband and I learned we were expecting twins, we laughed. On the drive home from the doctor's office, I realized it was Grandma Mead's birthday. I felt it was a sign she was there with me. The twins were born exactly six months later and were very difficult babies. They seemed to cry often and were not easily settled. They seldom slept. Two years later they both received an autism diagnosis, which explained some of their difficult behaviors. I missed her and wished she could meet my boys. It was a demanding full-time job caring for the twins. Sometimes I spoke to her aloud. I hoped she was guiding me.

When the twins were three and a half years old, my son Henry was born. He was quite vocal at an early age, which was music to my ears since my twins were receiving speech therapy. Isaac didn't speak at all, while Noah repeated words again and again. Henry, on the other hand, was speaking in full sentences before he was two years old. He loved to talk.

One afternoon, after Henry's nap, he was sitting at the table eating a snack. "Grandma Mead played with me today," he stated, matter-of-factly. I tried not to act surprised because I wanted him to tell me more about the experience. I had talked to him about Grandma Mead, but he only knew she was a special grandma.

"What happened?" I asked. "Was she in your room?"

"She told me stories," he said, as he took a few bites of his banana.

"Was it The Three Little Pigs?" I asked.

"No," he said. The conversation was over.

I had read about children having the ability to see those who had passed. Could Henry have interacted with Grandma Mead? Over the course of several months, he consistently reported her visits when he was in his room for a nap.

One afternoon he said to me, "Grandma Mead likes to ring doorbells."

"Yes," I answered, a bit in shock. "She likes to ring doorbells. What else did she say?"

"She lives in a house."

"Henry, she lives in heaven now, but she used to live in a house," I explained.

"Her house is red and white," he said.

I almost fell off my chair. He couldn't have possibly known any of that information. The red and white house was the one where my brother and I stayed each New Year's Eve.

When Henry was two and a half years old, he and I were outside one summer morning while the twins were at preschool. I was watching him toddle around our back patio area. As he was running, his sneaker hit an uneven patch of cement. I was too far away and knew I wouldn't be able to get there in time. I felt helpless.

As he was falling forward, he shouted, "Grandma Mead!" I was surprised by his exclamation. He landed face down on the cement. I remember thinking his injuries could be pretty severe because he hadn't put his arms out to brace his fall. I felt sick to my stomach. I picked him up and held him as he cried. I expected his shirt to be torn or his face to be bloody. I took him inside and tried to calm him down while I examined him. He didn't have a scratch on his body anywhere! It appeared as though someone had cushioned his fall.

I rocked with Henry in the glider for a long time while tears ran down my cheeks. I looked down at my little boy, nestled in my protective arms. Wonderful, wonderful, I thought. Thank you, Grandma Mead, for keeping him safe. I imagined her putting her arms around me and whispering, "God bless you."

~Tyann Sheldon Rouw

Miraculous
Messages from Heaven

Miraculous Messengers

Answering the Question

Life is eternal and love is immortal;
And death is only a horizon,
And a horizon is nothing save the limit of our sight.
~Rossiter W. Raymond

My aunt Pattie waited at the crossing as one of the many freight trains roared through the sleepy hamlet of Bradner, Ohio. She was in a hurry to get home and check the status of her sister, my mother, who was having open-heart surgery. The train passed. Pattie started across the tracks as she had a thousand times before. Another train traveling the opposite direction hit her car broadside and dragged the little blue car nearly a quarter of a mile.

It was a terrible, senseless accident. On that sunny fall day in 1983, the funny, energetic five-foot-tall bundle of energy, who laughed so easily, loved her family, and cared for everyone, was gone. She had been my favorite aunt, more like a second mother. I spent summers with her family as a child. My cousins were like siblings to me.

A train wreck in any small town is a major event. Everyone came to see which neighbor or friend was involved. Bradner's volunteer fire department rescue squad arrived at the scene within minutes of Pattie's crash. The train's engineer leaned against his massive machine, incapable of looking at the crumpled car. Within a month he retired, unable to continue the job he had loved for over thirty years. Luckily Pattie's ex-husband Don recognized the mangled wreck and was able to keep their adult sons and daughter away from the crash site.

My brother Mike and I went to help with Aunt Pattie's funeral arrangements. Barnet, the town undertaker, had tears in his eyes as he told us there was no way we could have an open casket funeral. Pattie's sons and daughter wouldn't be able to have a last goodbye.

A few days later, half the town was at the cemetery to remember the fiery woman who had touched so many lives. Even horses at the farm next door watched the ceremony from a nearby field.

Everyone missed Pattie, but life went on. Pattie's new grandson was born to her son Kent a few months after the accident. Her daughter Debbie gave birth to a daughter who became Pattie's namesake. The only nagging question for our family was whether Pattie had suffered in the crash. Nightmares about their mother's final moments haunted her children.

Years later, on another sunny fall day. I was living in Nashville, Tennessee, over four hundred miles from the train tracks where Aunt Pattie had lost her life. I'd taken a walk among the rolling hills of Beaman Park. The forest floor was carpeted with fall leaves in all hues of the rainbow. Birds were busy in the trees. I heard the raucous laugh of a Pileated Woodpecker, so I sat on a bench beside the trail trying to spot his swooping flight. The warm sun filtered through the trees making a kaleidoscope of light on the trail.

A few moments after I sat down, a slender blond woman jogged past in a blue outfit and gray running shoes. As she passed, she gave me an odd look, but kept on down the trail, her ponytail swinging with her stride. About a hundred yards away, she stopped and stood with her back to me for a few moments, her shoulders squared, her muscles taut. Then her shoulders slumped, and she turned, walking quickly back to me. I smiled at her, wondering if she was someone I should recognize.

"Hi," she said. "You don't know me. I don't usually do this, but she's being very insistent."

I looked around. The woman and I were the only people in sight. I stood in case I might need to get away from this deranged woman.

"I know this may sound a bit strange, but do you have an older female relative named Pat, or Pattie?"

How did this woman know who I was? "I had an aunt named Pattie," I replied hesitantly.

"I know she's passed on but…" a distracted frown creased her brows, "… she says to tell everyone she didn't know what hit her."

I sat down abruptly.

The woman frowned again. Her eyes were looking off in the middle distance. "Yes, that's what she wants to say. I don't know if this means anything to you. I just needed to give you the message, that she didn't know what hit her."

I looked up at the woman not knowing what to say.

She continued, "I don't want anything from you, and I won't bother you again." With a smile and a shrug, she jogged off down the trail. The laughter of a swooping woodpecker followed her. I never saw her again.

The family always knew Aunt Pattie cared for her family more than anything else. It seems she cared so much, she sent a message from beyond to alleviate our lingering anxiety concerning the last moments of her life.

~Leslie Gulvas

Picture Perfect Pseudonym

*The role of a writer is not to say what we all can say,
but what we are unable to say.*

~Anaïs Nin

L ittle did I know that I would be tagged with a new name from a spirit in the afterlife. A name other than what was on my Social Security card. At birth I was given the name of Sylvia Jane Bright. When I married, I loved my name change to Sylvia Bright-Green. I likewise loved my other nametags through the years: wife, mother, grandmother, great-, and great-great-grandmother.

So I was surprised a few years ago when I was labeled with an unusual pseudonym. My new name came via a professional writer friend who I asked to edit my paranormal book. She readily agreed and I sent her the manuscript. After two months, I telephoned and inquired about the status of my book. She said her position at the daily newspaper became more involved than expected, but promised she would get to my book manuscript that weekend.

Two weeks later, I welcomed my book back with all its professional comments and corrections. While implementing the editing suggestions, I perceived an eerie feeling that someone else had read my manuscript. So I phoned my friend and inquired.

"No, Sylvia," she replied. "I wouldn't let anyone read your manuscript without your permission. Why do you ask?"

I then described who I sensed had read my book. I saw a woman who appeared to be in her early thirties, medium build, about five-foot-four with dark brown hair pulled back into a mass of long curls. Her complexion was flawless like a doll's. She was attired in a grand, black floor-length Victorian style dress.

I likewise informed my writer friend that while I was intuitively tuned into this female apparition, I received a message from her. This disembodied spirit said she admired what I wrote in my manuscript; and commented that she was a cloistered writer and a trance medium that yearned to have been allowed to use all her secret abilities. But in her era she would have been locked up as a lunatic.

She then gave me an inspiring message: "Remember to take daily trips from your mind into your soul… because there is a blossoming being within lovingly awaiting to progress and connect you to your divine power. Trust that inspired power and wisdom to guide you forward at the perfect time and in the right way. So heed your inner messages, and entrust the reverent flow of your life and you will make a difference that only you can make." She further stated that she admired my adventuresome nature and freethinking spirit, and added, "Never give up on you… like my family forced me to do."

Upon informing my young newspaper friend (a logical, single, petite woman with short blond hair) about my eerie experience, she said, "This is even too weird for me. I don't believe in any of this stuff. I only offered to edit your supernormal book because we're friends and writers. But what you just described and told me is so way-out that it gives me the willies."

She told me that when she received my book manuscript in the mail she placed it in her hallway on an antique typewriter, and it stayed there until I reminded her of the editing. "The description you just gave of someone reading your manuscript," she noted, "matches the woman in the picture hanging over the 1900s typewriter. That old machine was hers. She was a great-great-aunt on my mother's side of the family who was often referred to as 'unusual.' You know my dear writer friend; you really are some 'Uncanny Granny.'"

After being given that Uncanny Granny title, it has become my nom de plume in all my paranormal writings. I even changed the title on my book to "The Uncanny Granny Chronicles."

I read somewhere that a mystic (or seer) sees from the heart and the soul to garner information and revelations from the hereafter. I believe this. I live this.

~Sylvia Bright-Green

64

An Answer from Heaven

Is death the last sleep? No—it is the last and final awakening.
~Sir Walter Scott

Nineteen is an age when boys are not only exploring their boundaries, they are pushing them. My son was no different and one of the things he was questioning was his relationship to religion, God and spirituality. I was in the midst of a spiritual search myself. I was reading a Bible commentary when he sauntered into the room one day and dropped down on the couch beside me.

"Isn't it boring in Heaven?" he asked.

I knew what he was thinking: harps, angels, endless singing and church... sounded pretty boring to me too.

"No, it's not boring," I replied. "You can do whatever makes you happy there."

I was improvising as well as I could; after all I had no idea what Heaven was like or even if such a place existed. I had to tell him something since parents are supposed to know everything.

A week later the unthinkable happened. My beautiful son died in an accident. It happened on the winter solstice, three days before Christmas, and my life slipped into eternal winter.

I knew somehow that my son's spirit was still alive. Anyone that happy and vibrant cannot just cease to exist. His body was buried in his grave but his spirit flew free.

After months of pain, I decided to visit a medium. She worked hard for an hour and had come up with my son's first initial and little else. She had resorted to telling my future mostly. I guess it was easier to fake the future than the past. I was disappointed after investing the time, the long drive and the money to go to see this medium. The worst of it was the lost hope. I had wanted so much to hear from Jay. I needed to know he lived on and he was okay.

As I got ready to leave she said, "I have an unusual message that your son wants me to give you." She had a very puzzled look on her face as if the message made no sense to her.

"What?" I replied eagerly.

"He says for me to tell you, 'Mom, I'm not bored!'"

I smiled for the first time in a long time.

~Marilyn Ellis Futrell

65

Road Trip with Dad

We are never so lost our angels cannot find us.
~Stephanie Powers

had just been dumped, I was fighting with my roommates, and I was incredibly depressed. I was desperate for a change. Thankfully, my coworker Abby, who had also been dumped recently, understood. She suggested we take a day trip to Atlantic City. We took Monday off from work and hit the road.

The drive from Baltimore to Atlantic City was about two and half hours, which gave us plenty of time to talk. Abby and I were friendly but didn't really know that much about one another's personal lives. So our conversation on the way to Jersey consisted mainly of ex-boyfriend bashing and assuring each other that we were better off without the jerks anyway.

Once we arrived in Atlantic City we wanted to take in a few of the sights before going in the casinos to spend what little money we had brought. It was a dreary day but we went to the boardwalk anyway. As we walked we kept seeing signs for five-dollar psychic readings. Having never been to a psychic, I was intrigued. Abby was less than enthused. So, we continued up the boardwalk, stopping for photo opportunities, perusing souvenir shops, and even having lunch at a classic fifties diner. The day was exactly what the doctor ordered to distract me from my hurting heart.

Once we decided to head back towards the casinos I suggested seeing the psychic one last time. Though a little apprehensive, Abby finally agreed.

The place we decided on wasn't very extravagant. In fact, it was just a tiny room with a curtain you stepped behind to meet with the woman who would tell you your future.

Unfortunately, my reading was less than stellar. She told me that my heart was broken and that for an extra $10 she could cleanse my chakras. I felt duped, promptly declined and headed out. Abby's reading went quite differently. The psychic told her she was cursed and would curse everyone she met, but for an extra $10 she could lift this curse. It was a horrible thing to say in a con to get money. Having had a string of bad luck over the last year, Abby thought the lady might have a point.

After the very disappointing scam we had just experienced we decided we were more than done with Atlantic City and headed home.

About thirty minutes after we hit the road Abby said something quite peculiar.

"Do you believe in mediums?"

Curious where she could possibly be going with this, I told her I had always considered myself a healthy skeptic. Having never had a personal experience I couldn't be sure, but I had been open to the idea that it was possible to communicate with people who had passed.

She then shocked me when she said, "I'm a medium."

She went on to describe how she had been seeing people that no one else could see since she was young. As she got older she began to think that she was just a crazy person hearing voices and seeing people who weren't there. But finally finding the courage to confess to her mother only assured her that it was a gift that ran in her family. Her mother sent her to a mentor, at a holistic center, who would help her better understand this gift. After meeting with her mentor she realized that it wasn't going away and accepted it as part of her. As years went by she would often receive messages from beyond that were intended for various people she encountered.

However, fear of the judgment that would often follow these types of communications kept her from sharing them with their intended recipients. Meeting with the psychic on the boardwalk had disturbed her so much because she had struggled with her gift, trying to decide if it was a curse or a blessing.

Then it happened. Again, she didn't know much about me, but she said something that made me an instant believer in mediums.

"Did your dad pass away when you were a teenager?" Abby asked.

"Yes, why?" I replied.

"Was he killed in a car accident?" Abby went on.

"He was," I said, my heart starting to race.

"Was he drinking at the time? Was he driving a Jeep? Did he hit some trees?" Abby continued.

I nodded, indicating she was correct. There was no way she could have possibly known these details.

"Did he have a beard? Did he have ruffles in his teeth similar to the ones you have?" Asking more questions, Abby begin to be equally as stunned by what she was saying.

"Yes, he always had a beard. And yes, our teeth are identical," I responded.

"Ok, don't freak out. But he is here," Abby said calmly.

What? My father who had been dead for ten years was suddenly making an "appearance." I had so many emotions running through me. I was excited but also terrified that this wasn't real. After all I was having a "conversation" with my dad who I thought I would never talk to again.

What occurred after that was a two-hour conversation with my deceased father.

She told me things that there was no way she could have known. She shared his feelings about decisions I'd made, accomplishments in my life, and how he laughed every time I would make an inappropriate joke that resembled his humor. She then told me things I needed to pass along to my mom: inside jokes between my mother and father when they were dating, things that he had observed since his passing, and sweet mementos he leaves for her.

Finally, she said to me, "Do you often cry alone in the bathroom?"

Because I was in the middle of a deep depression, I spent many nights in the bathroom sobbing. It was the only room my roommates couldn't hear me in. I would sit on the toilet with a box of Kleenex and just bawl, wishing I didn't feel so alone.

I nodded.

Abby said, "You cry because you are feeling alone, don't you? You curl up on the toilet with a blue box of Kleenex and just cry."

Tears began to stream down my face as I nodded again.

"He wants me to tell you, you aren't alone. He is always right by your side."

With that, she pulled into my driveway. She told me that he was fading and it was time for him to go. I told her to tell him I love him, and he said I love you right back. I hugged Abby, knowing what just happened to both of us was something that had cemented a lasting friendship, knowing that she had given me the best gift I could have ever received.

~Elizabeth K. Jaeger

Your Mom Told Me to Do This

We are each of us angels with only one wing,
and we can only fly by embracing one another.
~Luciano de Crescenzo

was largely unaffected by the Global Recession until I lost my job in 2011. That's when I decided to become a freelance writer. Inspired by a memorial to an American hero, 'Sparky', in my hometown of Princes Risborough, England, I started looking into the story.

That's how I met Maureen, who, in 1991, had campaigned to bring this brave young pilot the recognition he deserved. I went to meet her and she sent me away with a huge wad of paperwork and hours of video footage. As I waded through old letters, military magazines, and watched Sparky's memorial service on the television, I was welling up inside. Then, when I returned to speak to Maureen about it, she said she'd been guided to honour Sparky's memory by the spirit of his late mother, Miriam.

Maureen explained, "I was just eleven years old in November 1943 when the roaring engines of a B-17 bomber passed just inches from the roofs of neighbouring houses, where I lived in Princes Risborough. The experience was deafening and really frightening.

"My mother yelled hysterically, 'They're attacking the train!' My brother was waiting at the railway station to go to school and she was afraid he would be hurt in an imminent attack by the Germans.

"Fortunately local schoolboys recognised the plane's U.S. markings and shouted, 'It's American!'

"The plane was on fire with flames coming from the rear. I saw it lurch over the top of a bungalow before crashing into a field where it detonated on impact. I later found out that it had three tonnes of explosives on board. The pilot didn't stand a chance.

"The huge explosion shook the ground and sent shrapnel flying in all directions. I heard that a local farmer had been pinned to his milking shed by a piece of shrapnel that flew in whilst he was getting ready to milk the cows.

"I saw the whole incident unfold from my bedroom window and witnessing it had a huge impact on my life. As I grew up, I started to wonder about the identity of the pilot who had steered his stricken plane away from Princes Risborough, and in so doing, saved the town."

As I sat with Maureen, she explained that in adulthood she was told three times that a person called Miriam was trying to contact her from the other side. But she didn't know anyone called Miriam so she ignored it.

Fifty years after the crash, she met a gentleman on a flight to the U.S. and asked him to help her find the name of the pilot who died that day. He put a letter in a U.S. military magazine, which led to the uncovering of the pilot's identity. His name was Clyde Cosper—Sparky to his friends.

"I started to get letters from all around the world," she said, "from people who were interested in the story and from people who knew about the event.

"It was a strange time, as a series of coincidences occurred. I felt it was my purpose to bring honour to Clyde 'Sparky' Cosper in recognition of his sacrifice. I got in touch with the local newspaper, *The Bucks Herald*, in 1991, and they sent a reporter to research the story. He contacted Sparky's relatives in the U.S. and the paper also raised funds to build a memorial to Sparky in Princes Risborough town centre."

So now I understood how that memorial came to exist. Maureen supplied me with a lot of paperwork that explained the mission of the stricken plane. It included a letter from one member of the crew, Charles Vondrachek, describing the whole experience. Their mission in 1943 was to bomb German U boats at Brenham, but the mission was cancelled and they were told to turn back since a heavy storm was brewing. The radio signal came too late. They tried to turn back, but became embroiled in the storm and lost control of the plane. It was being tossed around in a thunderhead like a toy. The crew jumped out but Sparky stayed at the helm to try and guide the plane to safety.

The Bucks Herald reporter helped Maureen to track down Charles Vondrachek, who had bailed out when Sparky told them to evacuate over the intercom.

The subsequent unveiling of the pilot's identity captured the imagination of the world's press and Maureen collected all the newspaper reports surrounding the whirlwind of activity that ensued. It all now seemed to be out of her control and in the hands of fate.

Maureen showed me all the articles she had collected. One was printed in a U.S. newspaper called the *Bonham Favorite*, where journalists in America had picked up the story. Crewmember Charles told them, "I had no thoughts as I bailed out, things were happening too fast. I was busy dodging telephone wires. I'm sure he (Sparky) could have bailed out if he'd wanted to. I think he was trying to clear the town. He wanted to save those people and park the plane where it wouldn't take anyone's life. He guided it into a field where it blew up with three tonnes of bombs on board."

I felt incredibly privileged to be immersed in the whole experience decades later. Maureen explained how meeting the family had been such an eye-opener, "I was amazed to hear that Sparky's mother was called Miriam, and it brought back memories from my past when I was told 'Miriam is trying to contact you from the other side'".

Miriam had shot herself, committing suicide, in 1954—she was devastated by the death of her son and never recovered.

Maureen continued, "I felt that I had been led by Miriam to bring recognition to Sparky's actions and I embraced that role with great enthusiasm."

None of Sparky's relatives knew of his heroics. There were so many casualties in the war that the incident had passed with no particular comment. When they heard how Sparky's brave actions had saved the town they were very grateful to Maureen for bringing him the recognition he deserved.

She learnt more about Sparky through hearing the family's stories about him. He was just twenty-one years old and a jovial character whose ambition growing up was to be a fighter pilot. He trained at the Brady Aviation School (now Brady Airport, Texas) and was concerned about the math, but he needn't have worried—he proved to be highly skilled and was in the top ten percent of bomber fighters. This meant he was eligible to attend Bomber Flight School, where he completed his training and was awarded his Wings in February 1943. He named his plane 'Miriam' after his mother. He gave his mother a 'Royal' fly past her house in his B-17 bomber during the summer of 1943, just months before he died.

Maureen and I have both been in correspondence with Sparky's relatives in recent years, to bring honour to his name and to ensure that what he did for our town is never forgotten. Maureen's early communications resulted in a memorial service being held in his hometown of Dodd City, Texas, where a veterans home was opened in his name—The Clyde W. Cosper Texas State Veterans Home. Maureen was invited to attend the memorial service, which was an incredibly moving experience. I watched it on video ten years later and it had me in tears too. Charles Vondrachek was there, and those in attendance heard speeches from Sparky's relatives, from Charles, and from the Texas Land Commissioner at the time. Maureen also said a small piece and was asked to go on television.

All this time, Maureen felt that Miriam was leading her, influencing events, and making sure that she met people who could help. She said, "The whole experience seemed to carry me away on a wave of activity and strange coincidences. Curiously and unexpectedly, I was meeting people who helped bring recognition to Sparky's sacrifice, and I felt that someone was using me as an earthly guide to make things happen."

Maureen is in her 70s now, and I'm starting to wonder if it's my fate to continue telling this story, so that Sparky's ultimate sacrifice is never forgotten.

~Susie Kearley

Martha's Message

Angels can fly directly into the heart of the matter.
~Author Unknown

It's been said a million times, "When it rains, it pours." Well, during the early days of spring in the last year of the last millennium, my friend Tammy Rust, a schoolteacher from Delaware, experienced a Category 5 hurricane. But no storm lasts forever. And as it's also been said many times over, "Every cloud has a silver lining."

Graham Dill, Tammy's father, had a signature signoff for his daughter in every written e-mail, spoken voicemail, and face-to-face conversation. He would close by stating calmly, "Remember, God loves you, Tam, and so do I."

When Graham died unexpectedly, Tammy was devastated. She had been very close to her father.

After returning to Delaware for the funeral, Tammy visited her adopted teenage son, Robert, to deliver the bad news. Robert was a resident of the Sussex Work Release Program due to a substance abuse problem. He was also very close to his grandfather, who he affectionately knew as Pop. Through the difficult times, Graham had supported Robert as he battled his demons. He was both an inspiration and pillar of love for Robert to lean against, so the news was crushing.

Three days later, Tammy returned to work, depressed, but determined to move forward, and stay positive. The following morning the phone rang. It was Robert's natural aunt with more bad news...

Robert's birth mother had passed away. The aunt asked Tammy to inform Robert. She dreaded again being the bearer of bad news. She knew the visit would be one of the toughest chores in her life. But it had to be done.

So, two sleepless days later, Tammy again visited her only son, nervous and saddened. Robert's counselor joined them as they sat together around a small table in a colorless room. Above them fluorescent lighting hummed.

As expected, the news did not fall on happy ears. At first, Robert said nothing. Then, he stood up, stared deep into his mother's face with teary eyes, and without warning, slammed his chair violently into the table. Finally, he ran from the room, overwhelmed by his grief. Then, the counselor left without a word, leaving Tammy alone.

Several minutes later she left the room, feeling utterly hopeless and emotionally drained. She was still coming to terms with her father's passing and now she felt rejected by her child, a son she loved so much, at a time when she wanted to help him cope with upsetting news, but also a time when she needed him help her with her own loss.

Tammy made her way out of the building and across the parking lot to her car, oblivious to everything around her. Somehow she got into her car before she started sobbing. She sat there for minutes, crying and shaking, never feeling more alone in her life. Then, a knocking on her car window startled her. Partly embarrassed and partly annoyed, she glanced up through her swollen eyes to view the intruder.

Standing at the side of her car was a woman with a kind face and tender eyes. She motioned to Tammy to roll down her window. After Tammy did, the lady smiled and introduced herself simply as Martha.

Martha said softly, "I don't know who you are, but God spoke to my heart to come over to you." Tammy couldn't speak, so she listened.

Martha then added, "I don't know what is going on in your life right now, but be assured that things will get better."

Then, Martha leaned down closer and into the car to hug Tammy. Martha whispered into Tammy's ear, "And always remember, God loves you, and so do I."

Tammy crumbled, having heard the exact words her dear father frequently shared with her on every occasion, but now voiced by a total stranger. By the time Tammy composed herself, Martha was gone. Tammy looked everywhere, but the woman had disappeared. Tammy never saw her again, at the center, around town, anywhere.

~David Michael Smith

A Feathered Blessing

The union of heaven and earth is the origin of the whole of nature.
~I Ching

My husband Dave loved birds. It didn't matter what kind—robins, finches, blue jays, red-winged blackbirds, eagles, hawks—he loved them all. He was fascinated by their beauty, their seemingly effortless flight and their sometimes comic antics

When Dave was diagnosed with leukemia, he spent a large amount of time in hospitals enduring numerous rounds of chemotherapy, infusions of stem cells from his sister and medications to help him survive each procedure. Throughout his numerous hospitalizations, he missed seeing birds. Hospital windows don't often afford views of much except other buildings, air conditioning units and an occasional piece of the skyline.

Dave was always grateful when he was able to return home to some small sense of normalcy. Our home backs up to a farmer's field, and we are blessed with a beautiful stretch of open land behind us. When he was able, Dave would slather on sunscreen, put on his long-sleeved shirt and hat and sit out on our porch, soaking in every aspect of nature around him.

When smoke from fires in a neighboring state made the air quality dangerous for him, he would sit at our kitchen table and watch the birds through our bay window, as they swooped and soared through the yard. It restored his soul and lifted his spirits.

Dave fought valiantly for a year and half, but eventually passed from this life. It was an overwhelming time of heartache and sorrow for me and my adult children.

The first few days after someone dies, you are busy with the whirlwind of things that have to be done and decisions that have to be made. You move through the preparations for a funeral somewhat numbly. But we did it, and his funeral service was a joyous celebration of his life and his faith.

After the funeral, the reality hit me. I had lived with and loved this man for more than forty-one years. How was I going to make it through the days, months and years that loomed ahead?

I wandered aimlessly through our home, eventually coming to stand before our kitchen windows. Looking out on our back yard, I gasped at what I saw before me. There were birds everywhere. It was a gathering of feathered friends in numbers we'd never seen in our yard before.

Robins, who usually preferred to bath alone, lined the edges of the birdbath and splashed and played together as a joyous group. The top of our arbor was covered with six or seven beautiful flickers resting and sharing space at the hanging feeder with several blue jays. The wire fence that separated our yard from the field behind us was lined with masses of finches and sparrows looking like living notes on a musical scale.

More than twenty doves strutted about on the grass, while others rested on the wooden fences between our and our neighbor's homes. Birds of all varieties flew freely through our yard.

For about ten minutes a feathered miracle played out before our eyes, and then in one short instant, they all took flight and flew from our view. We had been given a beautiful, simple gift.

"Mom, do you think Dad sent the birds?" asked one of my children.

"Absolutely," I replied, as tears flowed freely down my cheeks.

Though my sorrow was overwhelming, I knew then that somehow, we were going to be okay. The Lord was allowing Dave to send us a special message. He would be close by to watch over us, and we would see him again. And when we do, I'm sure there will be birds.

~Jeannie Lancaster

A Pony for Tiana

The past is never dead, it is not even past.
~William Faulkner

A few days after our son Peter died, a friend we had not seen or heard from in a very long time approached us. Marino claimed he had a message for us from Peter. I was shocked. Was this his way of offering condolences? Did he not know that a mother who loses a son is beyond consolation? With the threat of hysteria in my voice, I excused myself, walked away, and left him to my husband Ralph.

Peter, our vibrant young son, had married Paula, a beautiful Laotian girl, and they had four incredible bouncy kids. Family and friends were always welcome at their home, which was surrounded by five green acres, sheltering all kinds of animals—dogs, chickens, rabbits, geese, and even turkeys. Peter loved kids; Peter loved animals; Peter loved life. But he died suddenly, at only thirty-seven. For me, days that had been full of love, laughter, and sunshine were reduced to hate, sadness, and darkness. I had crawled into a hole of nothingness and did not want to be consoled, least of all by a quack who claimed to be a messenger for Peter.

Still, I remembered reading once that as long as souls are still close to the terrestrial world they are connected by very powerful human love, and can, through some channels or mediums, give messages. Could it be then that Marino was a medium? No! Impossible. I was too much of a realist to believe such nonsense. Nevertheless, curiosity got the better of me and I did not silence my husband when he started to tell me about the message.

"Actually," my husband reported, "there was more than one message. The first one was for Christopher, and all Marino could see were white gloves."

"Oh sure…" I snickered. "Our oldest, our professor, can be a bit patronizing… at times. He could use some white glove manners… at times."

Ralph looked puzzled. "I thought you called Marino a quack," he reminded me. "I thought you said you didn't believe in messages from beyond."

"I don't… but you have to admit, it's funny how one can make things fit." I paused, reflecting on this. "So what was the other message?"

"The other message," Ralph continued, "was for Bobbie, and it said, 'we have to talk.'"

I was perplexed. Marino had no way of knowing that there were hard feelings between Peter and his sister Bobbie. Peter had confided in me that his sister was angry with him because he told her to get rid of her husband, that her husband was a bum. Could it be? No! Impossible! Still… somewhat intrigued now, I asked, "Was there a message for me?"

"No." Ralph shook his head.

"Was there one for Paula?"

"No." Ralph's voice hinted at regret. "Nor for his brother John."

"Well then…" I huffed. "You can see it's all a lot of foolishness. Paula and I were the closest to him." I shook my head vigorously to confirm my conviction. "If there was any truth to this, then surely Peter would have sent a message to his wife and his mother."

"There was a message for me," my husband spoke slowly, feeling his way.

"What was it?" I asked, and looked away in an attempt to hide my hurt feelings.

"Something about legal papers," my husband replied.

"Oh sure," I snapped, my voice edged with indignation. "Marino knows that Peter was your partner in the company, and so it is easy to fabricate a message about legal matters, but why? What on earth can his purpose be?"

Ignoring my question, Ralph continued, "Also... something about a pony." And that was when my heart stood still. Marino could not possibly have known that Peter had planned to buy his oldest daughter, Tiana, a pony. He had already built the barn; it just needed to be painted, it just needed a pony for Tiana.

~Christa Holder Ocker

Lady

Our perfect companions never have fewer than four feet.
~Colette

My husband came home from work that day, frantic and totally in love with a stray dog he befriended while working outside on a bulldozer. The black Lab and Springer Spaniel mix came out of nowhere, licking his ear and nuzzling his hand. He gave her water, tied her to a nearby tree in the shade, and promised she would come home with him later that day.

Unfortunately, an office worker noticed the stray dog earlier that day and had called the animal control offices to send someone to retrieve it. When my husband came out at the end of his shift, he was brokenhearted to find the dog was gone. Someone told him the animal control van was there not an hour before, and the stray dog had been taken to the pound.

That evening my husband repeated the sad story to me. It was easy to see that this stray had completely won his heart and he was totally devastated. I'd never seen my husband so enamored of an animal and we'd had plenty in our years of marriage.

He looked to me with tears in his eyes. "This dog is very special. We have to find her!"

"Then find her, we will," I agreed.

Five minutes later, we were in our truck and headed to the first of several locations where the animal control officers could have taken the black Lab. The third stop proved to be the right one; we'd found her. Before they led us back to the compound where she was being held, we were advised the dog would be held for seventy-two hours to give the legal owners a chance to retrieve her.

"We understand there is a waiting period," my husband said. "We want to be her new family, and we'll do whatever is necessary."

We followed the animal control officer to the rear of the compound where dozens of dogs were barking and snarling, along with dozens of cats mewing and pacing back and forth in cages.

Around another corner and the officer paused, looking to my husband. "Is this the dog you found earlier today?"

"Yes, yes!" He looked over to the black Lab and smiled. "I came back for you, girl."

The officer opened the gated door and gestured for us to enter. The Lab was curled up on the floor; her head drooped, big brown eyes hopeful but shy. I knelt down and lifted her chin, patting her head at the same time.

"Hello there, sweet girl."

My husband beamed. "Isn't she beautiful? I told you she was special."

"She is; I can see it in her eyes."

Those impossibly big brown eyes were so transparent; it was almost like she was conveying to us a promise that she would look much better once she'd had a decent bath, and that she was apologizing for her condition. It was also clear that someone had abused her, perhaps even beaten her and then thrown her away like trash. My husband and I were both touched deeply.

The next day I went shopping for a dog bed, collar, cans of wet food and bags of dry dog food, a half dozen treats and at least that many toys.

"So, what shall we name her?" my husband questioned when he arrived home from work.

"Lady. She's the perfect little lady." I hadn't even thought this out, but the name had come to my mind quickly and easily.

My husband agreed. "That she is!"

The next few days felt like weeks, the time dragging until the day came we finally brought Lady home. She walked throughout the house, sniffing as she went, eventually settling onto her plush round bed situated in our family room. We both sat in our recliners and just stared at Lady as she slept peacefully. Our two cats sauntered through the room, trying their best to look casual as they stopped and stared at the dark creature softly snoring in the corner. They approached her cautiously, sniffed a bit at Lady's feet, and carried on with their business as if this were not a momentous occasion. Everyone knew it was, however, sensing that our lives would never be the same and Lady had everything to do with it.

We lived in a rural area off a dead-end street and down a graveled road. Our property was just under two acres, and Lady seemed to know just where her boundaries were and what was off limits. She made friends with the neighbor dogs, and was especially kind to Ace, the big German shepherd next door who was fast losing his eyesight. Lady would walk with him, nudging him right or left along the gravel road if a car would approach, and she led him home in the evenings at about the dinner hour. Friends came to know and love Lady, recognizing her gentle, loving spirit and ever smiling face. One friend joked repeatedly about having her cloned; he loved her too!

One afternoon my husband and I were picking weeds in the front yard when a neighbor's chicken strayed into our space. Directly before us, Lady instantly froze, her body held in a beautifully poised point, her brown eyes locked on the bird.

My husband grinned at me and called out to Lady. "Go get it, girl."

Two seconds later, we had a dead chicken on our hands. That night my husband fried up that chicken, along with mashed potatoes and corn, serving a plate of everything to Lady. "This is for you, Lady. Tomorrow, we're going to take you pheasant and quail hunting."

And that became Lady's glory; she was magic out among the sagebrush. Pure beauty, pure instinct, and doing what she loved best. I went on every hunt with my husband, just to watch Lady dance with grace among nature's own.

The years went by and we loved Lady every day, month, and moment. She always had a bright smile and a spring in her step until the day came we learned she had cancer. We were devastated at the diagnosis and horrified at the prospect of losing our precious Lady, but that final day came and changed our lives forever.

We each had a chance to say goodbye to Lady, and friends, family members and neighbors all had private moments in which they shared with her. Then, exactly one week after Lady passed away, I was talking with a good friend on the phone. The friend was outside in her hammock, chattering away with me, when suddenly she stopped.

"That's strange," my friend said.

"What? What's strange?"

"A ladybug just landed on me."

"Nothing strange about that."

"Yes there is. This ladybug is gold in color."

Our conversation continued and later that same afternoon my son called, just to chat.

"So, how was your day?"

"Great," my son answered. "I went out on the lake today with a buddy and we water-skied. It was great, but guess what happened?"

"What happened?"

"A ladybug landed on me, a golden ladybug. I didn't even know there were golden ladybugs."

"I didn't know that, either."

That evening after my husband arrived home from work, he was eager to tell me what happened that day.

"I was outside working on a bulldozer." He grinned. "And this golden ladybug landed on me!"

I grinned back at my husband. "You and everybody else, it would seem."

I told him of the earlier calls where golden ladybugs had shown themselves.

"Wow, isn't that weird but kind of wonderful, all at the same time?"

"Yes," I agreed. "Our favorite nickname for Lady was Ladybug and I don't think this is just a coincidence."

We talked all evening of the special times we shared with our precious Lady. The next morning I was taking one of our cats into the veterinarian for his yearly immunizations. The doctor came in the waiting room and smiled warmly.

"I'm so glad to see you," the vet said to me. "Something happened to me yesterday and I wanted you to know."

I smiled. "Let me take a guess. A ladybug landed on you—a golden ladybug."

The vet grinned widely. "Yes indeed! Lady came to me for a visit. This is her way of letting everyone know that she's okay and she's sending love to all."

"They really do get a message through to us," I said. "Don't they?"

"Indeed they do," the vet answered. "I've seen this happen many times."

The tears that fell were happy tears. We love you, dear sweet Lady!

~Louetta Jensen

Whispers of Andrew

Angels deliver Fate to our doorstep — and anywhere else it is needed.
~Jessi Lane Adams

The way I found the house was strange to begin with. My husband and I were looking for a house to flip, and were having no luck at all locating a good prospect. The locations were poor, or the prices too high, or... well, let's just say there weren't any good matches and we'd been looking for months.

Then one day I was driving back to work from a meeting of all the guidance counselors in our area. I nearly passed by a side road I'd never traveled before when I felt an intense urge to drive onto that road. It was so forceful that I suddenly turned the steering wheel and found myself doing just that.

I drove past wetlands and saw nothing. "This is crazy," I murmured out loud to myself. "What do I expect to find here?" I resolved to turn around at the next drive, finally approaching a sad little white house on a knoll with an even sadder red barn across from it. I pulled into the driveway and saw the numerous "for sale by owner" signs. I got goose bumps all over. This was why I'd been brought here!

The place called to me so much that after we bought it, I thought it would be wonderful to live there. It had a history for sure, and certainly not the happiest kind. The farm family living there for years was plagued by alcohol issues and tragedy. Their teenaged son had died there in an accident with farm equipment. The parents were never the same.

One day, during the renovation, I pulled old wainscoting from a wall and a school photo fell out. It was a smiling boy with reddish hair. "Andrew," it said. I felt taken with the picture and kept it. Was this the boy who lost his life?

Not long afterwards I had a dream so real I couldn't shake it in the morning. The boy who had died came to me. He showed me a journal—a list of things he wanted to accomplish but couldn't. I knew somehow I was supposed to help him. He was asking for that—but I couldn't remember what was on the list, try as I might. The dream affected me so much that I went to the dilapidated barn where there were piles of papers and books strewn about and looked through them. I thought maybe, by some miracle, the list was real. Of course I found nothing, and gave it up to fancy.

Time wore on and I kept feeling the presence of the boy who died. Family members and neighbors spoke of the event and the troubles the family had faced.

A few years later two new children moved to the area—little reddish-haired urchins with dimples and big smiles. Their mother was facing hard times, and I got a phone call from another social worker asking me to help them. For some reason I felt compelled to make a home visit, which I almost never did. The mother's plight moved me more than anything else in my years of work. I spoke to others and we swept in as a team, befriended her, helped connect her with what she needed, reached out in every way we could. I was driven.

I sat with this young mother one day and listened to her talk about her history and her children. She said the name of the father—the same surname as the family that had owned the house I now lived in. Her ex-husband had a brother who died in a farming accident. "He's my guardian angel," she said shyly. "I know this may sound crazy, but he comes to me in my dreams. When I get so depressed I don't think I can go on, he comes and tells me it will be all right."

His name was Andrew. The boy from the farm. The boy from the photo. The boy who came to me and asked me to help him accomplish this list of things he needed to do. I faced this young mother, who had never taken her husband's last name, and told her everything. "He sent me to you," I said.

Although everything was far from solved, I know I was drawn there to help in whatever way I could thanks to the whispers of Andrew.

~Tanya Sousa

Chapter
8

Miraculous
Messages from Heaven

Dreams and Premonitions

No Offense, Grandma

Dreams are today's answers to tomorrow's questions.
~Edgar Cayce

I was twelve years old when my maternal grandmother passed away. The day we buried her was the very first time I saw my mother cry. Unable to deal with all the raw emotions, I retired to my room and hoped that sleep would bring me comfort. But it brought me far more than that. It brought me back Grandma Ruthie.

She came wearing the baby blue dress with the rose corsage that I had always seen her wear in the picture on my mother's bedside table. She sat at the edge of my bed and said nothing at first, as if she was waiting to see how I would react. I was scared of course and thought I must be dreaming. Perhaps I was. My grandmother told me that she was okay. She told me it was okay to laugh and to keep doing the things I usually do, as life goes on. She told me to be kind to my mother and to understand that she is doing the best that she can. And just as I was warming up to the idea that this was real, that I could ask her questions about what it was like on the other side, that she could explain to me what really happens, she was gone.

The next day I tried to tell my mother what happened but she was far too immersed in her own grief to hear of such nonsense. So I said nothing more of it to anyone.

I honestly did not give much thought to that incident until many years later. I was married and pregnant with my first child when my paternal grandmother passed on. I was sitting with my older sister sharing memories of all the wonderful times we had with our lively and mischievous Grandma Gertie. We laughed as we remembered her playful spirit. It was then that my sister nonchalantly mentioned how she hoped she would not visit her, the way Grandmother Ruthie had so many years earlier. I was shocked and asked her what she meant. She then proceeded to tell the story of how our grandmother had visited her that night so many years ago too. She described her wearing the exact same dress as I saw her wear and how she spoke the same words she had said to me.

The thought then came to us that perhaps Grandmother Gertie, who had just passed on, would try to pay us a visit as well. We both were a bit freaked out by this. Although I wanted to know that our grandmother was fine, I honestly did not think I could handle her visiting me. After all I was very, very pregnant. My sister joked that she did not want her to come to her either. We laughed and said into the air, "Grandma if you are listening… no offense but please go visit someone else." I had no dreams or nighttime visit that night and neither did my sister.

The next morning the two of us received a phone call from our cousin who lived out of town and was unable to come to our grandmother's funeral. She told us of a very weird dream she had the night before and how Grandma Gertie had come to tell her she was okay. She laughed as she said she did not understand the next part of her dream. "She told me to tell you both that you are chicken and that Sharon… I know you did not want to know, but you are having a boy, so there!" She then went on to say how real the dream was. My sister and I knew better but said nothing. That day we went shopping for baby boy clothes because we were positive that I was indeed having a boy… which I did!

~Sharon Fuentes

The Garden

Hundreds of dewdrops to greet the dawn,
Hundreds of bees in the purple clover,
Hundreds of butterflies on the lawn,
But only one mother the wide world over.
~George Cooper

I was still struggling with my mother's death. I still reached for
the phone to call her occasionally even though she had passed
almost a year ago. She was often on my mind. Nevertheless,
I seldom dreamt of her, and when I did, the recollection was
usually vague.

But this night, after falling asleep easily after a busy day, I had an
unusually vivid dream. I awoke about three in the morning with tears
trickling down my cheeks. Lying motionless, I tried to comprehend
the intensity of the dream. It was so surreal that I woke my husband.
The details I shared with him were quite clear. I recalled walking
through a winding flower garden and smelling the sweet fragrance
of roses. The garden bloomed with vibrant hues of red, yellow, and
purple. The luminescent colors seemed energetic in their own way.
Bluebirds perched on honeysuckle vines, softly chirped a soothing
song that offered hope and cheerfulness. Though I didn't recognize
where I was, the feeling that surrounded me was overwhelmingly
familiar. I was embraced by a powerful unconditional love.

In my dream, I was talking to someone, and we were walking
toward a wooden park bench at the end of the garden path. I turned

my head toward my companion and it was my mom. She was beautiful. Her short brown hair gently framed her face. Her smile gleamed as she expressed the depth of her love and joy for her family. She seemed very content and aware of the current events in our lives. It felt like she was telling me that she was watching over us from this incredible place of beauty and happiness. At the end of our visit, she whispered "I am always with you in spirit." Though my eyes filled with tears, I felt complete as she continued down the path without me. Then my eyes opened.

Shortly after, my daughter woke up crying. "I miss Nana," she wept. She too had been dreaming about my mom. While I held her close, I listened as she described the same garden that I had seen in my dream. I pondered sharing the coincidence with her but decided to let it be. Lulling her back to sleep, I softly spoke: "Nana's love is forever, my dear."

~Kathryn A. Beres

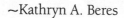

Prenatal Nocturne

The tie which links mother and child is of such pure and immaculate strength as to be never violated.

~Washington Irving

After my mother's death in 2007, I dreamt of her quite frequently. Some evenings I spent hours telling her how life had been treating me, and other nights consisted of dreams in which her death had never taken place. No matter the content, each dream gave me solace. Sadly though, as time went on the dreams were fewer and farther between. Several years after her passing, her visits only came every few months.

Then, in late 2012, my husband and I found out that we were going to be parents the following June. Although I was thrilled, the idea of going through a pregnancy without my mother's support made me anxious; I began to imagine all the milestones Mom would miss. My husband was supportive and as understanding as he could be, but my anxiety slowly turned into grief. Still, I took the necessary actions to confirm our pregnancy test results.

The following week, the evening of our first doctor's appointment, I fell into a deep sleep, filled with the warmth of seeing my baby for the first time. As my dream began to unfold, I found myself waking up in a hospital bed. I was alone in a sterile, dark room. A feeling of panic washed over me. Suddenly, the door opened and my mother entered. Her smile illuminated the tiny space. I couldn't help but smile back at her. I tried to get up and give her a hug, but realized

I was restricted by the IV attached to my arm. Mom motioned to me to stay on the bed, and she came to my side.

"Oh, I am so excited!" she began. She was glowing, but not because of some ethereal warmth. Happiness was simply oozing from her every pore. Mom pulled out a compact mirror, powdered her nose, and adjusted her hair.

"Where am I? What are we doing here?" I inquired.

"Silly, you just gave birth! The nurses have your beautiful baby in the other room, and I just can't wait to meet my granddaughter," she cooed.

"D-daughter?" I said, a tear coming to my eye. "But I don't understand. I was just four weeks this morning."

"Well, I can't explain that, but it's June 15th and you've just done a beautiful job delivering my grandchild. Oh honey, I'm so proud of you. Well, I'm off to meet my granddaughter!" With that she kissed my forehead and left the room as quickly and smoothly as she had entered, as if she was floating on a cloud.

My tears continued to flow, and as I woke up, my mother's warmth seemed to fill every fiber in my body. I felt closer to her that night than I had felt for so long. Still, my sleep was fitful for the remainder of the night as I wondered whether I had been granted a true visit with Mom or not.

The next morning, I pried myself out of bed and got ready for work. My mind replayed the dream over and over again as I began my commute. I was jarred from my thoughts a little over a mile from my house when, a few feet from the freeway entrance, a bus cut in front of me. I slammed on my brakes. At first I cursed the driver, but then I noticed the number and destination on the digital screen above my head. "152," it read, "No Longer in Service." I couldn't believe my eyes.

Mom was born in January of 1952, I knew in an instant this was yet another message from her. It was also confirmation that her visit the night before had been very real. "No Longer in Service." I chuckled lightly and felt empowered once more. I knew in my heart my mother was there with me, with my baby, and she was most definitely part of the incredible biological process I was embarking upon.

It wasn't until my twentieth week of pregnancy that my mother's visit was validated once more; my husband and I found out that we were having a baby girl, just as my mother had shared with me four months earlier.

~A.B. Chesler

75

Heavenly Introduction

You are my sonshine.
~Author Unknown

t was over; my baby was gone. It's never like television or the movies. Hospitals don't give you much time at all to sit and hold your child. As soon as they can, you are rushed out into a room, visited by a minister, and soon led out of the hospital. It's cold, and unfeeling, but... it's reality.

The next day, we quickly made whatever arrangements needed. The entire family was in shock. And then the crying began. And it went on forever.

I prayed every night for my sweet Bobby to visit me, that he would come and sit close, and I could give him a proper hug. How silly was that? I mean, he was gone, right? Nevertheless, I hoped, dreamed, and wished.

We were expecting four grandchildren all close together. It should have been a joyful time, waiting for new life. But one of those babies belonged to my son Bobby and his girlfriend.

Then, one night, I had the most fantastic dream ever. Bobby was there and a little girl with fiery hair stood between us. She was jumping up and down eagerly waiting for Bobby to answer her questions.

"What are these books about, Bobby?" she squealed.

"Ask Mom, Autumn, she'll tell you all about them," replied Bobby.

The books were pure white, so white the brightness was almost blinding. Those red curls bounced with every jump this little cherub made.

Bobby told me he couldn't stay, that he had much work to do. I awoke too soon. I wanted to grab hold of him and take him back with me, but it just wasn't possible.

A few days later, my husband Barry answered the phone.

"All ten fingers and all ten toes; nice weight; she's healthy, right?" He continued. "What did you name her? Autumn. Okay we'll be there later tonight to see her." Barry finished and hung up the phone.

The hair on my arms stood straight up and I felt chills. Was this the same Autumn? Could this just be a coincidence? At the hospital, they handed a beautiful baby. I looked under her little newborn cap and there was that fiery red hair. I took her in my arms, and softy whispered, "We have already met."

~Catherine J. Inscore

76

Papaw's Lantern

An angel can illuminate the thought and mind of man
by strengthening the power of vision.
~St. Thomas Aquinas

I agonized over the course of my future well after settling into the rhythm of college. I saw life as a wilderness with trails cut through it in all directions. So many paths were available, each one leading to a different outcome. But the woods were so thick that I couldn't see the end of a single trail. Which one was for me?

As I confronted the trailhead, my grandfather seemed to be nearing his trail's end.

"Papaw's taken a turn," Mom said on the phone. "You should come home for a few days so you can see him." She did not have to say "for the last time."

I sent e-mails to my professors, letting them know I wouldn't be in class. It was too late to head out that night, so I packed for the morning. Then I switched off the lamp on the nightstand and slid into bed. I was sure falling asleep would be impossible.

Instead, I tumbled right into a vivid dream where I stood in the dark by a road. Papaw came riding up in the fog, driving a small cart pulled by a single sorrel mare. A hazy ball of mellow, buttery light swung over Papaw's head. At first I thought it was some nighttime spirit, happily buzzing back and forth, until I realized it was a lantern swaying on its tethers.

The horse clip-clopped toward me, bringing with it the creaks and groans of the cart. Papaw whistled a jolly tune full of trilling notes that seemed to part the fog for him.

Papaw choked up on the reins and stopped the cart before me. He playfully tipped his old cap. When he held out his hand, I took it and slid onto the bench seat beside him. He clicked his tongue and gently slapped the reins. The horse set off, striding along on hooves that boomed.

Papaw and I rolled through the dark night air. The sway of the cart and the thud of horse hooves lulled us into a comfortable silence.

After a while, I said, "I thought you were sick."

Papaw shook his head. "I'm better now."

He flashed a wink and then an easy smile spread across his face. I had not seen that smile in many months, but now here it was, brighter than the lantern and illuminating for me the story of Papaw's life. His eighty years started at the tail end of the Great Depression and marched into the Second World War. Then he had amassed a fortune of experience mining for precious metals, loving a family, fixing cars, and whistling mysterious songs.

In that moment, I understood what a full life Papaw had lived. I asked if he had any advice to give me, just one pearl of wisdom.

Papaw considered the question for a while. Even when I was little—the youngest of four grandchildren—he took every question seriously. That's what I loved about him most.

"Don't worry about the forks," he concluded.

"You mean like on the dinner table?"

He laughed so hard that he had to let go of the reins to hold his belly. I laughed, too. I always had a way of thinking of things that left him "plum tickled." And when Papaw was plum tickled, he had a laugh that could not be reined in.

When our laughing simmered down to chuckling, he said, "I mean the forks in the road. Life puts plenty before you, and you won't always know which way to go. Don't worry and don't think. Just go. Make the best with the path you take. It's all one road anyway."

I nodded, thinking it was very good advice. But an aching silence followed.

"Tell me something," I urged, just so I could hear his voice and not the ache of silence.

"Tell you what?"

"Anything."

Papaw slipped out a little laugh. Instead of rambling on about fixing leaky radiators, crawling through mine shafts, or defending the coastline of Okinawa, Papaw apologized. He said there wasn't enough time for any stories.

"But we're in the middle of nowhere," I said. The veils of darkness were draped all around us. "There's plenty of time."

Papaw shook his head and pulled up the reins. "I have to let you off here. I can't take you any further."

The cart stopped, which I knew was my cue to hop to the ground. But I hesitated. I strained to see the road ahead, hoping to buy more time. If there was some landmark up ahead, he could take me that far and tell me a story just that long. But the pall was too thick. I could not see the way ahead. The lantern lit only us and the horse's haunches.

I started to protest. I refused to leave him. Papaw put on a patient grin.

"Of all my grandkids, you were always the stubborn one."

I looked down at my feet, feeling ashamed.

"Just like me, I guess," he added, which lifted my mouth into a grin.

Then he wrapped his arms around me and it was like a flood after a lifetime of drought. But the tighter I squeezed, the quicker my body slid down, until I was standing beside the cart with no idea of how I got there.

The cart was already trundling away. The lantern swung side to side, like a large ball of light. The farther away Papaw traveled, the bigger the ball swelled around the lantern, getting brighter with every swing. Then all I could see in any direction was bright light shining brighter.

I held up one hand to shield my eyes.

And that's when I woke up.

The lamp on the nightstand blared like sunshine. Hadn't I turned it off?

Then the phone rang. Mom called to say Papaw had passed away. Our tears did most of the talking until at last we hung up.

According to the alarm clock, I still had several hours before I could hit the road. I reached for the lamp to switch it off, but I stopped. Papaw had traveled a long way to give me that light. Somehow he'd known I would need my own lantern as I took life's many trails. So I touched the body of the lamp and said, "Thank you, Papaw."

~Jenny Mason

Prophetic Advice from My Father

There is a fine line between dreams and reality, it's up to you to draw it.
~B. Quilliam

Shortly after we moved to the small town in South Georgia where my husband and my father were born and raised, I began having a lot of trouble sleeping and periodic nightmares. Since I had never lived away from home, I attributed it to the stress of the move.

One such sleepless night, after I finally dozed off, I awoke to a terrifying dream that seemed so real I was in a cold sweat and shaking. It wasn't like a normal long rambling dream—it was just a flash of the headlights and grill of a tractor-trailer. The scary part, however, was that the first I saw of it, I was looking straight up to the giant chrome letters F-O-R-D across the front grill!

They say your body cannot tell the difference between real danger and perceived danger. It must be true because I felt the exact same fear and panic as if I were actually about to hit the truck head-on. I was so shaken by the dream that I didn't attempt to go back to sleep. I got up and sat in the living room, my mind going over and over it the rest of the night. Just before daylight, my husband got up to find me still shaken and sitting on the couch in the dark. "What's wrong, babe? Can't sleep?" he asked. In a fit of tears I told him about the dream, and tried to accurately convey the terror I felt and the fear that still lingered. He was sympathetic but thought little of it, telling me "It was just a dream. You are okay. What are you so upset about?" And honestly, I couldn't say except that it had seemed "too" real.

Well, unfortunately, that wasn't the end of it. About the time I thought I could get that picture out of my head and sleep again, I saw it again and a couple of nights later still again. This happened at least a dozen times over the course of a three-week period. It even happened twice in the daytime when I was wide awake. I was totally unnerved by it and constantly upset. I told my husband, "I know it is a warning. I am going to be hit head-on by a tractor-trailer! You don't understand—there is no time to get out of the path of it. I don't see it coming—it is just there!"

He tried to calm me. "Hon, you can't let a bad dream control your life like this." But I was convinced, to the point that I began to look for places where a truck could appear without adequate warning. It stayed on my mind day and night until I was afraid to sleep and afraid to get on the road with my children.

Finally the visions stopped. After a few weeks, the fear had somewhat subsided. I was beginning to relax and get my life back to normal.

One afternoon a couple of months later, we were heading north on Highway 29 towards Dublin, Georgia to do some shopping. I was driving, my husband in the passenger seat and all three children in the back. The speed limit was seventy, and I routinely drove at or very close to the posted speed limit.

Though I was not consciously thinking about the visions, they were never far from my mind. While speeding along, listening to the kids chattering in the back seat, I noticed we were approaching a long, gradual hill. I realized topping a hill would be exactly the kind of place where I would not see a truck until it was right in front of me. Although I did not see the vision that day, I certainly remembered it, which caused me to drop my speed to less than fifty. I stayed focused on the crest of that hill as I cautiously approached. When I was about halfway to the top, I looked up. I had to blink and look again, not believing what I was seeing. Not one but two tractor-trailers topped the hill, heading straight for me, one in each lane. Apparently one truck decided to pass the other on the hill and could not get up the speed to complete the pass, nor could he get back over before he topped the hill. Both trucks realized what was about to happen and hit the brakes hard, leaving a trail of black smoke and the deafening sound of thirty-six screeching tires, but to no avail. There was no time for the passing truck to get back in its lane.

In the next second, almost as if by instinct, I turned the car and we went bouncing into the fairly deep roadside ditch, plowing up dirt. As I fought to maintain control of the car, both trucks flew past—the one in my lane barely clearing my bumper.

As the car, finally under control, came rolling to a complete stop all three kids in the back seat were crying. Everything seemed to go black for a minute as I collapsed over the steering wheel in relief. When I raised my head and looked over at my husband, his eyes were big as saucers as he yelled out louder than he intended—"How on earth did you know what to do? I thought we were going to die!" When I finally found my voice I said, "Because I have lived this scenario over and over in my head for the past three months—that's how."

Had I not thought about the visions—I would have been driving the full speed limit and all three vehicles would have topped the hill at the same time. Still, I had not consciously planned what I would do, as in the visions I had no reason to believe I would have the opportunity to do anything.

Then suddenly I heard my daddy's voice repeating his unusual instructions from years ago…

My daddy had died six years earlier in a car wreck—but suddenly his words came flooding back to me loud and clear from when I was a teenager and he was teaching me to drive. After the usual "stay in your lane, always yield to pedestrians, don't forget to use your turn signal," I remember thinking his next words seemed oddly prophetic. "Remember, if you are ever faced with a head-on collision situation your first instinct is going to be hit the brakes and stay your course—but always remember not to do that. You leave the road—you hear me? Do not be afraid of hitting anything else. You get out of the path of the oncoming vehicle!"

Inexplicable visions kept me alert and served as a warning so that I was prepared, and unusual instructions blurted out at what seemed like an inappropriate time nearly nine years ago—saved not only my life but the lives of my entire family.

~Andrea Peebles

A Comforting Vision

While we are sleeping, angels have conversations with our souls.
~Author Unknown

The phone woke me up at seven. It was my mom. Grandpa was missing. Irritated, I thought: "She knew I was in the emergency room until 1:30 last night. He's most likely at the casino. I need sleep. Why did she wake me up?"

Later that morning, I called Mom to get the full story. The previous evening my grandfather had left his house, where he lives with my uncle, to fill up his tank with gas. He hadn't returned since. It wasn't unlike him to just head off somewhere without telling my uncle, so no one worried until several hours had passed. My parents called all of Grandpa's usual hangouts. Nothing.

My boyfriend and I drove to my parent's house to join my alarmed family. We got a teary reception. I remember sitting quietly on the kitchen stool watching in silence as my mother prepared dinner. I was thinking about Grandpa, his laugh and smile, and the way he would always sneak me candy before I went to school. Then I realized something and gasped.

"What?" my mom asked.

"I dreamed about Grandpa last night."

The wooden spoon she was holding dropped heavily to the stovetop as she turned to me.

"Where was he?" she asked, hoping the dream would reveal

some clue to his location. Although by now we were prepared for the worst.

I closed my eyes in an effort to recover the dream. I could only remember that it was dark; we seemed to be in a giant warehouse-type building with dim lighting.

My mom began to think about where that could possibly be. Maybe we could find him.

"What else do you remember?" she continued.

Suddenly the dream flooded back.

"I was walking toward him. He was in the middle of a big empty room, sitting there wearing his cowboy hat, his face turned down and slightly away from me as I approached. And I couldn't see her, but I knew that a woman was walking beside me. As we made it up to Grandpa, he turned to us and smiled."

"Mary," my mother spoke ever so softly.

My face twisted in confusion; I looked at her.

"Mary? His wife?" I questioned.

My mom looked back at me, her face calm and sad.

A day later we got the call. Search and Rescue had tracked down Grandpa's truck, which had been seen pulled off to the side of the road. Grandpa, whom doctors believed was suffering from dementia, had pulled over and left his car late the previous evening, according to the police. He started walking into the snowy wilderness of Oregon and eventually succumbed to the cold.

Grandpa suffering from dementia had been news to us. He had lived with my family for years and we had never seen any symptoms. This man who would wait for me to get off the bus and drive me up the hill to our house on his tractor; this man who would always want to play any game of cards at any time of day. How could this man have dementia, or anything else wrong with him?

After Grandpa was found, my mom asked more questions about my dream. I repeated only what I could remember. Then she asked me something new. "When was your dream?"

"It was the night Grandpa went missing, at 2:17 a.m. I remember because I woke up and thought how odd it was to dream about him and then checked my phone. Why?"

My mom had a funny look on her face. "The police said that his time of death was between 2 a.m. and 2:30 a.m."

I think I remember crying after she told me this.

I was confused and wondered what it meant. Soon after, my mom and I decided that it was never a dream at all, but a vision. I had this vision, it now seemed, at the exact moment Grandpa passed. I was there as he reconnected with his wife, who had passed two decades earlier.

It took quite a long time for me to heal from the wound of Grandpa's passing. Once I did, however, I began to see my vision in a brighter light. I am honored to be the one chosen to reassure my family that Grandpa is with his wife now and they are okay.

~Rachel Strickland

Ears to Hear

He wakens me morning by morning, wakens my ear to listen
like one being taught.
~Isaiah 50:14

Yesterday while visiting with my daughter Ari on the phone, she interrupted our conversation. "Elizabeth!" I heard Ari call to her six-year-old daughter. "Why are you making mud pies in your new school shoes?"

"I'm replanting flowers," Elizabeth announced. Ari whispered into the phone, "She's digging up dandelion weeds beside her playhouse and replanting them under her picnic table. You know the area where the ground has worn bare?"

"It's Earth Day," Elizabeth explained while she dug, "and tonight while I brush my teeth, I'm going to turn off the water. And if we have to go to Walmart we need to ride our bikes."

It surprises me how well children can "hear and heed" while we adults totally miss it.

Ari listened well at that age, too. In fact Ari was also six when we moved into a much-too-small house while the construction of our new house was being completed. Since there were no safe places to take our year-old Shetland Sheepdog, Spicy, for a walk, Ari and I discovered some great hiking paths in a nearby national park known as "The Gorge."

After each school day, Spicy and I retrieved Ari, and we escaped the familiar constraints of asphalt streets lined with overbearing steel and concrete. Soon we were enveloped inside a tunnel of trees with endless journeys on multiple trails, leading us up and around curvy inclined paths.

Spicy stayed close to my heels, that is until we reached the rocky cliffs. It was then an innate urgency guided him to run up and around each precipice with swift and secure maneuverability. Amazing how this dog knew what his greatest of grandfathers were bred to do: herd sheep through the treacherous cliffs in the Scottish Highlands.

Those hikes became the highlight of our days, especially as autumn's fluorescent colors flaunted their fiery blends.

That is until one memorable morning. Spicy was under my feet as usual while I prepared Ari's breakfast and sack lunch. His internal clock had him set to run down the hallway as he and I awakened Ari with my kisses, his licks and a few tickles and hugs. Laughter most always started our day, followed by a morning prayer for guidance and safety.

Except for this morning. Ari's shouting sent us scrambling to her bedroom, my heartbeat quickening with her escalating cries.

"Mom, we can't!" Ari screamed, sitting straight up in her bed, staring in front of her. "We just can't go!"

I wrapped my arms around her, but she continued her protest. "Mom, we can't take Spicy hiking. To that mountain. There's a murderer up there!"

"Ari! That's a wild thing to say." I pulled back to look into her face, a frightened face. "Where did you get such an idea?"

"I dreamed it, Mom. We were there on the trails, and this man was going to kill us. But I woke up before he could."

As much as I tried, I couldn't convince Ari it was only a dream. I figured that surely by the end of the day she'd realize how nonsensical it was, and we could resume our walks. Not so. She held strong to her conviction. Even the following day when Spicy and I picked her up from school, she adamantly resisted ever hiking in that area again. The dream was too real for her.

The following morning I opened the newspaper and almost dropped my coffee cup onto the front-page headlines. In bold print

I read "Dead Man Found on Gorge Trails in National Park." Stunned, I read the nightmarish details as though I were somehow a part of it. Hikers had found the dead man the afternoon before. Authorities believed the body had been there for at least twenty-four hours, within the time when we would have been there. The murdered man was discovered off the path, only a hundred yards from where we ventured every afternoon.

I can't explain it. I just know how grateful I am this little girl insisted we not allow that dream to come true. Ari had a few more dreams after that. None were as life and death as that nightmare.

One was an encouragement for our family. In another, Ari awoke from a dream, and after she described it to us, it confirmed the safety of a friend's husband who she said at that moment was stranded. The friend, who was at our house at the time, received a phone call an hour later, affirming her husband's safety and his reason for the delay.

I understand now those dreams were not meant to be spooky, something for another world, but a practical means of speaking to us in those still moments when we're more apt to hear Him. As a result, I now realize the practicality of dreams and how God still uses them to issue warnings and offer deep insights missed in our daylight hours... that is, if we have ears to hear.

~Ann Elizabeth Robertson

Safety Vision

Out of this nettle, danger, we pluck this flower, safety.
~William Shakespeare

Finally! I was back on my skis. In five minutes, I would reach the underpass and stop for a rest. I was winded, the aftermath of my holiday flu bug still lingering. I was approaching the highway up ahead where the ski trail broke through the east end underpass and into the dense pine stand on the other side.

I had never liked skiing that part of the trail. The entire structure shook and grumbled as transports and a steady stream of traffic sped across the bridge overhead. It had been marked for love overdue repair come spring.

Harsh Northern Ontario winters were especially hard on highways; frost weakened many stretches of road with time. This particular bridge showed its age, and each spring brought with it a new gaping hole or two in the crumbling cement. Travelers were glad that repairs would soon start, or so claimed the large Ontario Works sign now posted at the entrance.

It felt great to be back outside, back to my daily nature hikes. I chose to ski in the early morning. The trails were usually empty, and I cherished my solitude. Only today I heard another skier coming up behind me. Not wanting to push this poor old body just recovering from the flu, I decided to move to the side.

"Gloria, turn around. Go back home."

I gathered the flu bug had not left my body completely. I could hear the scrape of the skis behind me, I could hear the voice, but peering into the dark bush behind me, I saw nothing.

Over Christmas, I had been plagued with a vile fever that carried me in and out of delirium. I heard voices that didn't exist and spoke with people who weren't present. Apparently, I was not as clear of the illness as I thought.

"Go back home."

Yep. I was still pretty sick. That was my father's voice, and he'd been gone for decades.

I glanced back as I once again heard the scrape of skis. There stood my father, in winter garb, his face partially hidden by a ski mask, but his kind eyes visible. I knew his eyes so well. I felt tears on my cheeks, as I dropped my ski poles onto the snow.

"Daddy?" I had passed the point of wondering if I was still in the grip of my flu bug. My father, my beloved father, stood not a foot from my ski tip.

"Go home, my girl. You are not well enough to be out here. Go home. Please."

I inched closer to him until I could reach out. With that, his form started to fade.

Transfixed, I watched him disappear into the snowy scene behind him. I felt weak, and leaned against a poplar until I regained my breath. I looked around. The sun still shone in the sky above, the trees still glistened with newly fallen snow. The tears falling on my cheeks were real. So had been the vision of my father.

After some time, I bent over, pawed the snow for my fallen poles, and headed home. I saw nothing but my father's eyes as I skied to the car park. I was oblivious to the open water of the river, steaming in the early morning sun, to the beauty of the snow-laden branches, to all the sights and sounds I usually enjoyed on these morning forays.

Robot-like, I removed my skis and placed them in the car, my mind spinning with what just occurred. I barely remember the drive home. Soft music played on the radio. I was obviously still in the throes of this terrible sickness, and I craved the comfort of a hot bath and some medications. I decided to postpone my outings for yet another week.

As I opened the car door, I heard a news bulletin breaking into regular scheduled programming. Ready to close the door on yet another development in the war overseas, or another suicide bombing, or a faraway airplane crash, I was held captive as a staccato voice shouted over background noise, "Breaking news! Breaking news! We are at the scene of a fatal bridge collapse, the east end bridge on the outskirts of town." The voice went on to describe the utter devastation and the terrible casualties that resulted from the collapse of the overpass that I had narrowly avoided skiing under.

~Gloria Jean Hansen

Before I Go

We are not victims of aging, sickness and death. These are part of the scenery,
not the seer, who is immune to any form of change. The seer is the spirit,
the expression of eternal being.
~Deepak Chopra

I never thought of myself as psychic, even though I had more than one experience that might have caused me to at least consider the notion. I didn't connect the dots. I contemplated each incident and marveled at them separately. After all, they happened years apart. I see now they were each a gift that would become part of a fuller picture much later, when the time was right.

Three of my grandparents warned me they were going to die or let me know they had died (before my family was told). I was not told by them in the flesh, on the phone or by letter; I was told by their spirits.

I had no reason to believe any of them were near death when I received my "knowings." Two came by way of dreams. The third came via an image that felt real, even though I knew it was not.

When I was eight, I had my first knowing experience. I was very close to my maternal grandparents. I adored both my grandmother and her husband, my mother's stepfather. Grampy married Gram after my mother graduated from high school (her father had died when she was eight). Grampy treated Gram's children and their families as if they were his own.

Gram and Grampy lived a few states away but we saw them

many times each year. Our visits were always filled with love. Grampy was a particularly sweet soul. He had a great head of white hair, the kindest face and the best smile. In their apartment, he often sat in a rocker and would have one or more of us on his lap.

More than fifty years ago, when I was eight and sleeping, I had a dream that Grampy came to me. He told me he had died and that he had to go away. I kept begging with him to not go, telling him that he could not die.

I woke up and ran crying to my mother. "Grampy died, Grampy died," I cried out as I went running to her, telling her the dream. My mother assured me that it was "just a dream," that Grampy was fine. She held me, kissed me and reassured me that all was well. A few hours later, our phone rang. Gram called to say that Grampy had died of a heart attack earlier that morning.

Nearly fourteen years later, I had another dream. This time, it was about Gram. She and I had a very close relationship. Gram had been dealing with cancer for about a year. At the time, however, I believed she was doing better, that she was not in any imminent danger of dying. She lived in the same town as my mother. I talked with my mother at least once a week and got updates on Gram each time. I had just seen her six weeks earlier.

I dreamed that Gram came to me wearing the dress I knew she wanted to be buried in. She was standing in front of several doctors in white lab coats, my mother, and my mother's siblings. Gram called me by name and said, "I am dying. Please come to me." Again, as with my dream with my grandfather, I pleaded with her. "No, Gram, you can't die." She was calm and direct in her response. "But I am. Please come."

I awoke in tears. It was very early in the morning, well before my usual time to get up. I ran to the only phone in our apartment and called my mother. "Where is Gram? Where is Gram?" I cried. I had woken my mother up. It took her a few moments to respond. "I didn't want to worry you," she said. "You've been taking final exams. I was going to tell you once you were done."

"Where is she?" I pleaded.

"She's in the hospital and they say it might not be long now. She took a turn for the worse and had to be admitted. She's in a coma."

I was sobbing. My beloved grandmother was close to death and I had not been told. I needed to get to her.

Immediately after the call, I hurriedly threw on clothes, packed a small bag and headed for my hometown. A few hours later, I was at the hospital. I sat with my grandmother for hours, holding her hand. Because she was still in a coma, our conversation appeared one-way. But I knew she could hear me, even if her ears or brain were no longer working, and that she was sending love back to me. I told her, out loud, how much I loved her, how much she meant to me, and that it was okay for her go. I kissed her. It felt like she squeezed my hand. She died several hours later.

I was twenty-one then and I knew, in every fiber of my being, that my dream was a real communication with my grandmother, a communication that transcended the physical. I was so grateful to her for calling me to her side for one last goodbye.

A few years later, during a visit to my father's mother, I had my third knowing of imminent death. This grandmother was a petite woman, spunky and set in her ways. She wasn't a "warm and fuzzy" grandmother, but I loved her nonetheless. The day I visited, I had no reason to believe she was near death. She had not been ill. She was in her late seventies, and as far as I knew, she was doing fine... slower, but fine.

We had a good visit. When I went to leave her apartment, I opened the door and saw an old-fashioned, black, horse-driven hearse waiting for her in the hallway outside her apartment. Of course, I knew there really wasn't a horse or hearse there. Yet, the vision was perfectly clear. I knew, deep in my being, that it was waiting for her and that she would die soon. I also felt that she was the one providing me with this information, even though she was not conscious of it.

I drove home and called my mother. I told her of the visit and the vision, along with my interpretation of it. I said, as if I were a doctor with information about her health, "Grammy will die soon, within a week or so. You should go see her." Less than two weeks later, she died.

What a gift all three grandparents gave me: Grampy's special goodbye; Gram's call to her bedside; and Grammy's gift of knowing it was my last time to hug and kiss her, to tell her how loved she was. Those messages became the foundation for much greater knowings later. I am forever grateful to them.

~Valerie S. Libby

Chapter 9

Miraculous
Messages from Heaven

Divine Connections

A Message
from the Wall

Death ends a life, not a relationship.
~Jack Lemmon

My grandparents on my mother's side emigrated from Portugal through Ellis Island in the 1920s. Although they settled into life in the U.S., they loved returning to their homeland as often as possible. During one of my mother's many summers in Portugal, she met a man she would fall in love with and marry. My dad was unable to join her in the U.S. until he wrapped up family obligations. He finally made it here a few months later and settled into a typical immigrant's life. He worked very hard at two jobs and saved as much money as possible in order to achieve his dream... homeownership.

When I was five and my brother was three, my parents did it! They bought a two-family home, and we happily moved in. Although we didn't have much money, we had a great life. Our neighborhood was filled with kids, and we had daily pickup football, baseball, or basketball games until my mom called us in for dinner. We went on our annual vacation and stayed at the same motel in Cape May, New Jersey every year. My parents did all they could to support us, including finding a way to send my brother and me to college.

I learned so much from my parents about how to be a good friend, a good parent, and a good family member. They didn't preach;

they demonstrated by their actions. They set my brother and me on a good path.

When my brother and I moved out of the house, my parents were able to relax a bit, and my father dropped his second job. They were settling in nicely to the second half of their lives.

Then, the devastating news came. My father had a bad headache that just wouldn't go away. He finally went to the doctor and had an MRI. Our family was devastated to hear the result. He had a brain tumor and needed to have immediate exploratory surgery. I will never forget the discussion with the doctor after the surgery. My dad had an inoperable malignant tumor and his prognosis was for three months of life.

How could this happen to such a good man? Finally at the point in his life when he could begin to enjoy himself, he would be taken away. He was just fifty-eight years old.

Since I lived closer than my brother, I decided to move back home to support my mother through this ordeal. Over the next few months, I somehow made it through my job every day and drove to the hospital at night to see my father. After the initial brain surgery, he had changed slightly, but the man underneath was still there. We had many conversations with neither of us acknowledging the inevitable. Many of our conversations were about the importance of family. At that point in my life, I was a typical twenty-seven-year-old, enjoying dating, but not in a relationship. My dad told me that he wanted to see me in a happy family situation with children of my own. Unfortunately, he would never see it, because he died three months after his surgery.

A few years later, I met the woman who would win my heart, and together we built a family with two wonderful sons. My dad never met Lori, but he would have loved her. Although she was a midwestern girl from a family that had been in the U.S. for many generations, she loved the ethnicity of my family and was open to trying Portuguese food. She loved our large family gatherings.

At one of our family events, my VoVo (grandmother) talked about going back to Ellis Island to see where she had first touched

American soil. Almost ninety years old, she was unable to make it there, so Lori and I decided to give her a guided tour. We went for a day and filmed our visit for VoVo. The highlight of the visit was filming the American Immigrant Wall of Honor. This is a monument honoring immigrants to the United States. Families add names to the wall for a small fee. The funds support Ellis Island, and any immigrants' names can be placed there. Years earlier we had added the names of my grandmother, grandfather and father, so that future generations of our family could appreciate their incredible journey. We looked up their names in the computer, found the correct panel, and there they were:

MANUEL MIRANDA FERNANDES
NAZARE MARIA FERNANDES
FERNANDO ANTUNES FERNANDES

VoVo was overjoyed to walk through the visit by videotape, and she gave us a running commentary about her memories. She was especially touched to see her name on the wall.

A few years later, Lori and I were ready to start our family. We decided that if we had a boy, we would give him the same middle name as my father: Antunes. It was our way of remembering my father and honoring his legacy.

Lori went into labor two weeks early in the middle of the night, so we ran around and gathered our things and rushed to the hospital. One of the things we brought was our trusty video camera to film our child's birth. Unfortunately, in the rush to leave the house, I grabbed the first tape I saw and we were forced to tape over the Ellis Island visit. We filmed the thrilling moment that our son, Nicholas Antunes Fernandes, came into the world. It was a miracle, a joyous moment, something I will never forget. The only tinge of regret was that my dad would never meet Nick. But at least he would be in Nick's life, to an extent, through his middle name.

Two days later I filmed Nick and Lori as they entered our home from the hospital.

A few weeks later, while Nick was taking one of his rare naps, Lori and I decided to watch the video of his birth. We sat down, put in the tape and relived his birth. Next would come his first visit home. But before the visit, there was a split second gap that commonly occurs in old VHS videos between segments. Unbelievably, up on the screen came:

FERNANDO ANTUNES FERNANDES

The moment from the underlying Ellis Island visit when we filmed my dad's name had miraculously appeared just in that split second between segments. There is no way this could be a coincidence. I started shaking. Somehow my dad had sent us a message. He was there with us. He had met Lori and Nick, and it was as if he was telling me that he was happy for me and for my new family. He was still with us, communicating from heaven.

And he is still with me often as I go through life. I often think back to his parenting approach, his work ethic, and his supportive relationship with his friends to help guide me. I know he is no longer here, but he will never be gone. And through his message from the wall, he is telling us that.

~Rick Fernandes

Misty Moments

The greatest weapon against stress is our ability to choose
one thought over another.
~William James

Shara was a tall, lanky eleven-year-old with short curly auburn hair and eyes that glinted with mischief when I first met her that December. Her dad affectionately called her "string bean." Two years later, Shara and her younger sister became my stepdaughters. It was a busy home life with my own two daughters and visits from Shara and her sister on weekends.

Shara was the eldest of the four girls, upbeat about life. She was lighthearted and indulged in pulling pranks on her siblings. Her father and I were not immune to such tricks either. As the years went on she became a friend as well as a cherished daughter. During our conversations when we found some alone time, we would talk about matters that perturbed or frustrated us. Quite often she would just smile and say, "Don't worry about it, it's just small stuff anyway."

Tragically, two days after her thirty-sixth birthday, she was taken from us as a result of a workplace accident. A void was left in our lives that we couldn't fill. As the weeks went on, engulfed in a fog, I started to feel a presence in the house, nothing menacing, just a warm glow.

One evening as I was settling into bed and almost asleep, I startled as I sensed someone in the room. Turning around, I saw Shara, surrounded by a faint silhouette of light. She smiled at me with an impish look and spoke, at the same time laughing softly, "I didn't mean to scare you." I had heard that sentence many times when Shara was younger, as she would enjoy catching me unaware and try to get a reaction. I was about to speak, but she disappeared as quickly as she had arrived. That incident provided some peace of mind. I felt she was in a happy place; otherwise why would she be so mischievous?

As the weeks passed, my life took a bit of a downward spiral. My best friend for the past fifty years passed away. Any joy I had left quickly diminished as I focused more on the doom and gloom of life instead of the good. I had also been caring for an elderly parent the past six years and that proved more challenging each day. Minor irritations became huge in my mind and it was getting increasingly difficult to cope.

Trivial matters would upset me, such as forgetting something at the grocery store, or finding the car was low on gas, or getting my zipper stuck in my jacket and, oh yes, my hair required some major attention. That last thought brought a memory to mind. Shara sometimes messed up my hair to make it look free and easy, as she would say with a laugh. Her hair was quite often that way. She didn't stress about having a perfect hairdo all the time. Maybe I needed to calm down a little more. There were certainly more important matters that needed my attention.

One evening, my sleep was fitful. The frustrations of the day kept circling in my mind. Uptight, I got up to get a glass of water in the bathroom. The full moon was brilliant that night and shone directly through the bathroom window, eliminating the need to turn on a light. As I entered, I found Shara standing by the sink looking into the mirror. Again, that slight aura hovered around her. She was so close I could touch her, but instead I just stared, frozen, unable to utter a word.

At that moment, as if on cue, she turned around, eyes twinkling and smiling that beautiful smile. She motioned to her hair and then mine, and made a gesture with her hands as if to say, what can you do about it? I laughed and was just about to say something but she quickly faded. She was reminding me to let go of minor details.

Returning to bed, a strong feeling overcame me. I felt more at peace because I saw that no sadness surrounded her. I never had another visit from Shara, but those misty visions had provided me with some assurance that she had passed through on her way to a lovely place.

Life went on, with little details going wrong and still causing unnecessary frustration in my daily living. Then, one afternoon, as I organized some books on a higher shelf in my already bulging bookcase, a book wedged in the back came tumbling down, striking my nose in the process. Irked by this and my clumsiness, I angrily tossed the book across the room. Realizing the silliness of my reaction, I retrieved the dust-covered book and read the title: *Don't Sweat the Small Stuff*. I had forgotten about receiving that book many years ago and couldn't remember how I had acquired it. As I leafed through the dog-eared pages, curiosity got the better of me and I turned to the first page. My heart seemed to skip as I read the inscription, in beautiful handwriting, "Happy Birthday, Love Shara." A final message from heaven? I believe so.

Shara has been gone for four years, still touching my heart whenever I look at her picture, seeing the light in her eyes, reminding me to not stress about the little things.

~Christiana Flanigan

The Connection

A daughter may outgrow your lap, but she will never outgrow your heart.
~Author Unknown

I sat at my desk recording the week's stack of résumés when someone behind me shoved their jagged nails into the small of my back. The pain radiated into my kidneys. Even the natural childbirth I'd experienced recently couldn't compete with the debilitating strangeness of this attack.

The intensity pushed me forward and I gripped the edge of the desk. I needed it to let up — I didn't think I could stand it much longer. And then it was over. I took a deep breath and looked around. The clock on the wall showed 2:30 p.m. As I sat there, uneasy at the thought that the pain might return, I felt grateful that I could go home in two hours. I waited for the pain to return, wondering what could be going wrong with me that would cause such an onset of vicious discomfort. The pain didn't return and I finished out the day, retrieved my infant daughter from the babysitter and headed home.

In light of that episode, I asked my husband to watch the baby while I took a short rest, thinking maybe that's what my body was trying to tell me. Working moms pull out all sorts of stops to cover both the work front and the home front, and I do believe our bodies tell us when we've pulled out a few too many stops. We need to pay attention to the messages.

Several hours later I opened my eyes, feeling wonderful yet a bit guilty as I had slept way longer than I intended. My husband pushed the bedroom door open, baby girl on his hip.

"Are you awake yet?"

His tone was flat and I thought he was upset because I slept so long. We hadn't had supper, the baby probably had been fussing and I hadn't attended to any of it. And yet it wasn't in his nature to begrudge or complain about things like that. But something was on his mind.

"Yeah—I'm awake. What have you two been up to?"

He came and sat on the edge of the bed next to me. The room was dark and I couldn't see his face.

"Is something wrong?" I asked him.

"Your mother called. Elmer had a heart attack."

I sat up straight. Dad had a heart attack?

"When? Where is he? What hospital did they take him to?" I asked, kicking my legs over the side of the bed, as if my hurrying to get out of bed and get my shoes on was going to get me to him any quicker.

"He's not in the hospital."

My brain took a moment to process this fact, and it made no sense to me, of course. A person has a heart attack; the ambulance races them to the closest hospital. All the doctors and nurses come running and eventually the patient is stabilized and moved to their own room—right?

"He didn't make it, Bec." A quick hug and he and the baby left me alone with this, and my mind wrestled with those thoughts that bombard a person when they receive such news. He wasn't even sixty-two yet... he couldn't die. Was this really happening?

Downstairs I asked my husband why he didn't wake me up when my mother called.

"She said to let you sleep. There wasn't anything to be done. She'll call you later tonight."

"When did it happen?"

"Earlier this afternoon."

My father died in Minnesota, just over the state line from Iowa, and Minnesota state law at the time required an autopsy. The coroner's report arrived several weeks later. I had to look every other word up in my medical dictionary, but the gist of the matter was summed up in terms I understood... 90% blockage... 100% blocked... 85% blockage noted on the such and such... scar tissue observed... indication of possible earlier episode. Death was instantaneous.

What was it he'd told me at Christmas about feeling suddenly dizzy and having to lie down on the car seat until the sensation passed? He thought maybe he'd taken in a dose of carbon monoxide while waiting for my mother to finish her shopping.

There it was at the end of the report. The thing I'd been wondering about ever since they told me he died in the middle of the day. The official time of death on record.

2:30 p.m.

~R'becca Groff

Our Final Message from Dad

For death is no more than a turning of us over from time to eternity.
~William Penn

When we returned home from my husband Carl's funeral, our youngest daughter, Sue, checked her cell phone for messages. She let out a scream and collapsed against the refrigerator, crying hysterically. When we got her settled down, between her sobs, she said, "You won't believe this, I just got a message from Dad!" Then she played it back for all of us to hear. Carl's voice came through loud and clear on her cell phone: "I'm home, I'm free! I'm free! Thank God Almighty I'm free at last! Call Mom." It took all our breaths away.

We were all floored. How could this be? We tried to rationalize. My husband had been in a wheelchair from polio since age nine, although he'd never let it stop him. He always did everything and anything he could to help others. Could this be another time? He'd been in and out of the hospital and in such pain. Could it be somehow he called on one of his trips home and left that message on her cell phone?

But then, only in God's perfect timing, we got that call the day of his funeral. Somehow Carl and God figured out a way to send us one last message. We heard from him, in his own words, at a time when we all needed it the most. Through his love, a way to ease our pain, to let us know he was really all right. We received a wonderful heart-freeing message. Even though in our love and grief, we still miss him. We find comfort in his final words to us. Now Dad really is "Home," he is with God, and "Thank God Almighty, free at last!"

Timing is everything! Indeed he was finally free. Free from pain, free from his wheelchair, free from the body that held him prisoner all his life, free from the bonds of this earth. In Heaven, free for eternity with God Almighty, and he even called to tell us so!

~Gaye Loraine Kiebach

86

A Heart-Wrenching Goodbye

The reason it hurts so much to separate is because our souls are connected.
~Nicholas Sparks, The Notebook

That particular Wednesday in February seemed like most others. I worked at a job I liked. I went home to make myself something quick to eat before attending a night class at a local university. I got to class early to visit with fellow classmates. That is how it usually went on Wednesdays that winter.

I had no reason to expect anything would happen to a family member that day. My grandmother had been dealing with cancer, but she was in a good place and there was no imminent threat of her death. A few other family members had health issues, but nothing that was life threatening. I learned that night anything can happen in the blink of an eye and change your life forever. I also learned that the emotional bonds and connections we have with others are hardwired into our physical beings; and we can sense things happening to our loved ones even when we don't know of them with our minds.

I had always been close to my father. Although I loved both of my parents deeply and got along with both of them, I felt more in alignment with my father. Dad was a self-starter and a hard worker. He had overcome more than a few huge traumas in his life that would have emotionally crippled others. I looked up to him and appreciated how hard he worked to provide for his family. He loved my mother and lovingly referred to her as "my bride" throughout their marriage. He dearly loved his seven children. He was generous with his many talents, often helping family members and friends with their projects. He had his faults, as we all do, but he was a good man.

In the middle of my class that Wednesday evening, I felt, out of nowhere, a sudden and deep pain in my chest. It is nearly impossible to put into words the feeling I had, but I can still remember it to this day (nearly forty years later). It felt as if someone or something reached into my chest cavity and pulled out a piece of my heart, just ripped it from my body. This sudden pain caused me cry out, loud enough for the instructor to notice. He asked if I was okay as I rose from my seat. My response was one I gave without knowing where it came from—it just poured out from me as if I had been given the answer to speak. "Someone I know just died."

I barely have a recollection of leaving the classroom, or of driving home. I only remember grabbing my belongings and leaving, with tears running down my face. I felt a bit crazy. I did not know what was happening. What was that feeling in my chest? Why did it hurt so much? Even though the pain disappeared, an ache still lingered. I did not feel like anything physical happened to me, so I was not concerned about my health. Why had I blurted out that someone I knew had just died? Where did that come from? None of it made any sense. All I knew was it felt real, too real, and I could not stop crying.

I got home to an empty apartment. I do not recall where my husband was, but I did not feel he was the one to worry about. I called my parents' home. My parents and six siblings all lived together, and I was certain that was where I would get the answer to my burning question: "Did someone we know and love die today or tonight?" I called countless times over the next few hours. No answer. This was thirty-eight years ago, in the days before answering machines or cell phones, so I just had to keep calling.

About two hours after I got home from class and in between my phone calls to my parents, I received a call from my mother. She was sobbing. It took her a while to be able to speak. My father had died very unexpectedly that evening, at the age of forty-six. He had been home alone. When she got home from visiting my grandmother with my two youngest sisters, she found my father dead in their bedroom. According to the paramedics, my father died about the same time I felt something rip from my chest.

I felt then, as I still do today, my connection to my father was so deep that when he left this physical world, I could feel him leave in my body. I believe my body was reacting to the emotional pain of the loss before my brain was conscious of the fact that he had died. In the years since, I have felt comforted by the heart-wrenching feeling I had that night. It reminds me of our connection, in life and beyond this physical existence. I also like to believe that he might have wanted to take a piece of me with him, knowing that I would want it that way. I truly believe that wherever he is, I am with him, and that we are always and forever connected.

~Valerie S. Libby

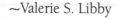

Music in My Heart

Music is well said to be the speech of angels.
~Thomas Carlyle

M y mother lived in a nursing home for seven years after suffering a stroke following surgery. Paralyzed on one side, unable to walk, she was confined to a wheelchair. I stopped by to visit her every afternoon after I got off work. Whenever possible, I ate with her. Three days before Christmas, in 1988, she joined my father in Heaven. For the first time in twenty-four years they would celebrate Christmas together. What a joyous reunion they must have had.

I wish I had been with Mom in her final hours. To hold her hand and tell her how much I loved her. To tell her she wasn't alone. If I had been with her, though, I might have missed her beautiful goodbye message.

On our final evening together, Mom said very little, where she usually chatted for hours about her grandkids, my sister and me. She was recovering from pneumonia and was so thin and frail I could feel the bones in her back when I hugged her. The nurse suggested I call my sister and brother and mention Mom was growing weaker, in case they wanted to visit with her.

After telling my family the situation, I hated the thought of leaving Mom alone and considered spending the night with her. But she had a roommate who I might disturb, so the nurse said not to worry, she would call if Mom needed me. I went home, planning to return early the next morning.

Unable to sleep in my bed, I carried my pillow to the living room and curled up on the sofa. Finally, as early morning light filtered through the curtains at my windows, I closed my eyes. I'd rest a few minutes and then go see Mom. As I drifted between sleep and wakefulness, a strange sound startled me. I sat up. Was I dreaming? No, I heard it again: music. Not the TV. Not the radio. The music reminded me of wind chimes in a gentle breeze.

My eyes drawn to the music, I looked up. Floating above me was a tiny, fluffy white cloud. Happy, tinkling music wrapped around me, like protective arms. Like Mom's arms. I sensed her presence in the cloud. Though no words were spoken, I knew. Leona (Lorena) Adele Chapter Young Stowe had gone home to her Heavenly Father. She was now free: no more pain, no wheelchair. She could walk again. She could play the piano the way she did as a child.

The cloud hovered over me. As the music slowly faded, a soft voice whispered, "I love you, Beverly Jean." Brilliant light sparkled from the cloud for a second then vanished.

Two or three minutes later, the nursing home called. I knew before the nurse gave me the news.

"Your mother went peacefully, a smile on her face," the nurse told me. "She said she loved you."

"Yes, I know."

Mom's physical body no longer is with me, but she left her music in my heart.

~Beverly Stowe McClure

88

And the Orchestra Plays On

Music is the mediator between the spiritual and the sensual life.
~Ludwig van Beethoven

Pum pum pum pum pum pum-pum, pum pum pum-pum-pum. Had I actually heard those notes coming from my piano or was I dreaming? I opened my eyes and realized it must have been a dream, as no one in my house would have been playing the piano so early in the morning. But what was that song? It seemed familiar but I couldn't place it.

My father had passed away recently at the age of ninety-six. When I tell people he was ninety-six, they nod and smile, and act as though that was long enough and I should be grateful to have had him around as long as I did. What they don't know is that we had a troubled relationship and there were times years earlier when I might have been ready for him to go. But at the end we had achieved equilibrium, a kind of peace that came with his decline and increasing need for care and my willingness to provide it. At first I cared for him out of a sense of obligation but at the end it was with genuine love and tenderness. We didn't speak of the past, but when he died I held him in my arms and told him I expected to hear from him again. Nothing else needed to be said. He was a different man by then and he knew that I loved him.

He died in his house, my childhood home, in a hospital bed

a few feet from his beloved Steinway piano. Everyone in the music community called him Maestro; they knew him first as a great concert pianist and recording artist and later as a conductor and university professor of music.

I didn't like being in his empty house at night. I could hear every creak, every groan the old house would make. But there was a lot of work to be done. The house had to be emptied. It made me sad that he was no longer there and sometimes the noises were a little scary. On more than one occasion I was sure that someone followed me up the basement stairs, but I couldn't look and would just run up as fast as I could. If I was there alone I wouldn't even go in the basement. On this particular evening, I was in the den listening to a CD of my father playing the piano to keep the noises of the house at bay. The CD player stopped and I heard someone playing the piano in the living room. Pum pum pum pum-pum, pum pum pum pum-pum-pum. Should I know that music? I thought my sister Kyriena had come over and I went to the living room to see her, but there was no one there.

A few days later my brother Mark and I were talking about our dad's memorial service. Mark, also a musician, planned to sing a favorite song of our father's from his concert touring days as guest artist of singer Paul Robeson. I casually told Mark that I had a tune going through my head lately that I couldn't place. I hummed it for him. There was silence on the other end of the phone; then Mark quietly told me that it was Dvorak's "New World Symphony," one of our dad's favorite orchestral pieces. Mark said I should try to get a recording of him conducting the piece with one of his orchestras and play it at the memorial.

Although I was raised on classical music and attended a lot of concerts in my younger days, my dad hadn't conducted for more than ten years and I rarely listen to anything but popular music anymore. There was only one way that piece could have come to me. He must have been playing it for me.

I worked hard to plan the memorial, gathered some of his musician friends, a former student, and a minister friend. Kyriena and I planned a reception. It was coming together and I was so happy that music would be the focus. I called someone from the orchestra to get a recording of the "New World Symphony." I also needed to choose which of his piano recordings to use at the memorial. One night at his house I heard the piano in the living room again. Not the same piece. It was more lyrical, sweeter, almost like butterflies in flight. What a beautiful piece. I wasn't as scared because this time I knew I wasn't alone. My father's ashes sat in an urn on his favorite recliner in the living room. Kyriena and I liked them there. We decided to keep his ashes in the house until the burial scheduled for the day before the memorial, which was two months after his death. So my father was there. But oddly, the piano was not. It had been moved earlier that week to be repaired before it was shipped to my sister Helena in Chicago. I was curious to know what this other piece was, but Mark didn't know.

When the cello player from the orchestra delivered the CD with the "New World Symphony," he told me that he'd decided to record another of my dad's favorite pieces, in case I wanted that one too. I played the CD in my car and had to pull over, stunned when I heard it. It was Smetana's "Die Moldau," the piece I'd heard playing on the piano that wasn't there.

I never told anyone how I'd known which pieces to play at the memorial. But when Kyriena told me she'd had a dream about our dad at a party, standing at the top of the stairs with a drink in his hand and raised to toast us, I knew he was happy that his message had been received.

On the day of the memorial, the university chapel filled with friends, family and musicians. My brother sang "A Balm in Gilead" and my father's piano recordings filled the hall. The organ, the string ensemble, solo violinist and pianists were all wonderful. But what moved me most was hearing the two orchestral pieces that my father had wanted to be played. I closed my eyes, and there he was in his white jacket standing in front of the orchestra with his baton. I'd heard the orchestra so many times before but never quite like I heard it now. As a child I sometimes resented having to go to all those concerts, but I wanted this one to go on and on.

The orchestra that he conducted for so many years is dedicating a concert to him. On the program? The "New World Symphony" and "Die Moldau." I didn't choose the music. The musicians did. I can't help but wonder if he has been visiting his old friends too. You can be sure that I'll be there and we'll all raise a glass to the Maestro as the orchestra plays on.

~Nina Schatzkamer Miller

89

Breathe

It is only with the heart that one can see rightly,
what is essential is invisible to the eye.
~Antoine de Saint-Exupéry

I first met Ralph when he was teaching a class at music college. His large, graceful hands described the physical stretches we as singers needed to do to fully develop our instruments. His deep, mellow voice established his authority: soloist with a major opera company, musical theatre tours and bass singer in a renowned quartet.

I was thrilled that he was assigned as my private voice teacher. Any concerns that his success had inflated his ego were put to rest immediately. At my first lesson, I asked, "What are you going to teach me?" He replied, "What would you like to learn?"

I loved him from that moment. It was the love you feel for a teacher who humbles himself in order to elevate you.

Ralph directed my strong personality in subtle ways. He trusted my voice, he trusted my judgment with song choices. Between the lessons and his Master Class, I learned faster than I ever had. He incorporated focused physical movement and visualization into his teaching, always encouraging an authentic voice to come forward.

With his guidance, I developed an acoustically fine, internal concert hall. What had been for years a mysterious maze of bone and muscle became stained glass panels that stretched with the notes. Polished rosewood walls and gilded balconies grew inside me, and resonated with the beautiful tones Ralph drew out with his gentle coaching.

When my uncertainty became vocal pushiness, Ralph told me to pull back, to "let the song sing itself." I'd always had trouble with that. I was a belter, a powerhouse who didn't know her own strength.

He'd say, "Breathe. You know how to breathe."

One month into our lessons, Ralph was rushed to Emergency. Word was that he would be in hospital for some time.

I took up a collection to buy Ralph flowers. On the way to the florist, an object hanging in the window of a metaphysical store caught my eye. It was a pewter dragon. Between its paws was a large, clear crystal. I had a strong feeling it was meant for Ralph. And it cost exactly the amount I'd collected.

Ralph looked worn and thin in his hospital bed. His breathing was laboured, his voice raspy. Handing him the wrapped dragon, I felt shy. It suddenly seemed sophomoric. As if I were a kid trying to interest him in science fiction. I needn't have worried. As Ralph lifted the little silver dragon from its box, tears sprang to his eyes. "Oh," he said.

I tilted my head. Ralph continued. "I died on the Emergency Room table," he said softly. "I have pneumonia from AIDS."

I felt numb. Tears formed in my own eyes. Then he said, "When I left my body, I saw the light people talk about. I went towards it. I wasn't afraid. It felt good."

He looked down at the dragon and tapped the crystal. "Then I heard your voice. And I saw a dragon with you, just like this one. You called me back, so I returned. We're not done."

My head spun. I clutched the side of his bed.

"I'd like you to learn everything I know," Ralph said purposefully. "And I want you to take over my class. Teach people how to sing. Let's have a meditation, right now. Breathe. Just breathe."

We closed our eyes. I visualized his aching lungs and willed his irregular breathing to deepen. I felt intuitive, solid information flow from Ralph into my mind, my body, my soul. I began to feel confident I could pass on his knowledge.

Ralph never came back to the college. He did some teaching from his rural home. He survived for three more years, often bloated and ill. I occasionally spent weekends at his home. In between his rest periods, we sat at the piano. The last song we worked on was "Swing Low, Sweet Chariot," one of my favourites. Again, he reminded me to pull back, to let my powerful voice cradle the song and not overwhelm it.

His wife quickly accepted me once she realized our relationship was purely musical. Besides, I was good with the animals, and always willing to work around the farm.

I planted their apple orchard, carefully placing manure from Ralph's beloved goats, Annabelle and Alice, into each hole. I quietly wept while planting, knowing Ralph would never eat from these trees.

Ralph's favourite place was his kitchen. He liked to sit around with friends and students, sharing tea, food and stories. He said he especially learned to love kitchens when he lived in Auntie Pearl's boarding house.

Ralph died while away visiting one of his spiritual teachers. I didn't get to say goodbye. When his memorial service was announced at a local church, I was anxious to pay tribute.

My turn came to speak. I was so devastated that when I reached the pulpit, I couldn't form words. I've never had stage fright; I love the stage. At this critical moment, I choked. I could only draw the shallowest breath. In the midst of panic, I hung my head and thought, "Ralph, help."

I felt two strong, graceful hands place themselves on my solar plexus and belly. I could sense Ralph's presence as clearly as if we were in the practice room. "Breathe," he said. "You know how to breathe."

His hands remained warm and solid over my midsection. Suddenly, I was able to draw a deep breath. I opened my mouth, and out came "Swing Low, Sweet Chariot." As clear and pure and "sung by itself" as Ralph had been trying to teach me. The room was hushed for several moments after I finished.

I said out loud, "Thank you, Ralph. Did I do it right this time?" I saw people wipe tears away. Ralph's students nodded their heads. I left the stage feeling complete. I was still sad, but a great burden had been lifted.

The minister stated that there was nothing more to be said after that.

We broke for repast. A woman took my elbow and guided me to an elderly lady, whom she told me was blind. The elderly lady said, "I could see Ralph. He was behind you."

I was startled, but reacted by taking her hand. She was Ralph's Auntie Pearl. Well, not his real aunt. She had rented a room to Ralph (and other travelling performers) for quite some time, and considered herself his adopted auntie. Pearl, was, in fact, Jimi Hendrix's "real" aunt, and a firecracker. She herself was a jazz singer, and we became friends that day.

For the next few years, Auntie Pearl and I visited and talked on the phone. What was the gist of our conversation? Ralph's frequent visits to our respective kitchen tables. He would arrive and just sit, as if again having a friendly cup of tea and sharing a joke. It was Pearl who taught me that we "see" our loved ones with our hearts.

It's over twenty years since Ralph passed. Auntie Pearl is gone as well. They're having a good time reminiscing. Ralph still visits my table. His coaching and ongoing support helped me have some success as a singer and voice teacher.

Every now and then, I get anxious about performing. About not doing it right. Then Ralph says, "Breathe. You know how to breathe."

~Reisa Stone

Reunions

To live in hearts we leave behind
Is not to die.
~Thomas Campbell, "Hallowed Ground"

My ninety-three-year-old grandmother would not have wanted to die four days before Christmas. She would not have wanted to ruin everyone's holiday. Little did she know that in her passing she gave us a wonderful holiday gift.

We women sat at a local diner having tea. My mother, my aunt Patricia, who we called Trice, and I were waiting to pick up what were rumored to be the best pies in town to bring back to my grieving grandfather. Mom was older and out of the house before Patricia was even a teenager, so this gave them some time to bond.

The only consolation we could think about the timing of this whole thing was that Grandma finally got to spend a Christmas with my Aunt Joanne, her middle daughter, who had died of lupus almost thirty years before.

My grandmother was an amazingly vibrant woman, who right on into her nineties was flying back up north from her beloved retirement community in Sun Lakes, Arizona, to visit us. Not long ago, she had stood in my Pennsylvania kitchen, baking Italian cookies like an artisan, holding out a hand and requesting a sifter full of powdered sugar like a surgeon asking for a scalpel. She was still dragging my grandfather, three years her senior, to dances at the community clubhouse until only a few years ago. She was at the casino playing slots three days before she died. I have photographs.

Joanne, the middle daughter, was smart, headstrong, funny—everybody's favorite the minute she walked into a room. She was the only one of the girls to go to college, a tall and athletic sister between two petite and more timid girls. She became an English teacher and married her college boyfriend, who whisked her off to Louisiana when he was offered a job as a Shell Oil engineer, where he eventually became a vice president. Joanne was diagnosed with lupus after her first baby, my cousin Addie, was born.

Doctors warned that the disease would progress if she had another baby, so she and my uncle decided to adopt. But she inadvertently got pregnant before the process was completed and called off the adoption. She died before my cousin Davy turned two.

Aunt Trice always claimed to be very sensitive to Joanne's presence. As we sipped chamomile in our booth at the diner, she described how during multiple stressful events in her life, Joanne appeared to her and told her everything was going to be all right. Joanne confirmed she wasn't sick anymore. Then after one visit, she told Trice she couldn't visit anymore, and the visions stopped.

My mother sighed, folding her arms dejectedly. "Why doesn't anyone come to see me?" she said. "I don't ever see anything like that! Does that kind of thing ever happen to you, Sue?"

"I don't see people when I'm awake," I said. "But sometimes, I'll talk to people during the day, people who have passed on, and ask them things. When I dream that night, they answer me."

Mom looked hurt. "I had this dream about Joanne once, but it didn't make much sense," she said. "She was running around this 1950s car in a beautiful white dress saying 'I feel so good, I feel great!' It was a turquoise '57 Chevy. She got in the car..."

Trice looked excited. She had trouble getting her sentence out. "That was my car!"

"What?"

"Daddy bought me a teal '57 Chevy after graduation!"

"I swear I didn't know that!" Mom gasped.

By the time her younger sisters graduated, my mother was married and struggling with two little kids in a one-bedroom apartment. So, sadly, she wasn't particularly involved in Patricia's adolescence.

"It was like this color behind you," Trice said, pointing out a toothpaste-hued stripe in the wallpaper behind us.

"Yes, and the dress was white with a sash and..."

"And one shoulder with a big bow? And the crinoline..."

"And the crinoline all around!" The two of them made the same gestures of tulle around the bottom of an imaginary skirt, laughing.

"I remember that dress," said Trice. "She loved that dress. She wore it to a high school dance."

"I always wondered why she would be running around an old fifties car in a party dress!" My mother bobbed her tea bag in and out of the glass cup, tears coming to her eyes. "Then she showed me her hands." Lupus caused painful swelling in Joanne's hands; she did hot paraffin treatments to soothe them. "She said, 'Look, they're better!'"

The back of my neck started to prickle.

"I hate to tell you this, ladies," I said, "but I had a dream about Joanne in a car and a white dress, too."

They put down their cups.

"I was walking along the side of the road, and she pulled up in a white car. It was a tiny, 1970s car, like a Volkswagen Beetle or something. We were both in big white dresses, like we were getting married. The car was filled to the dashboard with dress. We were driving through the mist, into nowhere."

"And what happened?"

"She was very mysterious. I asked where we were going. She said, 'Don't worry. It's okay.'

"I said, 'I'm scared.' She smiled and said, 'Don't be.'"

I turned to my mom. "Then I asked about you. I said, 'Can my mother come with us?' She said no. And that was it."

Of course, I once interpreted this to mean I would be driven to my death on my wedding day, but that never happened. And understand that, at five years old, I was a flower girl in Joanne's wedding, where we rode in black and white antique cars instead of limos, in big dresses. So it's not strange that I would associate these images with her—or that she would choose them to communicate with me, to ease my fears about what happened to her. Because in my youthful paranoia, I was afraid I'd be next to die from lupus.

At the table, the three of us rolled up our sleeves to show the hairs standing up on our arms.

We finished our tea. I felt nearly as drained as the cups. But we three women were united in the knowledge that Joanne had come to each of us. We just hadn't realized it until that moment when we compared notes. My grandmother's death had brought us together and allowed us to share these previously private moments. I miss my grandmother and my aunt Joanne terribly. But I can only imagine the beautiful Christmas reunion the two of them had. Perhaps they'll let the three of us know how it went!

~Suzanne Grieco Mattaboni

King Kong

My daddy, he was somewhere between God and John Wayne.
~Hank Williams, Jr.

"My Kong is falling from the building," I whispered into his ear as he lay dying in the hospital bed. Since I was a child, I called my father my Kong, after King Kong. I believed that he was just as strong as the giant ape. As he faced death, I did my best to help release him to the next life.

Two months after he passed away my sister called to ask if I would like to go see Lisa Williams, a well-known medium. I was familiar with Lisa from her show on Lifetime, and since I was eager to get a sign from my father, I agreed to go.

The center was packed, with every one of the nineteen hundred seats filled. We were in the second to the last row, way back from the stage.

I clutched my father's gold-plated watch (my sister suggested I bring a personal item of his) and listened as Lisa helped audience members communicate with their loved ones. I knew it was only going to be a matter of time until Lisa directed her attention our way. "I have a grandfather-like figure with me and he is speaking about his granddaughter Julie," she announced. The audience was quiet; no one raised a hand. I nudged my sister and whispered to her that this was Dad and he wasn't saying "Julie," he was saying "Jilly." My third child and my father had a deep bond and he called her Jilly, short for Jillian.

Although I sensed his presence, I wasn't confident enough to raise my hand. I needed something a bit more concrete, something undisputable.

"This man is letting me know he had cancer," she continued. I nudged my sister harder and assured her this was him. I raised my hand and was disappointed to see a woman in the middle row raising hers. Lisa asked both of us to stand so she could figure out which one of us she needed to speak to. She went on to say that this person died in June (my father had died June 8th). There was swelling of the legs (he had severe edema in the last few days that required special stockings). At this point she was still uncertain which one of us was the correct party.

"Important information," she called out. My heart pounded. I jumped up when she asked, "Which one of you is holding his watch?" I waved the watch in the air.

"Happy Birthday," she said. It was September 15th and my birthday was one week prior on the 8th. "He wishes you congratulations also." My fourth child was born three weeks after he died. I was in shock and could not believe I was getting a chance to hear from my father, yet I knew our bond was strong enough that if he could come through he would. She banged on her chest like an ape and apologized, saying, "I don't know why but he wants me to do this like Tarzan." It didn't resonate with me until my sister called out "King Kong!" I was convinced. No way could this woman have ever known a detail that intimate and single me out in a crowd unless Dad was communicating through her.

Each bit of information she gave us was just as meaningful. She ended our session by informing us that he would send us dimes. The very next day I found six dimes in various places; they seemed to have come out of nowhere. Even in death he is my Kong, and he remains an important of my life.

~Maribeth Graham

Miraculous
Messages from Heaven

The Power of Love

92

Strawberry Fields Forever

Strawberries are the angels of the earth, innocent and sweet
with green leafy wings reaching heavenward.
~Terri Guillemets

My parents loved strawberries. When I was a child they had a half-acre garden and one third of it was planted in strawberries. My mother would put quarts of berries in the freezer along with dozens of jars of jam so we had berries throughout the winter. When they moved from that house and gave up gardening, they bought berries from a local produce merchant or berry stand every few days all through the season.

My father spent the last months of his life in a nursing home and Mom made sure to bring him berries every day or two. He became ill from a case of the flu that was going through the home shortly after his eighty-second birthday. It was the end of July, but there were still strawberries available and my mother took him some, as usual, on the last day of his life. Before she left him for the night she fed him the last from the bowl. Two hours after she left she got the call that he was being taken to the hospital. He died before they got him in the ambulance.

The next spring I took my mother to visit his grave and place flowers for Memorial Day. Growing on his grave were about a dozen strawberry plants in bloom. They were the only berry plants in the whole cemetery. Groundskeepers had noticed the plants and deliberately mowed around his grave so the berries could grow. As the years went by the strawberry plants spread and grew out from his grave into the cemetery, but never over my mother's side of the plot.

Ten years after my father's death my mother was gravely ill. She was diagnosed with a type of blood cancer on her ninetieth birthday and wasn't expected to live more than a couple of weeks. With treatment she held on for four more months, until berry season. This time I was the one who brought her the berries. My husband had broken some ribs at the same time my mother was sick. We lived 150 miles from my mother and I had to divide my time between caring for my husband, caring for my mother, and caring for my eleven-year-old son.

The last time my mother was hospitalized for treatment they had given her a medication to reduce the amount of fluid in her body. That kicked off a major attack of her congestive heart failure, which severely weakened her and caused her to enter a nursing home, where she got steadily weaker. The last night I saw her I'd visited her earlier in the day and brought her berries. She had already been bedridden for a day or two. My husband wanted me to come home as I'd been gone several days and he needed me there. I stopped in to see her and tell her I was going home. She asked for some of the berries I'd left earlier. I gave them to her and kissed her goodbye, telling her I loved her very much and I would be back. My niece stopped by later and fed her the rest of the berries. I got a call from my sister the next morning telling me that my sweet mother was gone.

That was nine years and eleven months after my father passed away. They were married fifty-nine years, and survived the Depression, World War II, and raising four children. I always felt it strange that the last thing they both had to eat was strawberries.

At her funeral I sat in the front pew with my brother and sisters, wishing I could hug her just one more time. I felt her arms wrap around my waist where they usually did and give me a squeeze. I knew she was all right.

On the way home I started thinking about her things and what to do with them. My mother loved to read. She'd been through every book in the large print section of the library and bought several large print books of her own. She and a group of neighbors shared books all the time. As I was driving on the freeway I heard her whisper "Give my books to my friends," and I got the idea to start a library in the common room of her apartment building. We took two bookcases and all of her large print books to the common room and I sorted them by author. From time to time I bought more books and sent them to be added to the library.

I never had the courage and strength to visit my mother's grave. I missed her so much and I couldn't bear the thought of her there. Other family members went to do Memorial Day duty and I asked them about the berry plants. "Were there new plants on Mom's grave?" The answer was yes. The plants had never spread onto her grave while she was alive, but now that she was there, alongside my father, the plants had spread to her side as well. My parents were together, and their shared love for strawberries manifested itself in those plants.

A year after Mom's death, divorced for the second time, I was making plans to move 2,000 miles west with my son to start a new life with a wonderful man who had patiently waited for me. He was searching for a house for the three of us. He looked at dozens and finally found one with a big lilac bush out front. While there were bushes all around the house and some blackberry canes in the back, there weren't any other edible plants in the yard.

I arrived the first week of August, too exhausted from a weeklong drive across the country to look around until the next day. We were walking around, inspecting the various parts of the yard when we stepped outside the front fence. Under a bush, growing out toward the road, were a dozen strawberry plants that had not been there when he saw the house a month before. I took it as a sign that my mother was pleased with my new life.

~Joanne Fiestedt Babic

93

Grandma and Grandpa

Love is not singular except in syllable.
~Marvin Taylor

t was typical for Joey to call home and check in with me whenever he was out of town, but I immediately noticed something different in his voice.

"What's going on?" I asked him.

"Melissa, I have something to tell you," he answered carefully.

My heart sank. "Is everything okay?" I asked tentatively.

Four generations of Wootan men had left for a weekend getaway of male bonding. My husband, his father, his grandfather, and our fifteen-year-old son were together on the trip.

It had been three and a half years since we had lost our only other child, our daughter Kyley. She had been buried on December 23, 2008, her seventeenth birthday. It seemed like we were all just starting to make some progress with our grief when Grandma Wootan became ill. She fought long and hard. We prayed for an end to her suffering and on December 23, 2011, with the man she had been married to for sixty-five years at her side, she joined her great-granddaughter in Heaven. While it did bring us comfort knowing Grandma Wootan and Kyley had been reunited, it was heartbreaking to watch Grandpa Wootan mourn the loss of his beloved wife.

I wasn't sure if I could bear any more bad news.

"Everything is fine," Joey assured me. "Something happened. I… I almost can't believe it."

I breathed a sigh of relief and impatiently asked what he was talking about.

"You know how Grandpa Wootan says he talks to Grandma every night?"

Yes, I knew. Shortly after Grandma had passed away Grandpa shared with the family that he was "visiting" with her in the evenings. He explained to us that Grandma would come to see him every night before he fell asleep. We were grateful that he was able to feel her presence. Despite my own loss, I couldn't imagine losing the person you loved, the person you spent sixty-five years of your life with.

"Last night I was lying in bed," Joey began. "Grandpa Wootan and Dad were in the bed next to me. I hadn't fallen asleep yet and was just lying there with a pillow over my head. I heard Grandpa talking but I couldn't make out exactly what he was saying because the AC unit in the hotel room was running. I figured he was talking to Grandma. I wanted to hear him so I slowly moved the pillow away and looked out from under it." Joey paused. "Melissa, Grandma Wootan was standing there… right in front of me."

I tried to process what my husband had just shared with me. How could he have seen his deceased grandmother? Joey was adamant. He assured me he hadn't been sleeping and he had not imagined it. His grandmother had been standing right there in front of him, and as soon as he laid eyes on her, she was gone.

"What did you do?" I asked.

"I put the pillow back over my head."

I tried not to laugh at the thought of my big strong husband pulling a pillow over his head at the sight of his sweet grandma. I asked him what happened next.

"Grandpa said, 'Momma, where'd you go?' I lay still and after a few minutes I heard him start talking to her again," Joey finished.

I asked Joey if he had peeked out from his pillow to try and catch another glimpse of Grandma. He hadn't.

Wow! I was anxious to hear what Grandpa had to say about

all of this but Joey wasn't sure he should tell Grandpa that he, too, had seen Grandma Wootan. My husband was worried that Grandma might not visit anymore because he had seen her. I encouraged Joey to pray about it. The answer would come. I felt kind of bad, though… I don't think any of us truly thought Grandpa was really seeing his wife.

When Joey got home I asked him more questions. He still didn't feel like it was the right thing to do, sharing with his grandfather what he had witnessed. I had lots of questions for Grandpa, though: questions about Heaven, but mostly questions about Kyley and what she was doing. Had Grandma mentioned anything to him about my daughter? My questions would have to wait.

Grandpa Wootan had always enjoyed growing a garden and despite being in his eighties and not being able to see very well, he still enjoyed an active lifestyle outdoors. One afternoon, while out in the garden, Grandpa lost his footing and fell. His son rushed to his side and it became obvious they would be making a trip to the ER. We all feared he had broken his shoulder. He was in agony but the X-rays came back normal. He was sent home, his arm in a sling. For two nights Grandpa complained of not being able to sleep because of the pain. Nothing gave him relief and the slightest movement of his arm caused him to wince in pain.

Joey had made a trip to his parents' house to visit with Grandpa. When he returned home he walked through the front door silent, sat in the chair next to me, and shook his head.

"What?" I asked, straightening up in my seat. "Is Grandpa okay?"

Joey assured me he was fine… absolutely perfect as a matter of fact. I asked him about Grandpa's shoulder. Joey told me that Grandpa's shoulder was fine; there was nothing wrong with it.

I looked at my husband, puzzled.

"Apparently last night Grandpa was lying in bed in pain and Grandma came to visit him like he says she does every night. He says he told her he was sorry but he couldn't stay up talking with her any longer because he was in such pain and so exhausted from not being able to sleep the last few nights. He said he closed his eyes to try to rest and he felt someone grab his hand and a warm sensation go all the way up his arm to his shoulder. A sense of peace came over him and he immediately fell asleep. When he woke up this morning his shoulder didn't hurt at all and he had the sling off. He was demonstrating how he could move his arm all over the place... he was as proud as could be."

I looked at Joey, amazed. If only Grandpa knew that Joey had also seen Grandma!

Joey smiled at me. "I told him. He knows I saw Grandma. It felt like the right time."

I couldn't wait to hear Grandpa's response to the news that his wife really was visiting with him all this time.

"What did he say?" I asked.

Joey's voice was full of emotion. "Grandpa just sat on the couch, smiled, and said, 'Well, of course she is. I told y'all she was coming to see me.'"

~Melissa Wootan

94

Love Beyond
the Natural

Mother, the ribbons of your love are woven around my heart.
~Author Unknown

After the death of my stepfather, I thought it was best that my mother move in with me. Mom and I were not only mother and daughter, but also best friends. Her moving in with me at that time turned out to be the best thing for the both of us.

Mom cooked and kept the house while I worked and paid the bills. We had a system and a relationship that others envied. We went to bingo together. We went on vacations together. Her friends were mine and mine were hers. We laughed and talked. We argued and fussed. She spoiled me and I spoiled her more.

When Mom was diagnosed with cancerous brain tumors, I was told that she had approximately six months left. I was in denial and I decided that my mother's strength and determination would make her an exception to the rule; she would live forever.

Then one morning, I walked into Mom's room and found that she had passed away during the night. We didn't get a chance to hug or say goodbye. I indignantly questioned why she simply and suddenly slipped away. After doing everything together, why didn't we have the chance to fight death together? I was devastated and angry that she died alone. If only I had known that it would be her last night on earth, I never would have left her side. I questioned everything, including my worth as a daughter, a caretaker and a friend.

As time marched on, I longed for a sense of peace and closure, but they eluded me. I needed to hear from my mother that she was okay and that I had not let her down. Depression set in and I lost interest in everything, including my pride and joy—my aquarium. Mom had often mentioned how much she enjoyed it, how beautiful it was and how well I took care of it. Now that she was gone, my attentiveness to my hobby had gone also.

Nine months passed and Mother's Day rolled around. My grieving intensified. As I dressed for church, wanting to have something of my mother's with me, I decided at the last minute to use one of her pocketbooks. I sorted through them, looking for the one that best matched my outfit, and saw the simple black one that she often carried. "Just perfect," I caught myself saying out loud. Whenever Mom had a pocketbook dilemma, she always chose that one. I was running late so I hurriedly emptied out my pocketbook, threw my stuff in along with hers and left.

I sat in church and envied the children, young and old, sitting with their mothers. I thought about the last Mother's Day I spent with Mom. As tears streamed down my face, I smiled as I remembered working in my aquarium and her asking what I wanted for Mother's Day. Without stopping or looking up, I nonchalantly said that I wanted more fish. I knew she wasn't going to get them and I really didn't want her to get me anything. I didn't need a thing, and just having a mom like her with me was the best gift of all. However, Mom bought me a beautiful pantsuit, which I loved. And as trivial as this might sound, I wondered why she hadn't given me a card. She always gave the most beautiful, heartwarming cards, and I always looked forward to receiving them. Not wanting to seem ungrateful over something so minor, I figured she just forgot, and I never mentioned anything about it.

When it was time to give the offerings, the pastor said his usual, "Give and it shall be given, ask and believe, and you will receive." I took out my offering and silently asked for something, anything from my mother. Then, thinking what a ridiculous request that was, I walked up, put my offering in the basket and sat back down.

Later that night, as I emptied my stuff from my mother's pocket-book to put back into mine, I noticed a white envelope that had my name on it. Inside was a card. On the front it read, "For my daughter, may the Lord bless you always." When I opened the card, a fifty-dollar bill fell out. I picked up the money and read the inside of the card. On the left side she wrote, "Wishing a wonderful daughter a happy Mother's Day. Here's a little something towards your fish. Wish it was more. I appreciate all you do. I love you today and I'll love you always, Mom." On the right side it simply says, "I thank the Lord so often for giving me a loving daughter I'm so proud of."

Mom always dated her cards and May 2007 was in the upper right hand corner of the card. My mother had passed away in September 2006. Was this all just a mere coincidence with a mistaken date? I don't think so. To me, it was my mother's way of telling me she was in heaven. I finally had the peace and closure I needed. As tears streamed down my face, I looked up and whispered, "I'll always love you too, Mom."

Yes, I had lost interest in my aquarium. The few fish left and the condition of the tank reflected it. I took the fifty dollars and, adding to it, I bought what I needed for the health and welfare of my old fish. And of course, I bought new fish.

Even in death, Mom's motherly love saw to my needs. That card played an essential part in getting my life and my aquarium back in order, and both were beneficial and therapeutic towards my healing. But it was the card's wording and the "I love you today and I'll love you always" that was vital. I knew her love would always be with me. True love is an eternal, mystical force that can and will go beyond the natural. For the last time, my mother left something tangible to always remind me.

~Francine L. Baldwin-Billingslea

95

The Iris

Flowers are those little colorful beacons of the sun from which we get
sunshine when dark, somber skies blanket our thoughts.
~Dodinsky

The rain had finally stopped. Three days of Pacific storms had battered Northern California, leaving little doubt that we were headed into winter. It was November 30 — Thanksgiving had just passed and Christmas was a few short weeks away. I pulled my jacket tighter as I stepped out from my art studio where I held afterschool art classes for children. I wondered if the storm had left any lingering rainbows. As an artist, I considered rainbows to be Mother Nature's watercolor message of hope and promise.

I scanned the sky but there were only storm clouds, no rainbows. The yard was littered with storm-strewn leaves, branches, twigs and garden debris. The winds had been severe, causing moderate damage and power outages. A large potted tree lay on its side in the breeze-way, a casualty of heavy winds. I would need to add yard cleanup to my list of "things to do before I leave for the holidays."

I smiled thinking about my upcoming holiday trip. Travelling home to New Jersey always cheered me but this holiday season was particularly special — it would be my first Christmas back home with family in several years. It was a visit carefully planned as a Christmas Eve surprise for my mom and dad, but I really considered it a gift to myself. It had been a difficult year, starting a new business and struggling to build enrollment to make ends meet. I was looking forward to the holiday break but there was still so much to do before the trip: holiday shopping, Christmas cards to make and send, a holiday party for the studio students, and now storm cleanup. I made a mental note to call the gardener as I crossed the patio. As I turned to go back to the studio I stopped, startled by what I saw.

It was the color that drew my attention—deep purple and soft lavender in stark contrast to the drab brown leaves and twigs and ashen storm clouds. There in the middle of my garden, in obvious defiance of the winter weather, was an iris growing as lovely as a summer day. I was transfixed—it was, after all, late November and the temperature hadn't been above forty-two degrees for days. Irises don't bloom in Northern California in winter; they are a late spring perennial.

There was something magical about that flower growing with such magnificence at the wrong time of the year. The late afternoon sunlight filtered through the remaining storm clouds, causing water droplets on the petals to sparkle with rainbow fire. I didn't want to turn away for fear that if I did, the vision would vanish. I considered the flower a rare gift and perhaps a sign. It was a moment too special to let pass without sharing. I called my young student out of the studio and showed her the flower. I explained that irises are not winter flowers and therefore this bloom was a rare and special treat. "Why do you think it grew now?" she asked with five-year-old innocence. I had no answer.

I remembered the iris the next morning as I fixed my coffee and looked out the window to my back yard. The flower was still there and was even more dazzling than the day before. "So odd," I mused, and thought no more of it. By noon that day the iris was forgotten as was much of what I had planned to do for the rest of the weekend. A phone call from my tearful father and the shattering news that my mother had unexpectedly passed away left me numb and stricken. I could not imagine a world without my mother and I could not reconcile the thought that I would never see her alive again. There would be no Christmas surprise, no shared holiday dinner, the presents I bought her would never be opened, and the trip that I had so carefully planned would be made not for a joyous reunion but for her funeral services instead.

I didn't think about the iris again until the day of my mother's service. My brother was going to speak and suggested that perhaps I might want to pay tribute to her as well. I wasn't sure if I had the strength to bear it, and even if I did what would I say? My mother was an unforgettable woman. She was a force to be reckoned with, and was loved by all who knew her. She was "Mom" to many. She cooked and listened, lectured and comforted. She even threatened some with the disciplinary "wooden spoon." She had strong opinions, definite values and limitless generosity. All of us depended on her strength; she was the nucleus and anchor of our family. As I grew into adulthood my mother and I shared a special bond and despite the 3,000 miles that separated us, our relationship was a close and genuine one. It had been my mother who had always supported me through moments of grieving. How ironic that the one person who could help me through my worst sorrow was gone.

It was then that I remembered the iris and the determination of that single flower to bloom despite storms and wind and below normal temperatures. At once I understood the reason for seeing that unusual blossom. It was my mother's way of letting me know that her indomitable spirit could never be extinguished. In Greek mythology, the goddess Iris is the personification of the rainbow and a messenger of the gods. It was a rainbow that I was looking for the day I saw the flower in my garden. My mother provided me with a promise of hope and a reminder that she will be wherever I find beauty and love and grace in this world. Her essence is within all that is good and just and precious. All things, no matter how extraordinary, are ephemeral, but their imprint on our soul and in our hearts is everlasting.

The iris was still in bloom when I returned from New Jersey despite another round of Pacific storms that toppled a palm tree in my front yard. It is now March and tomorrow is my birthday. As no mother would let the day of her child's birth pass without recognition, mine has provided me with a gift; another out-of-season iris is blooming in my garden. Every blossom reaffirms her eternal presence. When my heart aches too much from the pain of missing her, when I desperately wish for one more hug or phone call or smile I remember the iris and how to look for rainbows where I may least expect them.

~T.A. Barbella

Viztin'

A grandfather is someone with silver in his hair and gold in his heart.
~Author Unknown

My grandparents lived only a block away when I was growing up. That's wonderful when they're as apple pie perfect as mine were. It meant that they would often walk over, just because, and visit. In their slightly rural drawls, they called it "viztin'."

I could always recognize my grandfather, Daddy Homer, as he slowly made his way to and from our house, walking with a cane, wearing his hat. A grandpa hat. A former teacher, he had merry, mischievous eyes and a way that transformed learning into a big game. In his seventies, this man taught a child the lesson of a lifetime: No matter what your age, seize the play.

He taught me to plant tomatoes and dive like an arrow and walk on stilts. He taught me sign language so I could talk to people in "secret code." We played jokes and checkers and card tricks. We laughed till our stomachs hurt.

I loved to hear his low, melodic voice, as if words lazed in his mouth like a long summer's day. The stories lolled there, too, just as easy and just as choice. One of my favorites was about his brother, Willie, who had died at nineteen. Those two brothers made a pact just before Willie died. If there were any way at all he could come back to visit, he would.

"Did Willie come back?" I always asked, knowing what Daddy Homer would say.

The story he told was that he'd waited and waited for his brother to come back. Nothing happened. Then one day, early in the morning, he awoke to see Willie standing at the foot of his bed, smiling. Daddy Homer groggily sat up to get a better look, and Willie was gone.

"Was that really him," he would ask, smiling with the mystery of it, "or was I just dreaming?" Like everything else, he made it into a game—into just another one of life's exciting questions—but he never answered those questions for me. Like any great teacher, he knew that the best education lies not in the telling, but in the asking.

Appropriate, I guess, that the man who taught me so much about the joy of life didn't stop even after his own death.

I was seventeen then. After the funeral, as life settled down to the stage of learning-to-live-without-Daddy-Homer-in-the-world, I had the first dream. It started with a knock at the door. I swung it open, and there stood my grandfather, grinning with mischief.

"Daddy Homer!" I exclaimed. "What are you doing here? You're dead!"

He laughed merrily at my bluntness—something he'd always appreciated. "That doesn't mean I can't come viztin', does it?" His eyes danced with the glee of the joke. But for the fact that I was asleep, it really wasn't much different from the way things had been when he was alive. We talked, told jokes, played checkers and cards, told stories. And then he left. End of visit; end of dream.

Except more dreams brought him back, again and again. It was always a different visit, but the theme was the same: My grandfather, in spite of being dead, came viztin'. And then he would leave.

Once I watched him leave, curious to see where he would go. Would he disappear with a poof at the end of the walk? Sprout angel wings and fly? He only walked just as he always had, down the street with his grandpa hat and cane, walking slowly home until he crossed Woolworth Street and rounded the corner till I couldn't see him anymore.

The dreams went on for quite some time. My dog died, and

Daddy Homer brought her back with him. I graduated from high school and started college. When I was lonely and homesick, he'd visit more. As I adjusted, he vizted less often.

Then one night, the dream was different. Instead of coming by, the phone rang. It was Daddy Homer. Did I feel like viztin' today? I felt horrible as I explained to him how busy I was. I was going out with friends and wouldn't be home that day. Could we make it another time?

There was a soft smile in his voice when he spoke. He sounded proud of me somehow. "That's just as it should be," he said. "That's what I've been waiting to hear."

I knew at that moment he wouldn't be viztin' again. When I said so, he gently explained that he wouldn't come back quite that way, but he would be there if I ever needed him.

I haven't had the dream again in the thirty years since, though I've often wished I would. There have been many times I hoped he was there, often catching a whiff of his trademark pipe tobacco. So many things I've taught my children and smiled, thinking of Daddy Homer.

There was even an incident when a beloved pet lay dying, and I thought I caught a glimpse of Daddy Homer scooping her tenderly into his arms. Just a flash and then gone, but I knew then, correctly, that she'd be gone, too. It was such a comfort to me. He would take care of her; of course he would.

Was that really him or was I just dreaming? It makes me smile to ask, though for myself, I know the answer. My grandfather may have taught me logic and skepticism, but he also taught me to find the playfulness—seize the play—in everything in life.

And even beyond.

~T'Mara Goodsell

Death Could Not Part Them

Love is a symbol of eternity. It wipes out all sense of time,
destroying all memory of a beginning and all fear of an end.
~Author Unknown

never knew Mabel when she was alive. I met her husband Al a few years after she passed away, at a time when he was looking for comfort beyond the physical. But, before Al ever crossed the threshold of my office, Mabel came to visit me. She came because Al was coming and there were things that I needed to know to make optimal use of my time with him. She came to set some things straight about how they disagreed about their one and only child. Mostly, she came out of love — to be there with and for him in the way that she could.

But let me start at the beginning. I am an intuitive. I give personal readings and teach individuals and groups about developing their intuition. This is not the profession I planned on. I practiced law for many years, and I was an educator before that. At the time I met Al, I had an office for my intuitive practice in a small town in Maine. One summer, during a town festival, I put out a sandwich sign with fliers on the sidewalk outside my office building. I offered shorter readings to walk-in clients (something I rarely did then and never do now).

Many years later, Al told me that on the day of the festival he was attracted to my fliers and took one home. He read it over, but intuitive work was unfamiliar to him… although somewhat intriguing. He put the flier in a drawer. He would come across the flier from time to time and think of calling me, but each time would simply put it away.

It was a little more than a year after Al first took my flier that he called, at a time when he was wrestling with his grief and really missing Mabel. When he called to make an appointment, he told me his name, his telephone number and only that his wife had passed away a few years before. I told him, as I do all clients, not to tell me more, not to tell me his story until after I had seen him and relayed the intuitive information I had gathered on his behalf. I did not want to know anything more about him or his wife until my preparatory work was completed (so he could really rely on the information received as valid and not influenced by what I knew). I did not know his age or the age of his wife; I did not know where he lived or what she died from, etc.

My intuitive process is to sit quietly for an hour or so (before I see clients) to ask for and receive the information they need. I am asking this of the Source that connects us all. I also invite loved ones, living and passed, to assist if they so choose. I am facile with this process. I can do it with my eyes open. I take pages and pages of notes regarding the things I see, feel, hear, and sense during each preparatory session.

Prior to sitting down to do the reading on Al's behalf, I noticed a large wisp of a filmy form at the corner of my office, by a window. At first, I wrote it off to strange lighting. The longer I looked at it, the more it took form. An older woman manifested out the wisp, with enough form for me to describe her. She was short, petite, had white hair and other specific physical features. She appeared to be standing before roses. Her energy was "spunky."

She showed me that when she passed away, it was very hard for her to breathe. She demonstrated that it was like having an anvil on her chest. She showed me Al caring for her and staying by her side through it all. She then immediately went into preparation mode for

Al. The message I received from her was that the reading was not to be about her. She would guide and have input (in fact, she pretty much directed the whole reading), but it was to be about Al.

She first told me that I would have to talk to him on his left side, because he had an explosion sort of an accident that made it hard for him to hear with his right ear. She showed me them together, as a couple through their lives, and very happy. I saw her playing the piano and an older tune I remember my mother singing, "Side by Side," was playing in my head. The song, I was told, was symbolic of their relationship; they were good partners who had lots of fun together and who had deep love for one another. Mabel's love for Al was tangible throughout the whole reading, in my preparatory time and while he was present for the reading. There were many personal messages relayed, too many to list.

After Al arrived and I had relayed to him to contents of the reading (which was mostly given to me by Mabel), he told me that they had a great relationship and marriage. He confirmed that Mabel looked as I had described her, and that she loved roses. She was spunky and had a mischievous side to her. Al and Mabel had traveled and lived in many places around the world. They rarely disagreed about anything, except for issues related to their daughter. Mabel, in my preparation, relayed an apology to Al about indulging their daughter perhaps more than she should have, for not agreeing with Al's suggestions for a more "tough love" approach, which might have allowed their daughter to gain more independence than the coddling approach Mabel took.

Al confirmed that he had a war injury to his right ear that involved heavy artillery; Mabel had played the piano (including "Side by Side"); she passed away from COPD (a progressive condition that decreases one's capacity to breathe); and he, indeed, was with her, side by side, through it all. He acknowledged the differences regarding their daughter and said it was comforting to hear how she was thinking "now."

Al was in his late seventies when I first met him. He is ninety now, and has been a regular client (and now friend) for more than ten years, generally having two "visits" with Mabel a year. Whenever he schedules a reading, Mabel shows up at my office (or sometimes my home the night prior) to be sure I am ready. Every time Al asks for a reading, Mabel is "front and center," as Al, a former career Navy man, likes to say.

Theirs is a love story that gives me hope for us all. It is the promise (and proof) that we continue to exist in some form after our death and that the connections and relationships we have here on earth are not broken in the least by our passing.

~Valerie S. Libby

Private Visit

We cannot destroy kindred: our chains stretch a little sometimes,
but they never break.
~Marquise de Sévigné

The insistent knock on the front door annoyed me. It was late and I had just fallen asleep. I kept waiting for my mother or husband to get out of bed and answer the door. I knew I needed to rest because we had to get up at the crack of dawn to drive to the hospital for me to have surgery.

Earlier in the evening I had felt restless and asked them to pray with me. I couldn't shake my fear even though I had already experienced way more surgeries than one human should have to go through. Each time I pulled through only to find out another one was necessary for me to regain full health. Eventually I calmed down and went to bed.

Now the knocking woke me and I found my husband Jim next to me snoring lightly. Mom's bedroom light was out and the house was silent; even the three cats were sprawled at the bottom of our bed.

By the third round of loud knocks, with the doorbell ringing, I went to the door shaking my head. I couldn't believe no one else heard this ruckus.

I opened it and started to speak, when all of a sudden my father danced in. He was happy and praising the Lord. He looked the same as the day we said goodbye to him at his funeral many years before. I couldn't believe what I saw; I pinched myself as I thought perhaps I was dreaming. No, here I was with the porch lights on and the bright kitchen lights beamed.

"Dad," I stammered. "What are you doing here?"

He answered, "I came to tell you that everything is going to be okay. You'll be fine. I promise." My father grinned. "It doesn't matter if you live or die tomorrow, you will live. Either you will live in heaven with Jesus and me or you will live on earth a little longer."

I began to weep. "Daddy, how did you know how scared I felt this time?"

"Because Mom, Jim, and you prayed. Then he said, "Wait, I have a surprise." He reached outside and grabbed someone by the arm and she jumped into the house.

I recognized his mother, my grandmother. I hadn't seen her for over twenty years. They were both grinning from ear to ear as if they had divulged the biggest secret of the century. Their infectious laughter caused me to join in. Then I realized we would wake everyone up, so I settled down and started to cry at the faithfulness of those we love and who love us.

Dad reached for me and hugged me and so did Grandma. Then they told me goodbye and not to worry anymore. I felt comforted as they let themselves out the door.

I wandered around the house full of deep thoughts and worship before I got a drink of water and returned to bed. Before I knew it, I was woken by my husband and mom. We left early for the long trip to the University of San Francisco and my major surgery.

Mom told me later that it was intense and the doctor believed that I wasn't going to make it through, but I had a strong heart and a positive attitude as I went under the medication. It had taken twice as long as expected and recovery was slow, taking several weeks.

When I told them the story one afternoon after a boring rainy hospital day, both of them were in disbelief. Then they shared that they had felt something must have happened overnight because I was so different in the morning. Neither my mother nor Jim heard the knocks on the front door.

~Paulette L. Harris

Wild Snapdragons

Every flower is a soul blossoming in nature.
~Gérard de Nerval

never believed in those "signs" from the dearly departed. You know, the pennies from heaven type stories that everyone tells. I did feel my mom's presence after she died, especially when I was recovering from my own cancer surgery and lying wide awake through the night. But to see real, tangible things sent from the dead seemed to be asking a bit much. Then my fiancé died.

I was the one who wasn't going to make it—I was the one with the cancer diagnosis. Bob took care of me through surgeries and chemotherapy. Two years after my diagnosis, when it finally felt like I would be a survivor, Bob left the house one day never to return. He died of a massive heart attack.

Along with shock and devastating sadness, I had survivor's guilt and an incredible anger. Just when our lives had started getting back to normal, he was gone. After sixteen years, my best friend and cheerleader, lover and constant support, was not coming back. We had built a life doing everything together—renovating houses, working on crafts, and most importantly landscaping and gardening. Although beautiful lawns were Bob's specialty, he had a way with flowers too—mostly the perennials that would come back year after year. I took care of the annual flowers, which he had been happy to turn over to me. Especially since each year he'd try to grow snapdragons and they would always die.

Early in the spring, six months after Bob's death, I was walking around the house when I noticed something green coming up through the landscape stones. A weed, I thought, and left it, deciding it was too early to be pulling weeds. A few days later, I noticed a similar weed growing back by the shed—again in stones, not in the garden beds. And then, on the other side of the house, in the sand between the red brick pavers—the same type of green weed. It took a while, but then I knew; they weren't weeds, they were plants. On the first warm spring day, albeit out of season, they bloomed. Snapdragons. I was surrounded by wild snapdragons, growing far from any flower gardens. They were different colors, vibrantly alive and showing up in the stones and between planks of treated wood and in the joints of the concrete driveway.

I'd ask everyone I knew—have you ever seen snapdragons grow wild? And always, people would say, "How could they? Although they are a gentle perennial, around this area they are grown as an annual flower. They don't come back." Since Bob died, they grow wild at my house. Of course, realistically speaking, birds could be getting the seeds and dropping them at my house—never in garden beds, of course, and only since Bob's death. But that is as strange as any other reason. Flowers from heaven? Three years later and I still have my wild snapdragons showing up here and there, in different places, from spring until fall.

There have been other little signs—lights that stop working, then suddenly have no problems, or tools that fall from their hangers just when I need them. One day I was walking in the snow, and suddenly was lying flat on my stomach, my face on the ground. I felt the hand that pushed me, yet no one was there. Bob had always pushed me down in the snow when I least expected it. By then I had started to understand that he was still with me, and my reaction was the same as when he was alive—I laughed and told him to stop pushing me around! And I know he was laughing, too.

But those snapdragons. Everyone can see them, not just me. How often Bob and I talked about them; how annoyed he was that he could not make them grow. Yet now they are my wild flower and my constant reminder that Bob still loves me.

~Dale K. Perry

A Message from Mama

knew from his childhood family photos and stories that Leonard had a younger sister. I had never met her. There had been some sort of quarrel between May and the rest of her siblings that caused her to break with them during their early adult years.

I met Leonard when we were both about sixty and widowed. He introduced me to his older sister and brother before we were married, but not May. I asked to meet her as well, but he said no. Leonard's refusal surprised me. Surely this old hurt, whatever it was, could be set aside after all these years. I pressed the point, but the answer was still the same. Leonard explained that his first wife Janet had felt as I did, so he had relented and let May back into his life. In return, May did something so spiteful to Janet that he could neither tell me about it nor ever forgive his sister again. "I won't let her do that to you," he said. "May is out of my life."

One morning, six years later, while Leonard was in the final stages of terminal cancer, the telephone rang. It was Paula, his older sister.

"I had a phone call from my sister May," she said.

It seemed a strange first comment. She usually began by asking about Leonard. Then I remembered. No one in that family ever heard from May.

"It's been forty years since we last spoke," Paula went on. "May said she had a dream about Mama last night. Mama told her she had to get in touch with her sister and brothers. May said the dream felt so real, she had to call me. She said she planned to call our brothers too. I told her Leonard was dying. She was upset and said she would write to him immediately."

As Paula talked I felt the hair stand up on the back of my neck. I had always thought that phrase was just a figure of speech, but this time it was real and happening to me. A message from their dead mother telling May to reconnect with her brothers and sister, after so many years of separation. Why now? Leonard and I lived two states away. How could May have known that soon it would be too late to reach out to him? What could have prompted such a dream?

I needed to ponder the phenomenon. A few weeks earlier, when Leonard was still lucid, he told me of a very real dream of his own. He was walking down a long, unfamiliar hallway when his mother appeared at the other end, waving her arms forward as if to say "Go back!" Leonard's reaction was joy at seeing her, but she rejected him, shouting, "You can't come here... not yet, not yet." Then he woke up, feeling hurt.

I put the two dreams together and came to the only conclusion I could. Although I'd always been skeptical about messages from the beyond, I had to wonder. Perhaps there is an afterlife, one from where a dead mother's power can work wonders to set things right among her living children.

May's letter arrived the day Leonard passed away. It was too late for them, but something good did happen as a result of that dream. May and Paula re-united and remained close. They were sisters again.

~Marcia Rudoff

A Promise
Is a Promise

It is not the oath that makes us believe the man, but the man the oath.
~Aeschylus

My grandson left in the early morning from North Carolina State University in Raleigh, where he was a freshman, to travel home to Statesville to vote for the first time. After having dinner with his parents he headed back to campus. It's an easy drive up Interstate 40 from Statesville to Raleigh. That night was different. He got as far as Exit 135 in Greensboro. Another driver hurled across all the lanes of traffic, flipped around and hit Russ's car head-on. He was rushed to Moses Cone Trauma Center nearby.

When I got to his bedside I wanted to scream. This couldn't be my grandson who glided across basketball courts with ease. This couldn't be Russ who stormed across soccer fields, blocking his opponents from scoring. No, this couldn't be the boy who was chosen every year since middle school as a Peer Mediator to intervene with kids who had problems with teachers or coaches. This simply couldn't be my grandson who, a few months earlier, marched across the stage to receive his high school diploma with honors and a scholarship for his work with troubled teens.

Now that boy lies still. No flutter of an eyelash, no wiggle of toes, no movement at all except for the unnatural rise and fall of his chest made possible by a ventilator. No broken bones but his head is twice its normal size. There's a big gash on his forehead. He looks nothing like the young man I know.

Family gathers and we hear the unthinkable news. Russ has suffered severe left and right brain trauma. He will not live, but if by rare chance he does, he'll require assisted living for the rest of his life. The neurosurgeon's words hang heavy in the room.

Hours stretch into days, days into weeks, and weeks into months. People come from everywhere. We cry. We pray. We hang onto hope. It seems strange how in the middle of a crisis one remembers things long past. As I keep vigil over Russ, I hear the words my mother spoke days before she died. "My dear, don't grieve. I'm going to Heaven but I'll return on a day when you will need me most." Is this just a fleeting moment of remembrance? Perhaps. Yet her words keep coming to me at the oddest times.

Each day I pull my chair close to Russ's bed. I talk to him as if he can hear and understand, because I believe he can. I tell him about the time when he was in fourth grade, how we climbed trees, built a tree house, rescued a dog, went shopping for school clothes, ate his favorite dinner, watched a movie until his bedtime. I remind him about the conversation we had after I turned the lights out.

"Grandma, we forgot to do something today you promised."

"What's that, Russ?"

"You promised we'd bake cookies."

"Don't you think that will be fun to do for breakfast?"

"Grandma, you know in our family a promise is a promise."

It was ten o'clock at night but I went to the kitchen to check for ingredients. No sugar, no eggs, no chocolate chips.

"Okay. Get dressed, socks and all. We're going to the store."

We bought our goods, went home, baked and ate cookies. As I turned out the lights I heard his voice again.

"Grandma, do you know why I love you so much?"

"No Russ. Why?"

"'Cause you're so flexible."

Sitting by his hospital bed now, I say, "Russ, flexible is a strong action word and so is a promise. Now it's your time to be flexible. I know you aren't aware what's happened to you but I need for you to keep fighting, 'cause a promise is a promise in our family and you promised me you'd finish college with honors. Please Russ, come back to us."

I put my head lightly on his chest and weep. I feel someone pat my shoulder. I think it's my son who has returned to the room. I look up in amazement. Somehow Russ has flung his right arm across his body and is gently patting my shoulder. Just as quickly, the arm goes back to his side. He doesn't move again for weeks. It's enough. I know Russ is still with us. He will live and come back to us all the way.

The healing is slow with agonizing and intense therapy. Russ has to learn to do everything again. Step by step, try after try he slowly recovers completely. All the while, I hear my mother's words. "Don't grieve. I'm going to Heaven but I'll return on a day when you will need me most." I can't get the words out of my mind. That's why I know somehow she's a part of the story. I learn how on Good Friday night.

On this holy night, a stranger calls my son to see how he and Russ's mother are doing. My son tells him Russ is alive and getting stronger each day. The stranger can't believe what he hears, so he shares the rest of the story:

"I never stop at accidents, but this night a higher force guides my car to a stop. I rush over to check on your son. He appears to be dead so I run over to the woman who causes the accident. She seems to be okay. I look up and see two eighteen-wheelers barreling down the interstate, certain to crash into the already tangled mess. I have a penlight flashlight on the end of my key chain. I pump it as hard as I can, directly aiming the beam at the trucks. They stop within a breath of the accident. I look back and see a woman who appears out of nowhere. She's a tiny woman with very blue eyes. She calmly goes over to your son, reaches in and gently places her hands on either side of his neck. She keeps his neck stabilized until the first responders arrive, then she disappears as quickly as she appeared."

I believe it's no accident the stranger is at the very spot where the tragedy happened. I believe it's no accident he stops. I believe it's no accident he has a penlight flashlight hooked to his key chain. I believe it's no accident the woman arrived to stabilize Russ's neck. Why? I can still hear her words. "My dear, don't grieve. I'm going to Heaven but I'll return on a day when you will need me most."

Yes, in our family a promise is a promise. This time the promise is made and kept by a tiny woman with very blue eyes. I know. She's my mother who comes back on a day when I needed her most.

~Nan Leaptrott

Meet Our
Contributors

Lorraine Bruno Arsenault lives among the rolling hills and lakes of New York with her husband Joel, daughters, nephew and rescue dog. She is the author of *The Long Run Home*, FootHills Publishing; has poetry published in *The Healing Muse*, and holds a Bachelor of Arts degree in philosophy from Marymount College.

Joanne Fiestedt Babic has been a freelance writer and photographer for twenty years. She has written newsletters, newspaper articles, a historical perspective and is currently working on two novels. She lives in Tacoma, WA with her son and their cats. E-mail her at babic_joanne@yahoo.com.

Francine L. Baldwin-Billingslea has been published in over twenty anthologies and magazines, including several in the *Chicken Soup for the Soul* series, *Whispering Angel* books, *Thin Threads*, *BellaOnline Literary Review*, and *The Rambler*, as well as authoring an inspirational memoir titled *Through It All and Out On The Other Side*.

T.A. Barbella is a writer and artist living in San Jose, CA. After thirty years in education, she currently runs a children's creativity center at her art studio. She enjoys writing and illustrating children's books, and she draws inspiration from the magic of children, her loving family and her indomitable terrier, MacGyver.

Kathryn A. Beres resides in rural Wisconsin, and has work appearing in over fifty different publications, including *Lifewise* (Focus on the Family) and *The Miracle of Sons*. Two-time recipient of the People's Choice Award, her inspirations are her husband Mike; four children, Kaytlyn, Andrea, Mitch and Tyler; and brother, Jeff. E-mail her at kathrynberes@hotmail.com.

In **Sylvia Bright-Green's** thirty-five-year writing career she has been published in fourteen anthologies and co-authored two books. She has published hundreds of manuscripts as well as newspapers and magazines. She has been involved for over thirty years with her local and state writers' clubs and the oldest spiritual/metaphysical group in Wisconsin.

R.W. Bryant is a mother of two, and grandmother of four. She has lived most of her life in northern Indiana, and has worked at a major medical center there for thirty-four years. She enjoys time spent with family, reading, writing, and painting.

A.B. Chesler is a writer and educator living each day to its fullest in sunny Southern California. Her favorite pastimes include reading, writing, learning, seeking new adventures, and spending time with her family, friends, husband, and baby girl. E-mail her at achesler24@gmail.com and she will happily respond!

Lisa Shearer Cooper graduated from the University of Colorado with a B.A. degree in English and M.A. degree in Education. After teaching ESL to adults for many years and authoring textbooks, she is currently engaged in memoir writing and teaching preschool. Lisa enjoys travel, hiking, gardening and yoga. E-mail her at lisa@sc3.net.

Michele Ivy Davis lives in southern California where she is a freelance writer and photographer. Her stories and articles have appeared in a variety of magazines, newspapers, and law enforcement publications, and her debut novel, *Evangeline Brown and the Cadillac Motel*, received national and international awards. Learn more at www.MicheleIvyDavis.com.

S.G. Desrochers is an educational assistant in Kingston, Canada. Her young students love hearing her numerous inspirational tales of her pug, Cuddles. She is in the process of self-publishing Cuddles' stories, as well as completing a musical of her adorable Pug. E-mail her at cuddlesthepug@outlook.com.

Inga Dore is a retired teacher and freelance writer who enjoys growing organic vegetables, walking, and visiting shut-ins.

Gillian Driscoll has a PhD in communication from the University of Colorado at Boulder. She is a wholistic life coach specializing in helping over-fifties visualize and plan their second half of life. Gillian is also a Reiki Master, inspirational speaker and writer. E-mail Gillian at gillian@gilliandriscoll.com.

Ginny Dubose lives out her dreams in Winter Haven, FL with her husband, Ray, and their two sons, Dan and Alex. A graduate of Florida Southern College, Ginny takes great joy in writing snippets of what she knows is a blessed and joyful life!

Judy Ann Eichstedt is the mother of six and grandma to five. She is an activist for the homeless and has co-written three books with her daughter Christina. She lives in Tulsa, OK, and enjoys reading and traveling. E-mail her at jeichstedt@cox.net.

Diana Creel Elarde, BA, MA. Diana consults and also teaches psychology for Maricopa Community College. Her husband Vincent edits and encourages her quest to become a successful writer. Amanda and Zdravko, her children, are her great sources of inspiration. E-mail her at dcgwest@live.com.

Melissa Face teaches high school English and devotes her free time to writing. Melissa's stories and essays have appeared in numerous magazines and anthologies. She lives in Virginia with her husband and son. E-mail Melissa at writermsface@yahoo.com.

Rick Fernandes has worked in the Internet world for many years, and has recently founded a website dedicated to good news and inspirational stories called Hooplaha.com. He enjoys reading, working out, and spending time with his family. Check out Hooplaha.com and e-mail him at rick@fernandeshome.com.

Christiana Flanigan lives in Mono, Ontario, Canada. She holds two diplomas from the Institute of Children's Literature. Several of her stories have been published in *Sideroads of Dufferin County*. Christiana enjoys reading, gardening, cycling, cross-country skiing and skating. Since childhood, writing has held a special place in her heart.

Johanne Fraser is a severely hearing impaired mother of two boys and blessed to be in a loving marriage. She works as an office manager in Surrey, BC. Johanne enjoys photography, reading, writing, gardening, walking, skiing and time with her family. She blogs at momwhearingloss.wordpress.com. E-mail her at momwhearingloss@ yahoo.com.

Sharon Fuentes is an award-winning author and special needs parenting expert. She writes a monthly humor column for *Westchester Family* magazine and her feature articles/essays have been published in numerous regional, national and international publications including *Chicken Soup for the Soul: Raising Kids on the Spectrum*. E-mail her at sharonbfuentes@hotmail.com.

Marilyn Ellis Futrell lives just outside Orlando, FL. She lost her nineteen-year-old son, John Robert Woodfin, in an accident in 2005. She was published previously in *Chicken Soup for the Soul: Messages* *from Heaven* and The Compassionate Friends national magazine, *We Need Not Walk Alone*. Tweet Marilyn at @MEFutrell.

Patricia Ann Gallegos lives in the beautiful Pacific Northwest. She inspires young authors through teaching writing classes at Evergreen School District, and works at Washington State University. She is a freelance writer finishing her first book, *In My Shadow: Inspirational Help for Goals, Dreams, and Legacy*. Contact her at pattygallegos@comcast.net or www.patriciagalwrites.com.

T'Mara Goodsell is an award-winning multi-genre writer who lives near St. Louis, MO. She has written for various anthologies, newspapers and publications and is working on a book for young adults.

Maribeth Graham lives in northeastern Pennsylvania with her husband and four children. Maribeth is the author of several picture books, a middle grade novel and YA novel. Her blog, Writing Like Crazy, (www.ninidee.wordpress.com) focuses on the craft of writing. She is on a journey, hoping for a good destination.

R'becca Groff is a former administrative assistant turned writer who enjoys writing from the perspective of her small-town Iowa upbringing. She supplies a business column for Cedar Rapids' *The Gazette*, and publishes in regional and national anthologies and magazines. She blogs about the writer's life at rebeccasnotepad.wordpress.com.

Leslie Gulvas is a high school science teacher, former scientific researcher, and freelance writer. Leslie is an avid traveler, horsewoman, hiker, sailor, and general collector of experiences who enjoys meeting new people and writing about her travels. She lives on a small farm in Ohio.

William Halderson is retired and lives in Tennessee with Monica and Max (wife and dog). He writes a column for his city's newspaper.

He is happy to have several of his stories published in the *Chicken Soup for the Soul* series. He is active in many church organizations. E-mail him at billandmonica1943@frontiernet.net.

Linda Texter Hall attended Temple University and Bread Loaf Writers' Conference at Middlebury College. Her career includes seventeen years at Winterthur Museum. She is a yoga and meditation instructor, and a founding board member of Cancer Support Community Delaware. Linda enjoys creative writing and exploring "inner space."

Gloria Jean Hansen is a nurse/bluegrass musician/author from Elliot Lake, and grew up in Kipling, Ontario, Canada. She has written several novels, articles, newspaper columns, and songs. Her spare time is spent camping with her family, writing and music. She will someday retire to a cabin by the river.

Paulette Harris is an author/speaker who has published nonfiction and fiction work. She belongs to several groups, including ACFW and CWG. She and her husband of forty-six years have three cats, two children, and five grandchildren. Paulette's hobbies are golf, gardening and culinary efforts. E-mail her at coloradopolly@yahoo.com.

Mariane Holbrook earned her degree from Nyack (NY) College and from High Point (NC) University. She and her husband John are retired teachers living in Kure Beach, NC. Mariane is the author of two books, *Prisms of the Heart* and *Humor Me*. She has two sons and six grandchildren.

Laura Hollingshead is a registered nurse, small business owner, and published author. Her current focus is a book for adult children of aging parents on the subject of starting the dialogue regarding health changes and planning for the mid and later stages of life. E-mail her at Medwoman@q.com.

Catherine J. Inscore believes everything happens for a reason; everything in life is a blessing. She is grateful to her husband Barry for all his support and encouragement. She thanks her thirteen children, twenty-nine grandchildren, four great-grandchildren, and many at Copper Mountain College where she works for their love and support.

Elizabeth Jaeger lives in her home state of Indiana where she works in a substance abuse clinic as Patient Scheduling Coordinator. She loves to read, hike, and travel, especially to Boston where she reunites with Abby once a year! E-mail her at elizabethkjaeger@gmail.com.

Jackson Jarvis is fourteen years old, into surfing and classic rock (he thinks he should've been born in the 60's) An aspiring music producer, he's also written three yet-to-be published books including *The Book of Bad Ideas* and *The Weird Stuff I Do*. He lives in New York State with his mom, Joelle, and his dad Eric is his guardian angel.

Janice Jensen, a well-traveled educator, has lived in or visited more than sixty-five countries. Her students have included a Saudi prince and children from a Colombian oil company. She's written about her adventures in Antarctica and Timbuktu, Mali. She dances ballroom, swing and tango for fun. E-mail Janice at jcjrealestate@gmail.com.

Louetta Jensen has written four novels and two screenplays and is a member of the International Women's Writing Guild and Women's Literary Guild. Her novel, *Bittersweet Serenity*, was among the winners in the North American Fiction Writer Awards, and received a Certificate of Merit in the Writer's Digest National Book Awards.

Laura Johnston is a lucky wife and mom who enjoys writing, reading, running, dancing (around the kitchen when no one is watching) and playing tennis. She graduated from Brigham Young University and aspires to publish young adult novels and children's picture books. E-mail her at laurajohnstonauthor@gmail.com.

Louise Tucker Jones is a Gold Medallion Award-winning author and inspirational speaker as well as a respected columnist for Oklahoma's *Outlook* magazine. Louise's work has appeared in numerous publications, including *Guideposts* and *Angels on Earth* magazines.

Susie Kearley is a British freelance writer, who writes for magazines and newspapers across the world. She has recently signed her first book deal on the topic of how to write for the health, food and gardening markets. Her hobbies include keeping guinea pigs and travel. Visit her at www.facebook.com/susie.kearley.writer or www.twitter.com/susiekearley.

Sally Kelly-Engeman is a freelance writer who worked for newspapers in Wisconsin, Montana and California. In addition to writing, she enjoys reading and researching and recently completed a historical novel. She also enjoys ballroom dancing and traveling the world with her husband. E-mail her at Sallyfk@juno.com.

L.A. Kennedy writes from her studio in Northern California. Her stories have appeared in *Guideposts* and various magazines. Also an artist, she created clay, macho, floral and fabric projects for magazines and holiday items for retail stores. She enjoys deer-proof gardening, working out and creative art. E-mail her at elkaynca@aol.com.

Gaye Loraine Kiebach is a retired disabled Licensed Practical Nurse who worked at a psychiatric hospital for over twenty-three years. Mother of three wonderful children and now four grandchildren. Hobbies are writing short stories and poems, designing and making quilts for the Veterans Hospital and a pregnancy center.

Melisa Kraft lives in Benton, KY, with her husband Steve and sons, Aaron-Jesy, 18, and Trig, 4. She has two other men in her life who she considers her sons and one grandson. Other than reading and writing, she enjoys relaxation time and worship, as well as being with her two rescued dogs who get treated like kings.

Freelance writer **Jeannie Lancaster** believes wholeheartedly in the tender mercies and miracles that occur in our lives. She is grateful that even in the midst of incredible adversity, there can be moments of great joy.

Nan Leaptrott is a popular motivational speaker, communication coach and author. She is actively involved in her church, community, and family. Her hobbies include designing floral arrangements, cooking, and listening to the pine trees sing. She is currently writing an inspirational book and a novel. E-mail her at nleap@pinehurst.net.

Joan Leotta has written many books, articles, and poems for adults and children. Her two recent novels, *Giulia Goes to War* and *Letters from Korea*, are available as ebooks. Joan also performs shows of storytelling and history. Her motto is "encouraging words through pen and performance." E-mail her at joanleotta@atmc.net.

Valerie S. Libby is a Personal Coach and Organizational Transformation Consultant with a highly developed intuition. A former lawyer, who has been psychic since childhood, Valerie leverages her intuition to guide clients internationally through roadblocks, accessing their previously untapped wisdom to achieve their personal and professional goals. Learn more at www.valerielibby.com.

Linda Lohman, BA, a frequent contributor to the *Chicken Soup for the Soul* series, doesn't just believe in miracles, she relies on them. Family, friends, and red hatting keep her busy. Living in Sacramento, CA, she is rebooting her life as a writer following two separate careers. E-mail her at lindaalohman@yahoo.com.

Jenny Mason is an award-winning author. She received a Master's degree from Trinity College Dublin and an M.F.A. from Vermont College of Fine Arts. She dwells in the side of a gingerbread mountain in Colorado, but previously lived on the breadcrumb shores of Sandycove, Ireland. E-mail her at jen.michelle.mason@gmail.com.

Suzanne Grieco Mattaboni is a writer and public relations consultant from Pennsylvania. Her work has appeared in *Seventeen*, *Newsday*, *Child*, *Long Island Parenting* and various trade magazines. She is working on a middle grade novel. Suzanne is inspired by a supportive and hysterically fun extended family. E-mail her at Suzanne@mattaboni.com.

Karen McBride has lived in the Tampa Bay area for twenty-five years, raising her three children. She enjoys exploring beautiful nature parks, photographing wildlife, and going to craft shows. She has written numerous articles for a local newspaper and has written her first children's book. E-mail her at kmcbride320@aol.com.

Beverly Stowe McClure, an honor graduate of Midwestern State University and former teacher, lives in the country where she enjoys photographing birds, deer, and clouds. She has nine books for children and teens published. Beverly enjoys genealogy and playing the piano. She also teaches a Sunday school class.

Nina Schatzkamer Miller was Children's Area Specialist at Borders. Her book, *The Storytime Handbook*, enables parents, teachers, booksellers and librarians to provide a complete story time that includes music, art, movement, food and literature. Her dad encouraged her to write the book. E-mail her at nina-miller@att.net.

Margaret Nava writes from her home in New Mexico where she lives with a rambunctious Chihuahua. In addition to her stories in the *Chicken Soup for the Soul* series, she has authored six books and written numerous articles for inspirational and Christian living publications.

Tammy A. Nischan is a Christian teacher, writer, and speaker. As the mother of six, two of whom are in Heaven, Tammy's passion is ministering to other grieving moms. She would love to hear from you through Twitter @ilovepennies, Facebook, or her blog "My Heart His Words" (www.tammynischan.blogspot.com).

Christa Holder Ocker, a frequent contributor to Chicken Soup for the Soul, wrote *Auf Wiedersehen: World War II Through the Eyes of a German Girl*, a finalist for the ForeWord Book of the Year Award. It is in numerous libraries including the Holocaust Collection at Yeshiva University, the Leo Baeck Institute, and the New York Society Library.

Jeanne Pallos is the author of several published stories for adults and children. She is passionate about writing family stories and preserving the memories of loved ones for future generations. She lives in Laguna Niguel, CA with her husband, one Golden Retriever, and one rabbit. E-mail her at jlpallos@cox.net.

Chicken Soup for the Soul editor **Kristiana Glavin Pastir** earned a journalism degree from Syracuse University in 2004. When she's not reading, writing, or editing for Chicken Soup for the Soul, Kristiana enjoys reading, yoga, and adventures with her husband—especially their scuba diving trips around the world.

Andrea Peebles lives with her husband of thirty-six years in Rockmart, GA. She enjoys cooking, nature, travel, photography and freelance writing. She is an avid reader and frequent contributor to the *Chicken Soup for the Soul* series. E-mail her at aanddpeebles@aol.com.

Dale K. Perry, a New Jersey native, took an early retirement to focus on writing, gardening and living life with kindness and purpose. She is an advocate for animals and historic preservation. Dale encourages everyone to find their dream and live it. E-mail her at dalekperry@gmail.com.

Lori Phillips writes about spirituality, dreams, marriage and relationships. She received her Bachelor of Arts degree in communications and a Master's of Education. Her print and ebooks are available from Real Life Help Books. She lives with her family in Orange, CA. E-mail her at lori@reallifehelpbooks.com.

Dr. Barbara Poremba is a Nurse Practitioner and Professor of Nursing at Salem State University, MA. She earned degrees from Harvard University, Boston University and the University of Massachusetts Amherst and Worcester. Barbara enjoys international humanitarian work, photography, skiing, tap dancing, sea glass collecting and grandchildren. Learn more at www.salemstate.edu/~bporemba/.

Roberta Carly Redford received her Bachelor of Science degree from the University of Wyoming in 1985. She is writing a mystery novel set in the Black Forest of Colorado.

Ann Elizabeth Robertson's years teaching secondary English and art (M.A. in writing) continue in her love of combining artistic and written expressions: relevant symbols of our struggles and triumphs in God's powerful scheme of things. She and her husband have four children and five grandchildren. Learn more at www.annelizabethrobertson. com.

Laura Robinson, married mother of two, is an actress, author and co-inventor of the classic board game, *Balderdash*. Laura co-authored *Chicken Soup for the Soul: Count Your Blessings* and *Chicken Soup for the Soul: Hooked on Hockey*. She is currently co-producing a television game show for fall 2014. E-mail her at laurarobinson@rogers.com.

Sallie A. Rodman received her Certificate in Professional Writing from CSULB and has appeared in numerous *Chicken Soup for the Soul* anthologies. She loves writing about the mysterious and unexplained events that happen in our lives. She plans to write an inspirational book on life after widowhood. E-mail her at sa.rodman@verizon. net.

Amy Rodriguez is a mom of two who writes about parenting with humor, families, and mental health. She has been a physical therapist and teacher, and is now in school to become a school counselor. She loves reading, writing, trying to garden, and doing anything near the ocean.

Amanda Romaniello is a Syracuse University graduate. This is her fourth story published in the *Chicken Soup for the Soul* series. When not writing, Amanda is training for long distance road races, reading, taking photos and spending time with her Dalmatian, Louie. E-mail her at amanda.romaniello@gmail.com.

Robert Rome is a professional musician, writer and audio critic. He currently lives in New York.

Tyann Sheldon Rouw lives in Iowa with her husband and three sons. She is a previous contributor to the *Chicken Soup for the Soul* series. Visit her blog, Turn Up the Valium, at tyannsheldonrouw.weebly.com or follow her on Twitter @TyannRouw.

Marcia Rudoff, a writer and retired educator, lives on Bainbridge Island, WA, where she teaches memoir writing classes for the senior community center and writes a monthly column for the local newspaper, *Bainbridge Island Review*. Her personal essays have appeared in newspapers, magazines and numerous life story anthologies.

Jane Self is a freelance writer and copywriter. She retired as Features Editor from *The Tuscaloosa News* in 2007 after eight years and was previously Assistant Features Editor for the *Macon Telegraph* for twelve years. E-mail her at jane@janeself.com.

Jodi Iachini Severson earned her Bachelor's degree from the University of Pittsburgh and she now lives in central Wisconsin where she works for the State Public Defender. As a freelance writer, she has been a frequent contributor to Chicken Soup for the Soul since 2002. E-mail her at seversonjl@gmail.com.

Shelly Shevlin received a Master's degree in Human Resources from Lindenwood University in Belleville, IL in 2006. She is the Human Resources Manager for the Illinois Department of Transportation in Collinsville, IL. Shelly enjoys traveling and spending time with friends and family. E-mail her at haplap13@yahoo.com.

Lillie Shockney is an oncology nurse and a University Distinguished Service Associate Professor of Breast Cancer at Johns Hopkins. She is the Director of the Johns Hopkins Breast Center and of the Cancer Survivorship Programs. She has received forty-one national awards and is a national speaker and author.

Susan Simmons received her paralegal degree from the Community College of Southern Nevada in 1990. She retired in 2009 after working for the Federal Government for twenty-three years. She lives in North Carolina and enjoys volunteer work, reading and making jewelry.

Loren Slocum, mother of three, International Personal Development Speaker and Elite Lifestyle Coach, "daddy's girl" and author of *Life Tuneups*, which appeared in *People* magazine as one of the Top 3 inspiring books of 2010. Loren has also published *No Greater Love* and *The Greatest Love*. E-mail her at lorenslocum@gmail.com.

Christine Smith loves to relive memories by putting them on paper and sharing them with others. She is active in her local church, and lives with her husband of forty-five years in Atoka, OK. With three children, fourteen grandchildren, and five great-grandchildren, there is never a lack of story material.

David Michael Smith of Georgetown, DE, is blessed by the many true stories of miracles shared with him regularly, including his seventh story, "Martha's Message," published in the *Chicken Soup for the Soul* series. When he's not writing, David enjoys spending time with his family and serving God's people. E-mail him at davidandgeri@ hotmail.com.

Tanya Sousa is a prolific freelance writer and has published in magazines, anthologies and literary publications. Three of her children's picture books have been published with Radiant Hen Publishing, the stories focusing on encouraging the idea of growing your own food and sustainable living. She is currently working on completing a novel.

Gary Stein co-founded an NYSE-member investment banking division. He has been a strategy advisor to dozens of entertainment firms, and was Executive Vice President of a 30-time Emmy-winning kids' TV company. Formally a Nashville songwriter, Gary recently authored the personal and candid book, *Confessions of an Unfiltered Mind*. E-mail him at gm.stein@verizon.net.

Reisa Stone is an animal communicator whose practice focuses on pet PTSD and spirit world contact. She is the author of a book of humorous and heart-wrenching stories collected from Ukrainian immigrants, *Baba's Kitchen: Ukrainian Soul Food with Stories from the Village*. Contact her at www.reisastone.com and www.ukrainiansoulfood.ca.

Rachel Strickland received her Bachelor of Arts degree in English Literature from the University of Oregon in 2011. She lives in Oregon where she enjoys cooking, baking, and anything outdoors. She attributes her successes to her husband, Nathan Eckstein, for his unfailing positivity and support. E-mail Rachel at missrachel. strickland@gmail.com.

Jennifer Taylor holds degrees in creative writing and literature. She and her husband live in Wisconsin. She enjoys traveling, gardening, and dancing. Jennifer leads a writing critique group and is on the board of her local writers' guild. E-mail her at Jenniferch2000@yahoo.com.

Donna Teti loves to write inspirational stories and poems that will lift a person's spirit. She has previously been published in other *Chicken Soup for the Soul* anthologies, *Guideposts* magazine, and many compilation books. Read more of Donna's stories at donnateti.com and on Facebook at Twinpop Inspirations.

Ellen Tevault received her Bachelor of Arts degree in English from Marian College and her Master of Library Science degree from Indiana University. She'd like to find a job writing or editing. Ellen has had articles published in *Reading in Indianapolis*, *ISL Connection* and *The Encyclopedia of Indianapolis*. E-mail her at ellenteva@yahoo.com.

Marla H. Thurman lives in Signal Mountain, TN with her dogs Sophie and Jasper. The three of them try to write something of value every day, but some days really "are" better than others. Still, they strive for the best! E-mail her at sizoda1@yahoo.com.

Christine Trollinger is a writer from Kansas City, MO and has had several stories published in the *Chicken Soup for the Soul* series and other publications over the past twelve years. She is a widow with three children, two granddaughters, and three great-grandchildren who are the apple of her eye. E-mail her at trolleys_2@yahoo.com.

Marion Ueckermann's writing passion was sparked in 2001 when she moved to Ireland. She has published devotional articles in *The One Year Devotional of Joy and Laughter*. She blogs for International Christian Fiction Writers. Marion lives in Pretoria East, South Africa with her husband and their crazy black Scottie, Wally.

Megan LeeAnn Waterman-Fouch enjoys sharing her stories with the world. She currently writes a monthly column called *Paws and Reflect* for a local newspaper, and continues to submit her inspirational children's book manuscripts to publishing houses for consideration. Her biggest joy is spending time with her family.

Mary Z. Whitney is a regular contributor to the *Chicken Soup for the Soul* series, as well as to *Guideposts* and *Angels on Earth*. She now resides in Ohio with her husband John and their dog Max. She has also written an inspirational fiction work entitled *Life's a Symphony* available on Amazon.com.

Melissa Wootan resides in La Vernia, TX with her husband, Joey, and son, Josh. She provides "Inspiration for the Heart and Home" by the joining of her two passions: writing and transforming old, discarded furniture into one-of-a-kind, "wow" pieces. She's created a Facebook page to showcase both. Visit www.facebook.com/chicvintique.

Bill Young lives near Portland, OR with his dog, Jake, where he owns and operates a roofing business. In his spare time he builds doghouses and birdhouses with really good roofs. E-mail him at Bill.n.Jake@gmail.com.

Meet Our Authors

Jack Canfield is the co-creator of the *Chicken Soup for the Soul* series, which *Time* magazine has called "the publishing phenomenon of the decade." Jack is also the coauthor of many other bestselling books.

Jack is the CEO of the Canfield Training Group in Santa Barbara, California, and founder of the Foundation for Self-Esteem in Culver City, California. He has conducted intensive personal and professional development seminars on the principles of success for more than a million people in 23 countries, has spoken to hundreds of thousands of people at more than 1,000 corporations, universities, professional conferences and conventions, and has been seen by millions more on national television shows.

Jack has received many awards and honors, including three honorary doctorates and a Guinness World Records Certificate for having seven books from the *Chicken Soup for the Soul* series appearing on the New York Times bestseller list on May 24, 1998.

You can reach Jack at www.jackcanfield.com.

Mark Victor Hansen is the co-founder of Chicken Soup for the Soul, along with Jack Canfield. He is a sought-after keynote speaker, bestselling author, and marketing maven. Mark's powerful messages of possibility, opportunity, and action have created powerful change in thousands of organizations and millions of individuals worldwide.

Mark is a prolific writer with many bestselling books in addition to the *Chicken Soup for the Soul* series. Mark has had a profound influence in the field of human potential through his library of audios, videos, and articles in the areas of big thinking, sales achievement, wealth building, publishing success, and personal and professional development. He is also the founder of the MEGA Seminar Series.

Mark has received numerous awards that honor his entrepreneurial spirit, philanthropic heart, and business acumen. He is a lifetime member of the Horatio Alger Association of Distinguished Americans.

You can reach Mark at www.markvictorhansen.com.

Amy Newmark has been Chicken Soup for the Soul's publisher, coauthor, and editor-in-chief for the last five years, after a 30-year career as a writer, speaker, financial analyst, and business executive in the worlds of finance and telecommunications. Amy is a *magna cum laude* graduate of Harvard College, where she majored in Portuguese, minored in French, and traveled extensively. She and her husband have four grown children.

After a long career writing books on telecommunications, voluminous financial reports, business plans, and corporate press releases, Chicken Soup for the Soul is a breath of fresh air for Amy. She has fallen in love with Chicken Soup for the Soul and its life-changing books, and really enjoys putting these books together for Chicken Soup for the Soul's wonderful readers. She has coauthored more than six dozen *Chicken Soup for the Soul* books and has edited another three dozen.

You can reach Amy with any questions or comments through webmaster@chickensoupforthesoul.com and you can follow her on Twitter @amynewmark or @chickensoupsoul.

Thank You

We owe huge thanks to all of our contributors. We know that you poured your hearts and souls into the thousands of stories that you shared with us, and ultimately with each other. As we read and edited these stories, we were truly amazed by your experiences. We appreciate your willingness to share these inspiring and encouraging stories with our readers.

We could only publish a small percentage of the stories that were submitted, but we read every single one and even the ones that do not appear in the book had an influence on us and on the final manuscript. We owe special thanks to our editor Kristiana Pastir, who read the stories that were submitted for this book and narrowed the list down to a more manageable number of finalists. Our assistant publisher D'ette Corona did her normal masterful job of working with the contributors to approve our edits and answer any questions we had. We also had the able assistance of our college intern Madeleine Feinberg, who helped us find many of the stories in this book.

We also owe a special thanks to our creative director and book producer, Brian Taylor at Pneuma Books, for his brilliant vision for our covers and interiors.

~Amy Newmark

Improving Your Life
Every Day

Real people sharing real stories—for twenty years. Now, Chicken Soup for the Soul has gone beyond the bookstore to become a world leader in life improvement. Through books, movies, DVDs, online resources and other partnerships, we bring hope, courage, inspiration and love to hundreds of millions of people around the world. Chicken Soup for the Soul's writers and readers belong to a one-of-a-kind global community, sharing advice, support, guidance, comfort, and knowledge.

Chicken Soup for the Soul stories have been translated into more than forty languages and can be found in more than one hundred countries. Every day, millions of people experience a Chicken Soup for the Soul story in a book, magazine, newspaper or online. As we share our life experiences through these stories, we offer hope, comfort and inspiration to one another. The stories travel from person to person, and from country to country, helping to improve lives everywhere.

Share with Us

We all have had Chicken Soup for the Soul moments in our lives. If you would like to share your story or poem with millions of people around the world, go to chickensoup.com and click on "Submit Your Story." You may be able to help another reader, and become a published author at the same time. Some of our past contributors have launched writing and speaking careers from the publication of their stories in our books!

Our submission volume has been increasing steadily—the quality and quantity of your submissions has been fabulous. We only accept story submissions via our website. They are no longer accepted via mail or fax.

To contact us regarding other matters, please send us an e-mail through webmaster@chickensoupforthesoul.com, or fax or write us at:

Chicken Soup for the Soul
P.O. Box 700
Cos Cob, CT 06807-0700
Fax: 203-861-7194

One more note from your friends at Chicken Soup for the Soul: Occasionally, we receive an unsolicited book manuscript from one of our readers, and we would like to respectfully inform you that we do not accept unsolicited manuscripts and we must discard the ones that appear.

When our loved ones leave this world, our connection with them does not end. Sometimes when we see or hear from them, they give us signs and messages. Sometimes they speak to us in dreams or they appear in different forms. The stories in this book, both religious and secular, will amaze you, giving you new knowledge, insight and awareness about the connection and communication we have with those who have passed on or those who have experienced dying and coming back.

978-1-935096-91-7

Emotional

Chicken Soup for the Soul.

Grieving and Recovery

101 Inspirational and Comforting Stories about Surviving the Loss of a Loved One

Jack Canfield,
Mark Victor Hansen,
and Amy Newmark

Everyone grieves in their own way. While the hurt and sadness never completely fade, it eases with time. Contributors who have gone through the grieving and recovery process share their stories of what helped, offering guidance and support in this collection of personal and poignant stories. With its stories of regaining strength, appreciating life, coping, and faith, this book will ease the journey to healing.

978-1-935096-62-7

Support

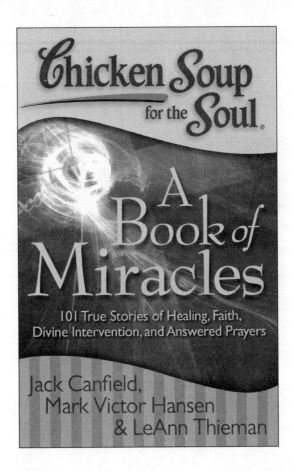

Chicken Soup for the Soul®

A Book of Miracles

101 True Stories of Healing, Faith, Divine Intervention, and Answered Prayers

Jack Canfield,
Mark Victor Hansen
& LeAnn Thieman

Everyone loves a good miracle story, and this book provides 101 true stories of healing, divine intervention, and answered prayers. These amazing, personal stories prove that God is alive and active in the world today, working miracles on our behalf. The incredible accounts show His love and involvement in our lives. This book of miracles will encourage, uplift, and recharge the faith of Catholics and all Christian readers.

978-1-935096-51-1

More

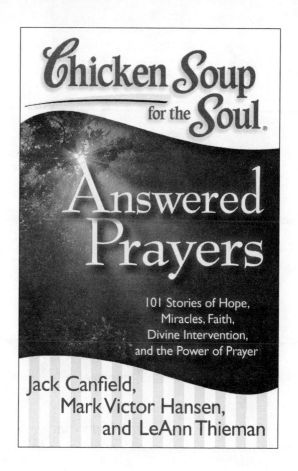

Chicken Soup for the Soul

for the Soul

Answered Prayers

101 Stories of Hope,
Miracles, Faith,
Divine Intervention,
and the Power of Prayer

Jack Canfield,
Mark Victor Hansen,
and LeAnn Thieman

We all need help from time to time, and these 101 true stories of answered prayers show a higher power at work in our lives. Regular people share their personal, touching stories of God's Divine intervention, healing power, and communication. Filled with stories about the power of prayer, miracles, and hope, this book will inspire anyone looking to boost his or her faith and read some amazing stories.

978-1-935096-76-4

Miracles

Chicken Soup for the Soul
for the Soul.

Angels
Among Us

101 Inspirational
Stories of
Miracles,
Faith, and
Answered
Prayers

Jack Canfield,
Mark Victor Hansen
& Amy Newmark

Celestial, otherworldly, heavenly. Whatever the term, sometimes there is no earthly explanation for what we experience, and a higher power is clearly at work. In this book of 101 inspirational stories, contributors share their personal angel experiences of faith, miracles, and answered prayers. You will be awed and inspired by these true personal stories from people, religious and non-religious, about angel guidance, miraculous intervention, and love from beyond.

978-1-61159-906-0

Divine